The practice
of university history teaching

MANCHESTER
UNIVERSITY PRESS

The practice
of university
history teaching

edited by
Alan Booth and Paul Hyland

Manchester University Press
Manchester and New York

distributed exclusively in the USA by St. Martin's Press

Published by Manchester University Press
Oxford Road, Manchester M13 9NR, UK
and Room 400, 175 Fifth Avenue, New York, NY 10010, USA
http://www.man.ac.uk/mup

Distributed exclusively in the USA by
St. Martin's Press, Inc., 175 Fifth Avenue, New York,
NY 10010, USA

Distributed exclusively in Canada by
UBC Press, University of British Columbia, 6344 Memorial Road,
Vancouver, BC, Canada V6T 1Z2

British Library Cataloguing-in-Publication Data
A catalogue record for this book is available from the British Library

Library of Congress Cataloging-in-Publication Data applied for

ISBN 0 7190 5491 5 *hardback*
0 7190 5492 3 *paperback*

First published 2000

06 05 04 03 02 01 00   10 9 8 7 6 5 4 3 2 1

Typeset in Sabon with Gill Sans display
by Servis Filmsetting Ltd, Manchester
Printed in Great Britain
by Biddles Ltd, Guildford and King's Lynn

Contents

III Learning and assessment

List of tables and figures

Tables

Figures

Acknowledgements

Many people have been involved either directly or indirectly in the production of this book. A particular debt of gratitude is owed to the higher education Funding Councils for England and Northern Ireland, whose Fund for the Development of Teaching and Learning enabled our 'History 2000' project to work at a national level on the development of teaching and learning in the subject between 1996 and 2000. This funding permitted the undertaking of research upon which many of the chapters in this book are based, and enabled us, and many of our contributors, to develop contacts with colleagues which helped to clarify issues and provided insights and ideas about enhancing the teaching of history.

Personal debts of gratitude are also due. Gerry Taggart and Caroline Bardrick at the Higher Education Funding Council for England were unfailingly helpful and efficient throughout the work of History 2000, and Graham Gibbs super-vised the project and provided strong support and strategic advice. George Brown, Jane Longmore and James Wisdom constituted a model Evaluation Board, invariably encouraging us and offering good ideas about the best ways forward. Nicky Wilson has been much more than the secretary to History 2000, facilitating every aspect of its activities with skill, good humour and a strong commitment to its goals, and also playing a major role in the preparation of this book. Finally, Jeanne Booth and Pauleen Hyland have provided support at all stages of this project, helping us to clarify our ideas and listening with patience to our accounts of the ups and downs of our efforts to develop and enhance the quality of teaching and learning in history.

Alan Booth
Paul Hyland

List of contributors

Hannah Barker is Lecturer in History at Keele University, with research interests in print culture and gender in eighteenth-century England.

Alan Booth is Senior Lecturer in History at the University of Nottingham, where he is also a University Teaching Enhancement Adviser. His research and publications are in the areas of popular culture in eighteenth-century England and the teaching and learning of history in higher education.

Susan Lovegren Bosworth is Assessment Coordinator at the College of William and Mary, Virginia, USA. Her current research interests include assessment in higher education, student socialisation and role enactment in the context of disasters.

Colin Brooks is Pro-Vice-Chancellor with responsibility for Teaching and Learning at the University of Sussex. He has taught seventeenth- and eighteenth-century British and American history at the University since 1970.

Janet Conneely is currently a PhD student at the University of Bristol and teaches modern and contemporary history at the University of Huddersfield.

Peter Davies is Senior Lecturer in History at the University of Huddersfield. He teaches modern European history, and his research specialisms include far-right politics and small-group teaching and learning.

Rhys Davies is a teacher of History at Longcroft School, Beverley, Yorkshire. He has a special interest in the use of visual sources and diagrammatic aids in the teaching of the subject.

John R. Davis is Lecturer in Modern European History at Kingston University. His research interests include nineteenth-century British and German history, and Anglo-German and international relations.

Ian Dawson is Principal Lecturer in History at Trinity and All Saints College, Leeds. He is also Director of the Schools Council History Project, a national curriculum development project for the teaching of history in secondary schools.

Joanne de Pennington is Lecturer in History at Trinity and All Saints College,

Leeds. She has experience of teaching Certificate of Education and Postgraduate Certificate in Education courses for adults entering teaching in further and higher education, and modern British social and political history.

Susan Doran is Reader in History at St Mary's College, Twickenham, and has published many books and articles on early-modern English history. She is a member of the History Benchmarking Group.

Christopher Durston is Reader in History at St Mary's College, Twickenham. He has published widely on seventeenth-century English history and is a member of the History at the Universities Defence Group's Steering Group.

Graham Ellis is Senior Lecturer in Educational Development at the University of Teesside. He has taught history in further and higher education and is course leader for the University's Postgraduate Certificate in Teaching and Learning in Higher Education.

Anthony Fletcher is Professor of History at the University of Essex, and the author of many books and articles on early and modern British history.

Peter J. Frederick is Professor of History at Wabash College, Indiana, USA. The recipient of several teaching awards, he has written widely on innovative teaching methods in higher education.

Guinevere Glasfurd is a PhD student in the Department of History at Lancaster University, and is currently working as a Research Associate at the University of Essex for the 'IN-TELE' Project (Internet-based Teaching and Learning).

Robert S. Gossweiler is Director of the Policy Studies Resource Laboratories at William and Mary College in Virginia, USA, a new facility that offers faculty technologically sophisticated research and teaching opportunities.

Jeremy Gregory is Head of History at the University of Northumbria. He has published several books and is currently completing *The Long Reformation: Religion and English Society, 1530–1870*.

Tim Hitchcock is Reader in Eighteenth-Century History at the University of Hertfordshire. He has published widely on the subjects of poverty, sexuality and religious radicalism in eighteenth-century England. His most recent book, edited with Michéle Cohen, is *English Masculinities, 1660–1800*.

Dai Hounsell is Head of the Department of Higher and Further Education at the University of Edinburgh. His many publications include *The Experience of Learning, Feedback on Courses and Programmes of Study* and *Reviewing Your Teaching*.

Paul Hyland is Head of the School of Historical and Cultural Studies at Bath Spa University College. His research and publications are in the fields of eighteenth-century Studies, Irish Studies and History in Higher Education.

Merv Lewis is Senior Lecturer in Economic and Business History at Sheffield Hallam University. He has published books and articles in economic history and computing for historians.

Roger Lloyd-Jones is Professor of Modern Economic History at Sheffield Hallam University. His two main research areas are personal capitalism and British business history, and Schumperterian long waves and British industrial capitalism since the industrial revolution.

Jane Longmore is Head of the School of Humanities at the University of Greenwich. Her main research interests are the social and economic development of eighteenth-century Liverpool and in the field of education.

Derek Lynch is Lecturer in Politics at the University of Huddersfield. His research and publications are in the field of International Relations and External Public Diplomacy.

Monica McLean is Lecturer in the Department of Education at Keele University. She is responsible for a programme for academic staff which leads to a post-graduate certificate in teaching in higher education.

David Nicholls is Professor of History and Head of the Department of History and Economic History at Manchester Metropolitan University. His most recent books are *The Making of the British Middle Class?* and *Gender, Civic Culture and Consumerism*.

Tony Nicholson is Senior Lecturer in History at the University of Teesside. His main research and teaching interests are in modern British social and cultural history. He is course leader for the University's MA in history: culture, locality and heritage.

Christine Peterkin is Senior Lecturer in the Department of History at University College Worcester. Her specialist interest is in the social and political history of the United States.

John Peters is Principal Lecturer in History and a Learning Development Adviser at University College Worcester. He has published on the financial impact of World War I and is currently preparing a book on World War I for Routledge.

Mark Roseman is Senior Lecturer in Modern History at Keele University. His publications include *Recasting the Ruhr 1945–1958*, and *Generations in Conflict: Youth Revolt and Generation Formation in Germany 1770–1968*.

Patrick Salmon is Professor of International History at the University of Newcastle upon Tyne. His most recent publication is *Scandinavia and the Great Powers 1890–1940*.

Robert B. Shoemaker is Senior Lecturer in History at the University of Sheffield. His publications include *Gender in English Society, 1650–1850: The Emergence of Separate Spheres?*, and he is currently researching public conflict in eighteenth-century London.

Kathleen F. Slevin is Professor and Chair of Sociology at the College of William and Mary, Virginia, USA. Her research interests and publications are in the areas of gender, ageing and feminist theory.

Alistair Thomson is Lecturer at Sussex University and Vice-President of the

International Oral History Association. He is editor of *Oral History* and co-editor of *The Oral History Reader*.

John Tosh is Professor of History at the University of North London. He is the author of *The Pursuit of History: Aims, Methods and New Directions in the Study of Modern History*.

Chris Williams is Lecturer in History at the University of Wales, Cardiff. He specialises in the social and political history of modern Britain, and his publications include *Democratic Rhondda: Politics and Society, 1885–1951* and *Capitalism, Community and Conflict: The South Wales Coalfield, 1898–1947*.

Michael Winstanley is Senior Lecturer in History and Associate Dean for Teaching in Arts and Humanities at Lancaster University. His publications include works on the development of shopkeeping, rural society in Britain and Ireland, radical politics, the textile workforce and working-class housing.

Abbreviations and acronyms

CTI   Computers in Teaching Initiative, established by the Funding
               Councils in 1989 to support the use of computers in develop-
               ing university learning.
CVCP   Committee of Vice-Chancellors and Principals.
Dearing Report Report of the National Committee of Inquiry into Higher
               Education, chaired by Sir Ron Dearing, July 1997.
EHE   Enterprise in Higher Education Initiative, funded by DfEE
               1988–96 to encourage innovation in university teaching and
               learning via institutional support.
GNVQs   General National Vocational Qualifications
History 2000   FDTL-funded initiative for developing good practice in the
               teaching and learning of History.
HUDG   History at the Universities Defence Group, a subject associa-
               tion for professional historians in Britain
ICT   Information communications technology
IT   Information technology
ILT   Institute for Learning and Teaching in Higher Education.
               Established in 1999, as the UK-wide organisation to enhance
               the quality and status of learning and teaching, and set the
               standards of good professional practice.
NEH   National Endowment of the Humanities (USA)
NGfL   National Grid for Learning
RAE   Research Assessment Exercise
SEDA   Staff and Educational Development Association. Leading UK
               professional association helping university staff to develop
               teaching skills.
SRHE   Society for Research into Higher Education. Professional
               association for stimulating and co-ordinating research into
               higher education.
THES   *Times Higher Education Supplement*
TQA   Teaching Quality Assessment exercise. Organised by the

	Funding Councils in UK universities to assess the quality of education provided to students.
TLTP	Teaching and Learning Technology Programme, established by the Funding Councils in 1992 to make teaching and learning more effective by harnessing modern technology.
UCoSDA	Universities and Colleges Staff Development Association. Leading national body for helping staff improve teaching.

1 Alan Booth and Paul Hyland

Introduction: developing scholarship in history teaching

In his study of the cultures of disciplines, Tony Becher analyses the beliefs and modes of behaviour of the disciplinary 'tribes and territories' which constitute the primary allegiance of academics in higher education.[1] Each discipline has its sense of community, its traditions, symbols, myths and rituals, its distinctive networks of communication, conceptual and methodological structures, truth criteria, and values and beliefs. Together these constitute the cultural framework and norms (often tacit) which act as the means of socialisation and as the arbiters of professional behaviour, status and career progression. In this sense an academic discipline is also a site of organised power; including and privileging some voices, and excluding, restraining or marginalising others. Through it we are disciplined, both by the claims to truth of dominant power-knowledge networks and by ourselves, into ways of thought and behaviour which over time have become almost second nature.[2]

Disciplinary cultures are clearly subject to temporal and geographical variation, and any glance at the international historiography of the discipline reveals this to be true of history. There is no culture-free history. Thus, for example, 'even if you take a strong and clearly defined ideology such as Marxism, the English Marxist historian differs from the German Marxist historian, and both in their turn differ from the Russian.'[3] Yet while history cultures differ, professional status – which constitutes the central motivating force for individuals within the profession – is, in the 'developed' world at least, almost invariably tied to research and publication. It is here that prestige and power reside, though, of course, this dominance of research over teaching, administration and public service is itself only a relatively recent phenomenon. Since the 1950s, the research model has become the norm and a finely calibrated scale of status is now in place, along which some research areas are regarded as more 'rigorous', some journals are more highly regarded, some types of work (in archives) are more respected than others and some forms of proof making (copious footnoting) are more compelling. Concomitantly, activities which focus upon the synthesis of knowledge or attempt to engage with public audiences have become viewed as inferior forms of activity.[4] This competitive status hierarchy largely determines each individual's reputation and the possibilities of future career advancement in the subject.

The dominance of one aspect of scholarly activity in the reward system has powerful implications for the teaching of history which, in truth, occupies an uneasy place within our discipline. On the one hand it is an activity which occupies a significant amount of professional time, and represents a strong personal commitment for many academics. Thus a recent survey of over a thousand American historians demonstrated that the desire to teach had been an important factor in drawing many into the profession, and that interacting with students was regarded as a primary professional satisfaction, with many recognising that they influenced more people through their teaching than through their (increasingly specialised) research publications.[5] On the other hand, pedagogy is marginalised in our formal systems of communication and recognition – in the conferences we hold, the history journals for which we write, the books we publish, the prizes and fellowships we award, and the whole pattern of career progression. Moreover, as Michael Sherry points out, 'if the academy shapes our values, it also reflects them. The truth is that many of us, even among those who prize teaching, still regard it as not only less rewarded but less sophisticated and demanding than scholarship – simply the easier thing to do, or otherwise less worthy of note.'[6] Such a belief is born of a general lack of systematic discussion of pedagogic issues, the roots of which lie in a postgraduate training which is still overwhelmingly research oriented. Even today, little systematic training is provided for graduate students in the teaching of their subject; still less in methods for researching and developing their teaching. Yet this is understandable given the competition for tenured posts and the high importance placed upon research by most appointment and promotion panels.

The dominance of research extends to the history curriculum itself, which tends to be viewed primarily in terms of appropriate subject content or 'coverage'. Thus curriculum development is often equated with the addition of new topics in line with the developing research interests of individual members of staff. By extension, expertise in teaching tends to be regarded as a natural corollary of excellence in research. This was nowhere more apparent than in the Teaching Quality Assessment for History, held in Britain during 1993–94, which demonstrated that peer assessors clearly equated excellence in teaching with departments highly rated in research.[7] Confirming this, a recent report of the History at the Universities Defence Group (HUDG) to the national Quality Assurance Agency remarked:

> In constructing their programmes, departments and subject groups draw heavily on the research interests of their members, believing that the achievement of excellent teaching is often best obtained by encouraging lecturers to bring together their research and teaching. This is borne out by the combined results in History of the RAE [Research Assessment Exercise] and TQA [Teaching Quality Assessment].[8]

In some ways this close association of research and teaching has benefits for the latter. Most notably, the continual feeding of new research areas and ideas into teaching undoubtedly helps to keep the subject sharp and vibrant for staff and students. Thus, for example, historical research, particularly in social history, over the last three decades has enlivened the curriculum through the development of knowledge, approaches and issues in areas such as the study of popular culture, ritual and belief, gender, ethnicity, consumerism, sexuality and language. Such subjects have given history a relevance to new generations and new kinds of student, led to greater use of interdisciplinary approaches and of a greater range of primary sources, and fundamentally refashioned the sorts of question historians ask of their material. We need to recognise, however, that research dominance has also diverted attention away from pedagogic issues, and has led to a focus upon discovery to the neglect of an understanding of student learning in the subject. As Roland Marchand observes: 'What most dismays me about our performance as academic historians . . . is our lack of acute curiosity about the process of learning itself . . . we are apt to give too little attention to the relation between our teaching methods and student acquisition of the skills we envisage.'[9] The challenge is therefore to re-emphasise the importance and scholarship of teaching, to bring a research perspective to history teaching and learning, and to encourage teachers, in the words of Peter Stearns, to 'apply some of the same enthusiasm and creativity to curriculum development that have for decades marked research'.[10]

Given the lowly status accorded to scholarship in teaching, it is not surprising that pedagogic issues have traditionally received so little attention. This does not mean, however, that history teachers have been unresponsive to change, especially in the face of increasing class sizes, modularisation and the commonplace demands to 'do more with less'. Indeed, faced with the rapid changes of the last decade some individuals and groups in Britain, the United States and elsewhere have been involved in rigorous and creative experimentation in the teaching of the subject. This has been particularly evident in the general areas of 'active' and 'independent' or 'self directed' learning, whether through refinements to traditional modes of teaching and assessment or the use of new technologies. Many initiatives have been concerned to make history teaching more 'student centred', particularly in encouraging students to take greater responsibility for their own learning, as, for example, in work on student-led seminars, self and peer assessment, learning contracts and portfolios. Other innovations have focused upon extending the range of transferable skills developed in a history degree, through experiments in, for example, collaborative project work, work placement, fieldwork, study and learning skills, and the use of multimedia. Most of those engaged in developing new modes of teaching have been concerned to make learning objectives and outcomes more explicit, to take account of student progression, and to introduce variety in learning activities and ensure that assessment tasks reflect the full range of skills to be developed.[11]

Such activity has helped to enrich and extend the scope of history teaching, and to raise its profile, but it has not displaced traditional assumptions and practices. Indeed, in the United States it has led to a counter-blast from those

committed to teaching through 'traditional' methods, who are keen to emphasise the centrality of subject over skills, the importance of teacher direction, the
lecture mode of teaching, and the individual essay and essay examination as the
principal means of assessing competence. Thus, for example, Daniel Trifan
writes:

> Our most important function as history teachers is to instil a fundamental under-
> standing of history, not the arcane and recondite niceties of 'group process'. How
> to get along and work with others could just as well be taught by working on a
> homecoming float as in a class in which students are supposed to be learning an
> academic discipline. [. . .] In history, the student engages in a one-to-one relation-
> ship with the material, and the success or failure of this relationship is reflected in
> the course grade.[12]

In the UK there has been similar controversy over the appropriateness of teaching skills, and latterly over the best ways to develop history students' skills. In its
submission to the Dearing Committee on the future of higher education in
Britain, the HUDG noted: 'The main issue dividing the profession is not whether
their subject should offer training in transferable skills but whether that training
should be explicit . . . or be left implicit.'[13] Clearly, the issue of skills in history
contains multiple threads and a diversity of deeply held and entrenched positions.[14] Frequently, however, disagreement is founded upon differing views of the
purposes of a history education, and, indeed, higher education in general. All
too often the dominant discourse posits a fundamental distinction between traditional 'liberal' notions of the subject (as a high-level intellectual discipline
committed to pure scholarship and aimed at the training of historians) and
'vocational' emphases (regarded as centred upon low-level transferable skills and
oriented to preparing graduates for the employment market). Tutors with more
vocational sympathies frequently resort to different stereotypes, and point to the
responsibility of teachers to their students given that a mere 2 per cent of UK
history graduates actually become professional historians or history teachers in
schools, with the overwhelming majority finding employment in commercial and
other professional occupations.[15]

   Given the recurrent emphasis by governments upon the vocational and instru-
mental in higher education during the last two decades, it is not surprising that
this tension has increased, with arts subjects naturally on the defensive and
fearful for their future.[16] It seems to us, however, that such a dichotomous view
is unnecessary and unhelpful both to our discipline and our students: that there
is no essential dualism between skills and knowledge, between the intellectual
and the practical; and that rather they are intimately related. A large number of
academic, personal and interpersonal attributes interact to produce the high-
level learning which should characterise a university education in history.
Moreover, it is neither necessary nor desirable to divorce the intellectual development of students from the practical and often compelling problems of the
world beyond the university. Indeed, it may be argued that to enable history

students (like those in many other intellectually demanding disciplines) to practise and develop skills that will enable them to put their knowledge and abilities
to effective use outside the academy is itself an important goal of a history education. Intellectual development need not be at odds with market forces.[17] The
multinational company Proctor and Gamble is not alone in emphasising that
successful applicants for its general graduate vacancies display, above all, 'imagination, creativity and sharp analytical skills'.[18] So, too, knowing how to communicate an idea clearly and cogently to others (a transferable skill) requires
mental flexibility and analytical rigour as well as interpersonal skills and an
ability to project the voice. In learning, as in life, distinctions between intellectual and practical, academic and personal, and skills and knowledge, soon dis-
solve. For us, therefore, the important issue is not 'skills versus scholarship', but
how we can help students to become high-level learners in a way which will
prepare them to be critical, creative, independent and reflexive; all key attributes
for academic, personal or career success in society today.

Where individual history departments place themselves on the long
liberal–vocational continuum is therefore, in our opinion, their own concern. It
will necessarily differ according to their culture and the experiences, expectations and needs of their students, though the recent history of history teaching
suggests that 'as a rule of thumb, prestigious departments and universities are
more likely to be liberal than vocational, and less prestigious universities to be
vocational rather than liberal.'[19] Whatever blend of purposes and priorities is
chosen, at the core of all history education must be a commitment to developing high-quality student learning. This in turn necessitates a commitment to
expressing openly, clearly and confidently what we, as a discipline, believe such
learning to mean. Articulating this in an explicit fashion for ourselves, parents,
employers, government bodies, the general public and, most importantly, for students is, we believe, essential not only to help students to learn effectively but
also to preserve and promote the integrity of the subject in the years ahead.

It is perhaps time to say what we think the characteristics of high-calibre
history learning are. The following list draws upon recent discussions by historians and educationalists in Britain and the United States, and if it seems redo-
lent of the contentious issue of 'standards' we should say that our intention is
not to suggest minimum thresholds, which we believe do nothing to encourage
teaching and learning development in the discipline. Nor are we saying that every
history graduate must possess all of these attributes at the highest level; indeed,
even the most able students would find this challenging. Rather, our purpose is
to encourage tutors to think in terms of the transformation of student learning:
a task which involves encouraging and enabling students to change their understanding of history and of themselves, and enabling them to influence their own
transformation in a process which is at once intellectual and skilful, personal and
interpersonal, subject based and transferable, academic and applied.[20] Here a
history education is not seen primarily as the incremental addition of particular
skills and attributes which are to be developed in isolation, but as a holistic

process in which many qualities interact and support each other through a continuous process of enrichment. Thus the distinctiveness of a history education is embodied in the quality and coherence of its many elements.

Characteristics of high-level learning in history

- *The ability to seek out knowledge.* This requires the development of a range of research skills which are at the heart of independent and effective learning in any context. They include not only the ability to identify and investigate many different kinds of sources of information (including electronic and statistical), but also the confidence to do so based on a critical awareness of one's own abilities and an appreciation of the range of strategies available.
- *The ability to manage large, disparate and often incomplete bodies of information from a wide range of sources.* This involves building up factual knowledge from primary and secondary sources, sifting and synthesising it, identifying key elements, considering provenance and purpose, discriminating between the essential and peripheral, and structuring material in a systematic and logical fashion. It also involves the ability to work analytically and creatively to combine different types of source (e.g. literary, visual, numerical, material or oral), and to assess their values in the context of a particular problem or issue. Evaluative and decision-making skills are therefore fundamental to the realisation of this attribute.
- *The ability to understand and evaluate the conceptual and methodological frameworks which form the basis of historical knowledge and interpretation.* This requires an awareness of the key concepts and methodologies which have shaped the discipline – particularly of the importance of historiography – and the ability to apply this knowledge in relation to particular topics of study. More broadly, it involves a sense of how histories are made and of the discipline as a whole as a continuously evolving yet contested field of knowledge. This in turn may be linked to a wider awareness of how knowledge may be created and defined, and how we come to understand the world.
- *The ability to describe and explain the nature of past societies, and the forces of historical change and continuity within them.* This requires an awareness of general models of agency and causation, and an ability to compare groups, societies and cultures. Identifying the principal factors which shape a particular society or historical period, understanding the complex interactions between individuals and social groups and their environment, being able to identify fundamental shifts or turning points for societies and individuals, and to appreciate the complex interaction of many different kinds of causal factor are all central to this. It also requires a wide range of analytical and interpretative skills, and the ability to appreciate both the distinctiveness of past societies and their relationship to the structures and values of the modern world.

- *The ability to use historical knowledge and skills to develop one's own insights and interpretations.* This involves being able to see different approaches and perspectives on a historical topic, that meanings are usually contested, and that evidence and arguments are often incomplete and uncertain. It also involves developing the ability to compare and contrast differing points of view, to evaluate their merits, and being able to question received judgements and historical orthodoxy in order to come to one's own judgements. In order to develop their own frame of reference, creating new knowledge from old, students will need to gain considerable self awareness and the ability to apply past experience and previous learning to that process.
- *The ability to address and resolve problems.* This involves linking new knowledge with existing knowledge, and using the one to inform the other; identifying and clarifying problems, formulating hypotheses and examining alternative methods of solution, and explaining, testing and evaluating the preferred solution. These activities require high-order analytical and decision-making skills, and are integral both to the learning of history and to the addressing of practical problems encountered in employment.
- *The ability to think creatively within and beyond one's historical studies.* This involves students developing a critical imagination which allows them to connect empathetically with the past, ask imaginative questions of their material and be able to shape a view of a historical topic which can overcome source deficiencies by employing a combination of critical rigour and creative use of the available resources. It involves the constructive application of analytical thought; not merely the ability to question but to generate ideas and apply critical thinking in a creative fashion. It also means being receptive to new and challenging ideas and evidence, and thus requires reflexivity and flexibility.
- *The ability to work and learn with others.* This involves 'knowledge in action', as opposed to the mere possession of knowledge. It encompasses a great range of communication and social skills, including the clear and cogent use of language in various kinds of written and oral presentation, the ability to present statistical information graphically, and the use of information technology and visual means of representation. Clearly, strong interpersonal skills such as active listening, responding, networking, negotiating and helping others will be essential. The development of the self awareness and self confidence to promote one's own views and persuade others will also be important.
- *The ability to manage one's own learning within and beyond academic studies.* This involves the ability to action-plan, and to reflect critically upon one's own experiences and learning. It expresses a commitment to self development and a desire to discover more. These in turn suggest an active willingness to seek feedback from others, and an ability to identify areas for personal and academic development and to devise strategies to achieve them based upon an awareness of preferred learning styles and a realistic appreciation of context.

- *The ability to use knowledge and skills in a socially responsible and constructive manner*. This requires an understanding and appreciation of the importance of ethical issues and problems within and beyond historical studies. It also involves sensitivity and tolerance towards different value systems, and an active sense of citizenship and civic responsibility based upon critical reflection and personal integrity.

Here, the development of understanding and skills is part of a single educative process. Just as skills are required to gain understanding, so understanding enables students to apply their skills more effectively. So, while focused upon the subject matter of the discipline, a history education can be equally concerned with 'developing general qualities of a personal and social kind as well as those of an intellectual kind. It encompasses outcomes including communication skills, problem-solving abilities, interpersonal skills, planning and strategic thinking abilities and critical and evaluative skills, including logic.'[21] Critical and creative, and individual and collaborative, activities are all essential; all part of a desire to help students to become more capable of learning and acting independently. Integral to this is the ability to reflect systematically not only upon one's subject but upon oneself – to 'make connections between knowledge, self-understanding and actions' in ways which make learning and life come together.[22] At its best, a history education encourages us to make sense of ourselves as well as making sense of disciplinary knowledge, and to acquire, in Radford's words, 'practical high level skills combined with wider awareness (educational, cultural, and so on), personal autonomy and social responsibility'.[23] If it can meet such a transformatory agenda, then history might truly consider itself both an intellectual and practical subject, and live up to the claim made on its behalf by Geoffrey Elton, as 'the only subject that makes you grow up and takes you past adolescence'.[24]

Such an ambitious agenda is, of course, highly challenging for students; though challenge is an integral part of motivation and a defining feature of higher education. It is also demanding for history teachers struggling with the demands of larger classes, more administrative tasks and the pressures of research performance. It requires not only a sensitivity to the value and potential of teaching but also careful planning – thinking through the conditions which can generate such student learning, and designing teaching and assessment practices which help and expect students to demonstrate high-order abilities. This order of reflexivity requires experience and commitment, demanding, in Paul Ramsden's words, that 'teachers should, in fact, become scholars of their own students' learning', willing to interrogate carefully their own practice and systematically uncover their own and their students' prejudices and assumptions, in a process founded upon continuous experimentation and development.[25]

A full discussion of the many strategies that can be employed to promote and deliver high-level history education is not possible here. But at an individual or departmental level a useful starting point would be to conduct an audit of current thought and practice, asking the following kinds of question:

- What kinds of thing do we want our students to learn (knowledge, skills, concepts, methodologies, applications, values, etc.)?
- What are the opportunities that are provided to develop knowledge, practice skills, etc. (lectures, seminars, tutorials, group projects, fieldwork, work placements, etc.)?
- What kinds of assessment task are used to test the achievement of the key objectives (essays, exams, oral presentations, posters, projects, reports, etc.)?
- Who assesses the learning (tutors, student self assessment, peer assessment), and what criteria are used?
- What do current students and former graduates think are the most important or useful things that they learn from a history education, and what are the best ways to achieve them?
- How does the department review its practices and keep abreast of new thinking and innovations in teaching and learning?

Asking how far the answers to the above are in alignment can provide some useful insights and issues for investigation. These can be explored in many ways, including keeping a journal or portfolio of teaching experiences, using self-evaluation questionnaires on particular aspects of teaching, using student feedback, informal or formal discussion with colleagues, peer observation schemes or, more ambitiously, researching one's own teaching using action-research methodology.[26] Reflexivity need not therefore be a purely individual or intellectual process, but can be an imaginative and creative one involving others in investigations of what Schon notes are often 'messy but crucially important problems' of practice, through 'experience, trial and error, intuition and muddling through'.[27] Indeed, given the entrenched views sometimes evidenced in discussions of new teaching methods, there is much to be said for the view that in terms of ensuring quality in history teaching and the spread of good practice, 'we could do with less pontificating and more experimentation and enquiry'.[28]

In developing history teaching, it is clearly necessary both to examine the effectiveness of the conventional practices of tutors and departments, and to assess the benefits (and costs) of introducing enhancements and innovations. This process of evaluation, however, needs to be centrally informed by careful consideration of the extent to which current and new activities promote the attainment of the key goal of improving student learning in the discipline. Yet measuring how teaching processes affect the kind of learning that history students seek and attain within a particular course or programme is neither simple nor always comfortable, especially when it is one's own practices that are the subject of attention. Building teams of tutors who can share their experiences and opinions in a spirit of mutual support and cooperation can both help to reduce the sense of isolation and trepidation that tutors sometimes feel in relation to their teaching, and to ensure that as good practices and innovations are identified they are well understood by colleagues and can thus be more readily applied to a variety of other settings. Working with colleagues to review, research and innovate in history teaching therefore helps not only to promote the realisation of good practices and their testing under various conditions, but also to ensure that findings are more widely disseminated and embedded in the work of whole departments and the traditions of the discipline. Many of the essays which follow here are based upon such collaboration, through which tutors have addressed issues that are of common concern in history teaching and offered findings that can be used both to make improvements and to provide a foundation for further research and reflection.

To understand how teaching practices and contexts can be enhanced to improve the quality of learning, it is clearly necessary to listen to and examine carefully the views of history students. How they see their experiences of learning, what is expected of them, what problems they confront and how any changes introduced are likely to affect them are key questions that help to keep student learning at the forefront of attention in any review or development of teaching. These kinds of question have been asked by many of the contributors to this volume, using questionnaires, interviews, focus groups and class discussions to gather information and opinion. Some of the work reported here has also deliberately drawn students into the whole process of planning, testing and evaluating innovations, thereby helping to create a sense of common purpose and a shared responsibility for learning, and enabling students to gain valuable experience of working with their tutors through all the challenges and pleasures of research.

As in historical research, learning from other people's experiences and achievements is an essential ingredient of good scholarship in history teaching. This involves not only learning from the ideas and practices developed by tutors in other disciplines and institutions, but also from the vast array of research on teaching and learning in higher education. Such a prospect may, at first, seem daunting, particularly as some of the epistemology and methodologies of educational research may seem alien to the ways that most historians think and talk about their teaching. Yet there are considerable benefits. For while high-quality learning in history requires a distinctive kind of education, many of the challenges faced by history staff and students are generic problems to which much scholarly attention has been given. As Ramsden points out, 'there is consistent, replicated, research-based evidence that certain teaching approaches and strategies are associated with higher quality student learning',[29] and these findings offer both practical and time-saving ways forward for historians. Moreover, in representing a discipline of such fundamental importance to society and higher education, it is vital that as historians we should not only address the common issues and concerns of higher education, but use our scholarship to influence and contribute to the future patterns of its development.

In the essays here, many of the general principles of good teaching have been used to guide the research and development work that has been undertaken. Yet they also reflect the practical realities of developing teaching and good practice in the discipline – the 'swampy lowland where situations are confusing "messes" incapable of technical solution'.[30] They are the product of research, reflection and experimentation by individuals, and groups of individuals, facing particular problems or thinking critically and constructively through issues of disciplinary practice. There is therefore no attempt to produce absolute solutions or universally agreed practices, for in teaching none exist. The book does, however, offer advice on a wide range of issues of central importance to the teaching of history, and provides a starting point and aid to reflective practice for others interested in developing their teaching, whether as individuals or departments. We would like to think also that this volume of essays will provide a reference point for the development of good practice in the teaching of history as the subject enters a new century, and encourage the adoption of good practices and the development of scholarship in history teaching.

Notes

1 T. Becher, *Academic Tribes and Territories: Intellectual Enquiry and the Cultures of Disciplines* (Buckingham, SRHE/Open University Press, 1989). On disciplines and disciplinarity, see also P. Bourdieu, *Homo Academicus* (Cambridge, Polity, 1988); R. Usher, I. Bryant and R. Johnson, *Adult Education and the Postmodern Challenge* (London, Routledge, 1997), ch. 4; and D. Ryan, 'The impermeable membrane', in J. T. E. Richardson, M. W. Eysenck and D. W. Piper (eds), *Student Learning: Research in Education and Cognitive Psychology* (Buckingham, SRHE/Open University Press, 1989), pp. 185–97.

2 See M. Foucault, *Power/Knowledge: Selected Interviews and Other Writings* (Brighton, Harvester, 1980).

3 Anonymous historian quoted in Becher, *Tribes and Territories*, p. 22.

4 For a critical view of current views of scholarship and an attempt to address them, see C. Glassick, M. Huber and G. Maeroff, *Scholarship Assessed: Evaluation of the Professoriate* (San Francisco, Jossey-Bass, 1996).

5 See the *Journal of American History*, 81:3 (1994), the whole issue of which is devoted to a discussion of the results of this survey of 'The Practice of American History'.

6 M. Sherry, 'We value teaching despite – and because of – its low status', *Journal of American History*, 81 (1994), pp. 1051–4.

7 For a critical analysis of this exercise, see G. Brown, 'Assessing the quality of education in history departments', in A. Booth and P. Hyland (eds), *History in Higher Education* (London, Blackwell, 1996), pp. 298–319.

8 *Standards in History*, Final Report of a Working Party of the HUDG to the Quality Assurance Agency (London, HUDG, 1998), pp. 9–10.

9 R. Marchand, 'Further comment on Daniel D. Trifan's "Active learning: a critical examination"', *Perspectives*, 35 (1997), 29–33.

10 P. Stearns, *Meaning over Memory: Recasting the Teaching of Culture and History* (Chapel Hill, University of North Carolina Press, 1993), p. 111.

11 For examples of development work in History, see Booth and Hyland (eds), *History in Higher Education*; and R. Blackey (ed.), *Innovations in the Teaching of History* (Long Beach, University of California Press, 1993).

12 D. Trifan, 'Active learning: a critical examination', *Perspectives*, 35 (1997) 23–8. See

also replies by Oberly and Marchand in the same issue, and C. Meyers and T. Jones, *Promoting Active Learning: Strategies for the College Classroom* (San Francisco, Jossey-Bass, 1993).

13 HUDG, *Submission to the National Committee of Enquiry* (London, HUDG, 1997), p. 3.

14 For this debate in the humanities, see A. Assiter (ed.), *Transferable Skills in Higher Education* (London, Kogan Page, 1995); P. Cole, 'Transferable skills in the humanities', *New Academic*, 3 (1993); and no named editor, *Skills versus Scholarship in Arts and Humanities Higher Education: Proceedings of a Conference Hosted by the Humanities and Arts Higher Education Network*, Open University, 11 October 1997. For a critique of the language of skills, see R. Barnett, *The Limits of Competence: Knowledge, Higher Education and Society* (Buckingham, SRHE/Open University Press, 1994).

15 The returns on UK graduate employment are to be found in the annual publication *What Do Graduates Do?* (Manchester, Association of Graduate Careers Advisory Services).

16 On the ebb and flow of this debate, see H. Silver, *Education and History: Interpreting Nineteenth- and Twentieth-Century Education* (London, Methuen, 1983), part 2; and M. Allen, *The Goals of Universities* (Buckingham, SRHE/Open University Press, 1988).

17 For an interesting discussion on this subject, see the Council for Industry and Higher Education's *A Learning Nation* (London, CIHE, 1996).

18 *The Independent*, 9 April 1998, 'Fast Track' supplement, p. 7. For similar views see the Council for Industry and Higher Education's *Towards a Partnership: The Humanities for the Working World* (London, CIHE, 1990); and L. Harvey and S. Mason, 'A Quality Graduate', in J. Tait and P. Knight (eds), *The Management of Independent Learning* (London, Kogan Page, 1996), pp. 13–28.

19 Brown, 'Assessing the Quality', p. 306. For confirmation of this view, see C. Boys *et al.*, *Higher Education and the Preparation for Work* (London, Jessica Kingsley, 1989), ch. 2.

20 For discussion, see P. Nightingale and M. O'Neill, *Achieving Quality Learning in Higher Education* (London, Kogan Page, 1994); R. Barnett, *Improving Higher Education: Total Quality Care* (Buckingham, SRHE/Open University Press, 1992); Association of Graduate Recruiters, *Skills for Graduates in the 21st Century* (Cambridge, Association of Graduate Recruiters, 1995); HUDG, *Standards in History* and *History Subject Benchmarking Statement* (London, HUDG 1999); and Stearns, *Meaning over Memory*.

21 Nightingale and O'Neill, *Achieving Quality Learning*, p. 53.

22 Barnett explores this in *Higher Education: A Critical Business* (Buckingham, SRHE/Open University Press, 1997). He identifies eight types of self reflection: self reflection on disciplinary competence; educational reflection; critical reflection; reflection as metacompetence; the reflective practitioner; reflection as self realisation; reflection as social transformation; and societal reflection.

23 J. Radford, K. Raaheim, P. De Vries and R. Williams, *Quantity and Quality in Higher Education* (London, Jessica Kingsley, 1997), p. 178.

24 Elton quoted in the *Times Higher Education Supplement*, 17 January 1986.

25 P. Ramsden (ed.), *Improving Learning: New Perspectives* (London, Kogan Page, 1988), p. 13.

26 For useful practical introductions to a range of reflective practice methods, see L.
    Beaty, *Developing Your Teaching through Reflective Practice* (Birmingham, Staff and
    Educational Development Association, 1997); and T. Angelo and K. Cross,
    Classroom Assessment Techniques: A Handbook for College Teachers (San
    Francisco, Jossey-Bass, 1993).
27 D. Schon, *The Reflective Practitioner* (New York, Basic Books, 1983), pp. 43–4. Schon
    is the pioneer of reflective practice work. See also his *Educating the Reflective
    Practitioner* (San Francisco, Jossey-Bass, 1987).
28 Marchand, 'Further Comment', p. 33.
29 P. Ramsden, *Learning to Lead in Higher Education* (London, Routledge, 1998),
    p. 171.
30 D. Schon, *The Reflective Practitioner* (New York, Basic Books, 1983), p. 42.

Part I

Context and course design

Teaching and the academic career

After a decade in which the most prominent driving forces behind change in the higher education system in the United Kingdom have been the Research Assessment Exercise (RAE), increasing student numbers and the declining unit of resource, the last few years have seen suggestions of a change of emphasis. As the United Kingdom has moved away from an elite system of higher education (even if it has not yet developed a truly mass system), and as the course of economic and cultural change has raised ever more difficult questions about the skills of the labour force and the uncertainties of employment in an era of rapid technological development, so social and governmental pressures have been exerted upon higher education to ensure that an undergraduate degree represents more than purely academic certification (or the certification of retained knowledge). Governments have worked, over the past generation, to erode the privileged position of (especially) the old, chartered, pre-1992 universities.[1] And, over a longer period, academics have shifted from an institutional to a disciplinary loyalty.[2] These developments have taken place alongside the growth of the notion of the student as customer and consumer. Students, it is alleged, purchase a range of educational services appropriate to their particular needs and interests. But what guarantee does the student have of the quality of the product – the teaching – on offer? This, it has been argued, cannot be left to the market. Instead, teachers in higher education, as with their colleagues in primary and secondary education, should receive some formal certification. The degree programmes which they offer should be publicly accountable and audited. Over the last five years there has, too, been a rather belated realisation among government funding-bodies of the need for formal support and encouragement of improvements in teaching methods and in the understanding of student learning.

The Higher Education Funding Council for England/Department of Education for Northern Ireland's new Fund for the Development of Teaching and Learning has accorded some finance for the investigation and implementation of improvements in curriculum delivery and, more broadly, in teaching and learning. The National Committee of Inquiry into Higher Education, which produced the Dearing Report (1997), while by no means ignoring the research role of universities, placed unprecedented emphasis on the quality not only of teaching, but (and more importantly) of the learning to which that teaching contributed. Not least, the Report suggested the establishment of an Institute of Learning and Teaching in Higher Education (ILT), and began a debate as to whether membership of that Institute or associate membership might not be a precondition for the holding of a teaching post in higher education. Much has subsequently been made of the need to create a teaching profession in higher education, and the Dearing Report emphasised that there was a need for further research into teaching and learning – a call which others have revised, suggesting that what is needed is not so much more research as more understanding of the implications of the research already completed.

The consequences of these developments for universities and for the careers of individual academics remain uncertain. On the one hand, the RAE was established in 1988, before government attention turned to teaching and learning. It confirmed (or, occasionally, conferred) status. It brought money, or threatened to take it away. The Teaching Quality Assessment (TQA) system, as introduced in England in 1993, did not, and behind this disparity of treatment lay entrenched prejudices and assumptions. Teaching in higher education was something that came naturally – something that did not need to be, or could not be, taught.[3] The former assumption was the more comforting; the latter largely derived from suspicion of the discipline of education and the practices of staff development units. It appeared, too, to be more difficult to decide upon criteria for the recognition of excellent teaching and on their application in practice.

At the same time, largely led by the expansion in student numbers, aided and abetted by the decline in the unit of resource and given some added zest by the seeming determination of many institutions to allow a research culture to flourish (with the implication that this would be at the expense of thought about, and emphasis on, career progress in teaching), the 1980s and 1990s have witnessed a significant increase in the proportion of teaching undertaken by temporary and part-time tutors.[4] Viewed from one angle, this represents a cutting of costs, a casualisation of labour and a further degradation of the status of teaching. Viewed from another angle, it represents an opportunity to develop in graduate students an experience of teaching and a determination to enable gifted teachers, for whom permanent posts could not be found, to deploy their skills for the benefit of the student community.

On the mainland of Europe, the picture of higher education, its funding and priorities, and its juxtaposition of teaching and research, are very different. The relevance of developments in the USA, however, is much more immediate and far reaching. There, on the one hand, much more experience (and no little grief) has been accumulated in addressing the question of the preparation of graduate students for college teaching careers, while, on the other, a series of initiatives, originating in the Carnegie Foundation work of Ernest Boyer,[5] has recently been undertaken with the general aim of reviving undergraduate teaching in research-led institutions. In the absence of a national Funding Council, and with a proliferation of private colleges and universities (and now, for-profit institutions), it is the market that holds sway. Moreover, in the USA the number of institutions granting doctoral degrees is only about one-tenth of the number of those that award undergraduate degrees.[6] In the UK, almost all institutions award undergraduate, master's and doctoral degrees. Almost all, that is, have a claim to be preparing future members of the profession.

What follows here is an investigation of the relationship between research and teaching at the critical moments of appointment and promotion, and of the importance given to teaching in career training. Our research was set in the context of the actual circumstances of appointment and, indeed, promotion, as practised by higher education institutions, their history departments[7] and the heads of those departments in the late 1990s. We circulated a lengthy questionnaire to 100 heads of history departments and received 58 replies: 29 from old universities, 13 from new universities, 10 from university colleges and 6 from respondents who did not indicate the title of their institution.

Teaching and the appointment process

Two-thirds of respondents to our questionnaire reported that teaching issues were 'very important' in the specification of their most recently advertised junior post; one-third that they were 'moderately important'; none that they were 'unimportant'. Only two institutions had advertised for a post without specification of the content of the teaching required. Interestingly, positive replies were received from 60 per cent of the institutions in answer to the question, 'Did the job specification relate to teaching style and methodology?', and new universities were more likely to include such specifications. This seems a surprisingly high proportion, given that such matters rarely appear in advertisements, and we conclude that these are specifications developed internally and perhaps sent to candidates as 'further particulars'. Similar questions were asked with respect to the advertising of senior appointments: here the number reporting the specification of content fell to about three-quarters, presumably as a consequence of the departmental urge to 'get the best person regardless', while over 40 per cent claimed to specify issues of teaching style and methodology. Fifty-five per cent of all respondents reported that senior appointments were designed to produce the best research candidate; 24 per cent that this was not the intention. In general, a focus on research area and quality was a characteristic both of pre- and post-1992 universities, but less so of colleges of higher education.

In relation to the process of appointment itself, while almost three-quarters of departments reported that all their members were involved, 40 per cent also asserted that only the formally constituted panel was involved. This contradiction may reflect uncertainties about the precise procedures involved in the appointment process, particularly with regard to permanent as against temporary posts. Only 14 per cent of respondents reported using formal advertisements for the appointment of hourly paid staff. These tutors more usually were selected by the head or members of the department in half of our institutions. Nearly 60 per cent of departments asked referees for specific comment on the teaching experience and quality of candidates.

With regard to the conduct of interviews, three-quarters allocated responsibility for asking questions about teaching to one member of the appointment panel, yet it was striking that 14 per cent of respondents did not require candidates to outline their teaching experience and strengths during the interview. Over 90 per cent of departments required candidates to give a presentation and about the same proportion specified its nature and form. The information on teaching strengths and skills most likely to impress interview panels was that provided by the presentation, followed by the reference, and then the evidence of the interview and the 'general ability to communicate'. Only three replies mentioned the 'quality of ideas about teaching' or evidence of 'thought given to the learning process'. Responses from the three types of institution suggest that, as a general trend, old universities are more likely to emphasise references, whereas new universities are more likely to emphasise performance at the interview and presentation, and the ability to communicate well.

Of those recently appointed, only one had no experience of teaching and, given the recent expansion of various types of teaching for postgraduate students, many noted that current applicants are now better prepared for teaching than was the case five years ago. Thus one respondent noted: 'In general, young staff are less arrogant and more aware of the importance of teaching for the health and development of their subject than previously. Widening access and non-standard entry students have also posed real challenges. It is a healthy culture-shift which enhances both teaching and research.' Half of the forty-two respondents who gave reasons for this change referred to the growing proliferation of temporary teaching posts. Eight attributed the change to 'formal teacher training'; six to 'more commitment to teaching' or 'more interest in new approaches to teaching'; and four to the 'increased competitiveness of the job market'. One respondent pointed to the 'higher average age at appointment'.

Training of new teachers

Among newly appointed staff, permanent colleagues were given reduced teaching loads in three-quarters of responding departments. The corresponding figure for temporary staff was about 10–12 per cent. Of the nineteen institutions with stipulations as to how this reduced teaching time should be spent, seven already required teacher training and four expected participation in curriculum development. Eight institutions, by contrast, currently required their new staff to attend primarily to research and publication. The difference between old universities (which tended to require or encourage research) and the new universities and colleges (which tended to require or encourage teacher training/curriculum development) was statistically significant. Only one of the old universities reported that it looked for teaching development during the reduced teaching time; none of the new universities and colleges required that time to be devoted to research.

Even where there was reliance on hourly paid tutors, those colleagues were likely to be given some training. Forty-two institutions provided some training in teaching and examining for hourly paid tutors. While this appears to be a reassuringly high figure, such arrangements appeared to be very much *ad hoc*. For new permanent faculty, induction programmes were nearly ubiquitous, and in about a third of institutions departmental programmes supplemented those offered on an institution-wide basis. The consistency of practice with respect to mentoring was less clear. Old universities were rather more likely to offer departmental induction, but this may reflect more varied practice in combining departments at other institutions. With regard to the role of the new ILT in the training of new staff, opinion was (predictably) divided. About a third of all respondents opposed the idea of the ILT accrediting a generic programme for new teachers, and the proportion of those opposing the accreditation of discipline-specific programmes was slightly higher. Rather surprisingly, views as to whether or not completion of associate membership should be a prerequisite for appointment were quite evenly balanced. In general, there was little sign of respondents believing that the art of teaching was something with which one was born, and support for training was widespread. However, one respondent stated that, 'we have allowed training to pass into the heads [sic] of educationalists, who "train" staff in "ideal" methods, not in (a) departmental methods (b) realistic methods given constraints (c) subject-specific methods'.[8] Another noted that 'quality teaching requires time more than anything else',[9] a view that appears to be widely held.

In relation to staff development more generally, over three-quarters of departments had their own staff development policy and two-thirds had specific staff development requirements. Old universities were least likely to have such a policy, but still the majority of them did. This suggests that the idea of up-dating skills to maintain membership of the ILT may be easier to introduce than has been thought. Encouragement, whether formal or informal, for the continuing professional development of faculty seems likely to have as much impact on the enhancement of the status of teaching and the quality of learning as does any requirement for membership of the ILT. The practice of peer observation of teaching has been accepted in just over half of the institutions surveyed: 40 per cent of old universities and as many as 70 per cent of the new institutions. There will, no doubt, continue to be debate as to the relationship between enhancement and judgement, collegiality and hierarchy, in the observation of teaching, but its potential in terms of its ability to foster the 'pedagogical conversation' remains considerable.

Promotion and career progress

Promotion is clearly predicated upon excellent performance, yet about two-thirds of departments surveyed did not have an agreed understanding as to what constitutes either competence, professionalism or excellence in teaching. Of the remaining third, five departments had a definition of competence, four of professionalism and six of excellence. Definitions included reference to university guidelines (3), approval of external examiners (1), record of innovation (3), student performance/evaluation (5) and 'general teaching quality' (9). One department reported that it related 'excellence' to 'creative achievements recognised at national levels'.

About 60 per cent of respondents could recommend colleagues with distinguished records in teaching (however defined) for promotion.[10] This was most clearly the case in old universities: indeed, different institutional types ensured that the responses on this issue were among the most polarised of any in the questionnaire. There was some evidence that heads of department themselves were uncertain of the institutional procedures and priorities.[11] The ability to recommend discretionary increments was available to almost the same proportion of department heads, though it was heads in old universities who were most likely to have this opportunity. In submitting materials on candidates for promotion, twenty heads required a critical self analysis of teaching; thirty-three did not. In rather more cases there was encouragement to provide such a document. In judging teaching skills there was a reliance on internally generated opinion: only three institutions required a reference specific to teaching, and in over a quarter it was not the practice even to ask referees for an opinion on teaching issues. Even where formal internal references were sought, those who did not ask for an opinion on the candidate's teaching experience and competence outnumbered those who did by a ratio of two to one. By contrast, thirty-one departmental heads and colleagues used student evaluations in their consideration of candidates, while twenty-two did not. In a few cases, the inclusion of student evaluation was at the request of the candidate, and more than half of our respondents thought that the emphasis which their institution placed upon such student evaluations was increasing.

The vast majority of promotion committees and procedures considered each candidate's record in teaching, research and administration, and a few institutions also considered the rather American concept of 'service' (though to the institution rather than to the wider community). Very few operated a formal weighting system: those that did were most likely to be from within the old universities. In almost a quarter of institutions, promotion could be achieved as a result of excellence in one area regardless of achievement or performance in the others. One respondent reported: 'I'm inclined to say yes, with regard to research – in practice', hinting at what, anecdotally, many historians believe: that whatever promotions criteria require and procedures specify, not much more than token acknowledgement is paid to teaching. It was noted: 'Lip service is paid to teaching but status and promotions, and the resource allocation to Departments is based on research.' In this respect, it is tempting to assume that little change has been effected since the early 1990s. The lesson drawn from the first round of quality audits by the then Higher Education Quality Council was that despite statements of criteria, 'excellence in teaching was still not afforded the same weight as research when promotions decisions were being made'.[12] Only one respondent suggested that 'careers can be made from the rhetoric of "learning and teaching"'; on the other hand, a number of institutions reported the imminent introduction of specific recognition in career progress for teaching excellence.[13]

Our attempt to ask about the professionalism of the treatment by promotion committees of materials submitted on teaching was vitiated by the variety of procedures involved and the small size of the sample. Questions about perceptions of the conduct and the predilections (not to say biases) of promotion committees also produced poor response rates. But they did show that research performance was thought to be heavily weighted: twenty-seven respondents thought this was the case, with only three disagreeing. A mere six believed teaching to be more heavily weighted, and only three administration. In old universities, unsurprisingly, eighteen believed research to be favoured by career progress committees, with only one respondent doubting that. Seven of forty-six institutions reported that professorships might be awarded on the basis of teaching excellence. Twelve (of which two were old universities) awarded professorships for pedagogic excellence,[14] but there was some hesitancy in describing how 'excellence' was defined, which may be due to the ignorance of departmental heads as to the nature of discussions in promotion committees.

Conclusions

We have investigated some of the attitudes, priorities and practices of historians as expressed at a time of considerable change and uncertainty. Like colleagues in other disciplines, historians are apparently being pulled in a number of directions. In a number of places, heads of department feel that institutional difficulties are constraining their ability to respond positively to teaching issues. However, it was notable that neither in the questionnaire nor in the interviews did we ever gain the impression that improvements made for TQA, or subsequent to it, had been other than permanent. The complex impact of the RAE and the TQA on staff commitment to, and the quality of, teaching, was described by one respondent as follows: 'The commitment to teaching remains strong, but there is a greater tendency to employ teaching assistants as a means of freeing up time for research by full-time members of staff . . . Paradoxically I can see no evidence that the quality of teaching has declined. It certainly is much more imaginative than ten years ago.' The same respondent's general comments continued:

Successive principals of the university have gone out of their way since the early 1980s to emphasise the importance of research, though the university remains officially committed to promoting research and teaching at the highest levels. This has been accompanied by a sharp deterioration in staff–student ratios. Nevertheless, in my opinion standards of teaching have probably risen. Several new colleagues appointed in the last five years, though chosen primarily for their qualities as researchers, have proved to be remarkably diligent, imaginative and effective teachers. Teaching assistants, with very few exceptions, have also won widespread student support for their work.

What, a number believed, was most needed was time: 'The main point I should like to make is that despite RAE emphasis on research output, teaching issues are more seriously considered than ever before. The only (!) conflict is in relation to the *time* which colleagues have for all their duties. Pressure is high in all areas.' This emphasis upon time was striking. The gloomier view was rare, though in one new university it was reported that, as a result of the RAE:

> There has been a marked increase in casual and hourly employment, with little or no institutional support for the individuals doing this work. Training systems and staff development are restricted to permanent members of staff, creating a kind of casualised ghetto of insecure employment, undertaken by extremely dedicated, but largely untrained recent post-graduates.

Distinctions between old and new universities and colleges were more complex than might have been expected: the number of occasions in the questionnaire in which there was a statistically significant difference in replies was small. The willingness of new universities and colleges to enter the research competition, and their insistence that new, even temporary staff, should be full participants in that, are sufficiently evident from the language of job advertisements in the *Times Higher Education Supplement* (*THES*). One college respondent remarked that 'development of teaching skills is now "compulsory" . . . but a few exceptions are still allowed for staff with urgent RAE commitments'. There is, equally, evidence of a sense of regret among department heads and individual faculty members at the insistent pressures of the RAE. Moreover, while research strength brings (or ought to bring) financial reward to departments and to individuals, teaching strength is not similarly acknowledged. At present, it barely brings financial reward to departments, and this reinforces an institutional reluctance to reward excellence in teaching at the individual level. Thus one new university respondent concluded that 'in this department and university, research has been prioritised recently but that has really been to partially redress an earlier imbalance. Across the university as a whole, teaching (rightly) predominates. In this department, we are approaching a more even balance of attention, though not reward.' Whether such balance can be maintained in the absence of specific and individually accessible rewards may be doubted. Much as one might wish to rely upon collegiality, this seems, in the current climate, a thin reed. Pressures upon new teachers are clearly increasing. This can be gauged, at its crudest, from the advertisements for posts published in the *THES*. A substantial proportion are for temporary appointments, and are often fractional appointments at that.[15] Sometimes the language used (perhaps by the personnel office, perhaps by the department) is anything but welcoming: 'You must be worthy of submission as research active in the next RAE and will be expected to develop and teach modules at both honours and sub-honours levels.' This was for a two-year post in medieval history.[16] One part-time, half-year post sought an 'ideal candidate [who] would have a Ph.D and teaching experience'. Research is most often emphasised, not only in permanent but even in temporary posts. An early-modern religious history tutor was sought for one year by a department which wanted someone to

> teach and examine BA and MA courses at both undergraduate and postgraduate level; provide seminars as required and carry out advanced research. The successful candidate will have some teaching experience and ideally will have been awarded a doctorate or will be close to submitting their dissertation. The department places emphasis on the fostering of a 'research culture' and the successful candidate will be able to demonstrate a strong commitment to research.[17]

This was for a post covering staff leave. It is rare indeed (and refreshing) for a department simply to invite 'applications . . . from outstanding scholars to meet the Department's teaching needs'. One twelve-month post, covering research leave, was to be filled by someone who, 'in addition to offering replacement teaching on certain undergraduate courses . . . will be expected to develop and teach undergraduate and Master's degree courses which reflect her/his specialist interests. Applicants should have a strong research record, together with experience of teaching and administration.'[18]

The evidence is largely that appointees are already better prepared (even if it is a matter of learning-by-doing) than they used to be in meeting the demands placed upon them. But of longer-term significance is the relationship between the demands placed upon temporary post-holders and the preparation which they will have to have acquired during their doctoral studies. The emphasis on 'proven teaching experience' will, perhaps, translate, in a few years' time, to associate membership of the ILT. How will that be gained? Doctoral studies may have to include, alongside the completion of a research dissertation, training in teaching – and teaching in practice. One consequence might be that a number of institutions – those which produce a large number of entrants to the profession – subsidise the rest. However, so long as a very broad range of institutions offer doctoral degrees in the UK, the level of subsidy will not be as great as it is in the USA, where only a very small number of the total higher education institutions award doctorates. That minority thus provides teacher training to entrants: and many entrants to the profession, trained in research universities, find themselves employed teaching in institutions with little or no research facilities or commitment, and with an understandable and justifiable teaching mission.[19] The commitment to teaching *and* research in all UK institutions helps to mitigate the problems – especially the disillusionment of young faculty – that afflict the USA.[20] But it remains the case that young professionals, who have had their first experience of teaching in a (comparatively) well-resourced department and with students who are, in terms of educational qualifications, highly qualified, are likely to find that most posts require rather different skills. It also appears to be the case that graduate students/temporary appointments are more likely to be undertaking the teaching of courses in the first year of a degree programme, precisely at the point at which the differences in preparation and expectation between students will be greatest. Those responsible for the development of the remit of the ILT have taken on the question of the importance of transferring the credits acquired by aspiring associate members: it might also be worth considering whether it should be a requirement that such members acquire experience in more than one institution. Certainly, cooperation between institutions, locally or regionally, ought to be encouraged.

There is a need for departments, in their appointments policy, to shift the emphasis away from knowledge of *content per se* to a broader consideration of *method* and *purpose* in the context of institutional and departmental missions and of student preparedness and expectation. Institutions still shy away from the thoroughness with which American colleges and universities approach the task of advertisement, screening and interview. Telephone discussions, meetings between members of a search committee and, perhaps, eight or ten candidates at the American Historical Association Convention, followed by three or four finalists visiting the campus for two days of presentations, discussions and interviews: that is a characteristic routine, and not only for tenure-track posts. By contrast, one major institution in this country gave an applicant for a temporary post the blessing of a mere twenty-minute interview. The depth and collegiality of the Pedagogic Colloquium, as outlined by Lee Shulman when he was President of the Carnegie Foundation for the Advancement of Teaching, and as developed at, for example, Stanford, is absent from UK practice.[21] Even David Gosling, in his meticulous review of the ways in which appointing committees might ensure that they hire a 'good teacher', refers to the 'relatively short space of time' and the 'limited time available on the interview day'.[22] It is hard to avoid the impression that, while pressures of time might be the proffered justification, the whole process of appointment is still lodged in the assumptions of an elite and amateur educational system – in which all doctoral supervisors were known and trusted (or otherwise).

In the UK, appointment practice – and timing – currently seem often to be driven by the need to plug a hole in the curriculum. Equally, 'performance at presentation' seems to reflect a rather narrow judgement. It is obviously important to judge the strengths and weaknesses of a candidate's 'preparation, level, delivery, and clarity'. One old university looked for 'enthusiasm first; interest (novelty) of content . . . and style, second equal'. But these surely need to be set in the context of an understanding of pedagogy. Only one return mentioned 'ability to foster student-centred learning' as an element in their departmental definition of the professional teacher. Another new university noted the need to 'assess whether a candidate could deal with teaching requirements for our types of students'. That clearly is crucial, especially given the recruitment of new teachers from universities which have high numbers of graduate students and atypical undergraduates. But a conversation in which the department went to some lengths to outline the strengths, weaknesses, needs and interests of its students might be a more productive approach.

More broadly, we believe that there is quite a pressing need for departments to give collegial attention to teaching and learning issues. Much of the focus of recent discussion has been geared to ways of recognising excellent teachers. We would underline what Gibbs and others have stressed: that excellence in teaching involves discussion and planning, as well as delivery.[23] Teaching is still viewed by some faculty as the last bastion of rugged individualism.[24] We did not, in our questionnaire, ask whether departments were increasing the time they spent talking about teaching and learning, though anecdotal evidence suggests that they are. More attention is being paid both to the reports of external examiners and to the discussion of annual monitoring exercises. Whether more planning is taking place is doubtful. The extent of the deployment of 'course teams', their remit and responsibilities, and their reporting routes, is currently unclear.[25] So are the respective advantages of departmental conversation and course-group structure. A number of recently appointed faculty members told us that they found teaching almost a private matter, in contrast to the extensive discussion of research plans and achievements, and in a number of cases this contrasted with their experience of graduate work. Their research had been an (often unhealthily) private matter: it was in their occasional teaching that they had been able publicly to express their fascination with the discipline and to talk about it.

There is widespread support for training in teaching for new entrants to the profession.[26] This is, though, combined with a continuing hesitation as to the most effective, relevant and economical method of training. Doubts over the suitability of educationalists and, indeed, of staff development units, in leading these programmes are widely shared. This poses a difficult issue for the ILT and for universities as they draw up their courses for the accreditation of teachers. We are moving, though slowly, towards definitions and understandings of teaching excellence; and rather more deliberately towards a summary of professionalism and competence. We have yet to bring the educational research on this into departmental practice.[27] 'Conscientiousness, punctuality, preparedness, availability' was how one college understood excellence; another put it in negatives: 'no complaints and no noticeable exodus from units'. We lack a common understanding of excellence: as one respondent replied, 'who knows [how excellence is defined] – it seems very idiosyncratic'. Equally, we need more understanding than we currently have as to the range of strengths and weaknesses that a teacher may have – and of the range of strengths essential, and weaknesses tolerable, according to student and institutional interests and concerns. We lack an accessible language for discussing pedagogy. An unwillingness to accept the language of educational researchers has been as characteristic of departments of history as it was of the last Conservative governments. Worse, the language of accreditation and accountability, of assessment and of audit, has been thrust in front of academics; the historians among them no less disdainful and fearful than others. By no means always, but, we suspect, too often, we have taken refuge, while discussing teaching, in the anodyne, in the apologetic. It is striking that the range of 'scores' in the TQA exercise is much more compressed than that in the RAE, and it is symptomatic of the failure of language and of nerve that the TQA procedure has now reduced the role of the observation of teaching. One of the key tasks for the future will be to carry forward the debate as to the nature of excellence in teaching. The much-lauded dissemination of good practice will clearly be necessary, but it will not be sufficient. It will inevitably have to be tested against the specific circumstances of each group of historians and history students, and in that process the heads of history departments will have a crucial role to play.

Notes

1 Hereafter, these institutions are referred to as 'old'; 'new' is used to describe the polytechnics which became universities in 1992.
2 See U. Teichler, 'The conditions of the academic profession', in P. A. M. Maassen and F. A. Van Vught (eds), *Inside Academia: New Challenges for the Academic Profession* (Utrecht, Centre for Higher Education Policy Studies, 1996), p. 51.
3 Compare Elton's view that 'Inevitably, in an untrained profession, excellence is likely to be extremely rare': L. Elton, 'Dimensions of excellence in university teaching', *International Journal of Academic Development*, 3 (1998), 8–9. For an American perspective, see R. M. Diamond, *Serving on Promotion and Tenure Committees* (Bolton, MA, Anker Pub. Co., 1995).
4 There is a great need for consistent terminology. Part-time tutors may have permanent contracts; full-time tutors may have temporary contracts. The UK has, strikingly, seen an increase in teaching undertaken by temporary and part-time staff. It has not seen increasing use of confirmation of appointment as a hurdle which substantial numbers are expected to fail. There has probably, too, been a decline in mobility between institutions other than in terms of movement to professorships.
5 E. Boyer, *Scholarship Reconsidered* (Princeton, Princeton University Press, 1990).
6 A recent survey by Ted Margadant (presented to the American Historical Association Convention, January 1999), which looked at the 140 programmes which produced at least two PhDs over the period 1987–98, shows with brutal clarity just how the institutions with the twenty largest doctoral programmes dominate the rest. Of the 3,194 PhDs they produced, 1,218 secured tenure-track positions, compared with 377 of the 1,373 PhDs from the next twenty largest programmes.
7 One of our problems in following through this project has been the multiplicity of organisation within institutions, which has meant that history can, and on occasion is, submerged, and lacks, not least for the purposes of our enquiry, administrative autonomy and disciplinary coherence.
8 See T. A. Angelo: 'Faculty needs are often problem-centered, while faculty-develop-

ment programs typically are topic-centered', in 'From *faculty* development to *academic* development', American Association for Higher Education, *Bulletin*, June 1994, p. 5.

9 This claim might be thought to run counter to research findings for the USA at least. See J. Hattie and H. W. Marsh, 'The relationships between research and teaching: a meta-analysis', *Review of Educational Research*, 66:4 (1996), 507–42: 'time on teaching is unrelated to teaching evaluations'(p. 516) and 'time on teaching is not related to quality of teaching' (p. 528). But note the reliance on student evaluation as a measure of teaching quality.

10 Interpretation of the responses on promotion was rendered difficult by the varying practices and terminology used across the sector. One respondent put the point forcefully: 'I suspect that this questionnaire assumes standardisations that do not exist, and that its findings will be vitiated either by apparent similarities which conceal differences or by the reverse. It is impossible to explain procedures or indeed values in terms which are so generalised on the one hand, and so particular on the other.'

11 For an unusual review of the impact of one institution's system, see R. Emanuel's two articles, both entitled 'Does teaching really count towards promotion?', in the University of Glasgow's *Bulletin*, April 1991 and June 1992.

12 *Learning from Audit* (London, 1994), quoted in G. Gibbs, 'How can promoting excellent teachers promote excellent teaching?', *Innovations in Education and Training International*, 32 (1995), 75.

13 Reporting the findings of an international survey, Teichler noted that 18 per cent of 'middle-rank' and 23 per cent of 'junior staff' at English universities, across the disciplines, believed that 'teaching effectiveness should be the primary criterion for the promotion of faculty' (n.b.: 'effectiveness' not 'excellence'): 'Conditions', p. 36.

14 For a summary and evaluation of recent developments in the USA, see M. T. Huber *et al.*, *Scholarship Assessed* (San Francisco, Jossey-Bass 1997).

15 A number of respondents confessed to difficulty in replying to parts of the questionnaire as no, or very few, permanent appointments had been made in the 1990s.

16 *THES*, 5 June 1998. A sister department at the same university sought a person for *five* months 'to contribute to the teaching and assessment of Old and Middle English language and literature, chiefly at undergraduate level, and also to contribute to the School's research'.

17 *THES*, 26 June 1998.

18 *THES*, 17 March 1998. The notion of developing courses within a one-year appointment is an odd one. To rub salt into the wound, the department went on to 'welcome applications for half-year appointments' within the twelve months.

19 Thus 54 per cent of PhDs from the twenty largest programmes in the USA awarded in 1987–98, who had secured tenure-track posts, were teaching in institutions without PhD programmes. That figure rose to 73 per cent for the next twenty largest programmes. *ex inf* Margadant, n.6 above.

20 There is an interesting, if indirect, comment on this point in M. Shattock, 'The challenge ahead', *THES*, 14 August 1998. One of our respondents argued that 'a glut of highly qualified young staff is currently available': a straw in a wind blowing from the USA.

21 See, for example, P. Hutchings, 'The pedagogical colloquium: taking teaching seriously in the faculty hiring process', in D. DeZure (ed.), *To Improve the Academy* (Stillwater, OK, New Forums Press, 1997), pp. 271–94.

22 D. Gosling, 'Recruiting good teachers', *New Academic*, 6 (1997), 11–15.

23 Gibbs, 'Promoting excellent teachers', pp. 74–84, and his 'Promoting excellent teaching is harder than you'd think . . .', *Change*, 27:3 (1995), 16–20.

24 Compare the situation reported from Australia in 1992: 'many academics feel threatened by the thought of seeing their teaching activities as being open to scrutiny and debate in the same way as research activities are. There is a sense that teaching is a more private activity than research': C. McNaught and J. Anwyl, 'Awards for teaching excellence at Australian universities', *Higher Education Review*, 25 (1992), 38–9.

25 See, for example, Elton, 'Dimensions of excellence', pp. 4–5.

26 Indeed, it is arguable that the ILT has arrived just in time. Without it, the UK might have reached the American position in which undergraduate programmes depend upon teaching assistants, but in which those assistants receive financial support but, often, distressingly little pedagogical training. The situation obviously varies from institution to institution and from campus to campus, but while the Pew Charitable Trusts now fund a 'Preparing future faculty' programme which operates in fifteen institutions (and extends from these centres to regional partners), we also find (e.g. at the University of California, Los Angeles) that 'veteran teaching assistants teach the courses on how to be a T.A.' (*Chronicle of Higher Education*, 13 November 1998, p. A11). For recent comment on 'Preparing future faculty', see American Historical Association, *Perspectives*, January 1999; for its web site, see <http://www.preparing-faculty.org/>; and for a sample report of the position in the past decade, see R. M. Diamond and P. J. Gray, *1997 National Study of Teaching Assistants* (Syracuse, Anker Pub. Co., 1998).

27 See, for example, Elton, 'Dimensions of excellence', or Gibbs, 'Promoting excellent teaching'.

3 Alan Booth

Creating a context to enhance student learning in history

In the early part of this century, the principal objective of history teaching was the transmission of an agreed body of knowledge to students who, in the provincial universities at least, were often destined to become schoolteachers. As one literary historian put it: 'The student learns a subject that he may teach that subject in order that that subject may continue to be taught.'[1] Learning the subject meant that the student's role was essentially to assimilate thoroughly, and reproduce in examinations, the knowledge imparted by tutors. This, in distilled form, was represented in what has been termed the 'great tradition' of history teaching in schools, where, as David Sylvester notes:

> The history teacher's role was didactically active; it was to give pupils the facts of historical knowledge and to ensure, through repeated short tests, that they had learned them. The pupil's role was passive; history was a received subject. The body of knowledge to be taught was also clearly defined. It was political history with some social and economic aspects, and it was mainly British history, with some European, from Julius Caesar to 1914.[2]

Implicit in this 'transmission theory' of teaching and learning is the conception that if the person imparting the knowledge knows the material thoroughly, and delivers it competently, then students should learn. If students fail to do so, then it is likely to be their own fault, the result primarily of lack of interest or ability.

Although such crude conceptions have disappeared from teachers' declared objectives, what is actually practised in lectures and seminars is not always so dissimilar to the transmission model. This difference between 'espoused theory' and 'theory in use', between what teachers say they do and what they actually do, has often been remarked upon.[3] In terms of learning, much research into student learning over the past twenty years has pointed out that learning is a process in which what students do themselves is more important in determining what is learned than what tutors do.[4] Teaching is therefore fundamentally about making student learning possible. This has several important implications. First, it puts the student at the centre of activity. Second, it emphasises that teaching and learning are part of a single dynamic process. Third, it suggests the need for tutors to adopt a facilitative rather than a transmissive role, employing methods which encourage students to engage actively with learning tasks. Finally, it indicates the importance of understanding how students themselves think and feel about learning.[5]

In terms of understanding the factors influencing student learning, as Tennant points out, most explanations emanate from perspectives which either take the person or the social environment as their point of departure.[6] Thus there have been prominent attempts over the last twenty-five years to explore students' 'learning styles' – whether, for example, a student is reflective or impulsive, a converger or diverger, a serialist or holist – and the influence of personality traits on learning.[7] Such approaches underline the importance of the individual student, and thus acknowledge tutors' own experience that students differ markedly in how they learn. However, they can, if too narrowly interpreted, be taken to imply that individual preferences or traits are fixed. Most influential in the recent literature, therefore, have been approaches which recognise that, while students do have particular preferences and habits of learning, most are likely to adapt their approach to learning according to their understanding of the task demanded, the assessment practices employed, and what they generally perceive is required and likely to be rewarded by tutors in a particular course setting.[8] As Nicol puts it in a review of this research: 'Learning is now understood to be "situated" in academic and disciplinary contexts that influence not only how students construct their subject knowledge, but also how they construct interpretations of how they are supposed to learn, what is worth learning and what it means to be a student.'[9] This learning context is, at the undergraduate level, still largely departmental or subject based. It includes not only module and programme content, teaching methods and assessment procedures, but also physical features such as layout of teaching rooms and access to equipment, and indeed the whole culture of a department or subject group – including implicit power relations between teachers and learners, and tutors' often tacit conceptions of teaching and learning. How each student experiences this great web of interacting elements will help to determine whether he or she adopts deep or surface approaches to learning at various times throughout his or her studies. [10]

It is therefore important for history tutors and departments to understand what students value and how they experience learning in their subject, and to use this knowledge as the starting point for the development of learning environments which can motivate students and encourage a deep approach to learning. This is the focus of this chapter. It is based upon student responses to questionnaires administered to students at the beginning and at the end of their degree programmes. The questionnaires consisted of two parts: the first a series of rapid-response questions; the second, open questions intended to provide a more textured picture of student perspectives. The views recorded were drawn from a sample of approximately 300 history students at the University of Nottingham and of 120 students at Bath Spa University College. While 90 per cent of the Nottingham students were traditional eighteen-year-olds with high grades at A-level, those at Bath were from a greater diversity of backgrounds, with approximately 40 per cent being mature students, many of whom had arrived with 'Access' or related qualifications. Taken together these groups comprise a broadly representative sample of students studying history in British higher education.

The rationale for studying history

'From the student perspective', Ylijoki observes, 'the most prominent element in their experience in university is the rationale of studying, the internal logic of their studying. The answer to this question forms the basis of what they get from university, and what kinds of experiences they will want to have during their study time.'[11] Choosing to study history is commonly expressed in terms of a keen long-term 'interest in the subject', and this seems to be as true of the mature students at the Open University as it is of those at Bath and Nottingham. Indeed, it is equally apparent in students' choice of history at the age of sixteen.[12] While this response undoubtedly needs unpicking, overwhelmingly those beginning university history courses talk about their aims in terms of developing critical thinking, acquiring new ideas, sharpening their skills of constructing and presenting arguments, and gaining expertise in handling historical source material. In addition, 86 per cent of first-year entrants to both Bath and Nottingham feel that personal development is a very important aim for them in their course, with less than 2 per cent regarding it as unimportant. This emphasis upon subject and personal achievement does not mean that entrants are not strategically motivated. Indeed, 86 per cent of those at Nottingham and 75 per cent of those at Bath think that getting a good job is very or quite important. However, only 3 per cent claimed that career factors were very important in their decision to enter higher education, and this contrasts very markedly with the 97 per cent in a recent study of engineering students.[13]

In the study of history, students place a premium upon the personal. As researchers discovered in the 1970s, whereas students in science or professional subjects typically described learning tasks as demanding logic, the careful following of a clear hierarchy of common rules and methods, and the empirical observation of relationships between phenomena, Arts students tended to see their subjects as requiring personal interpretation, generalisation and comparison, and felt less constrained by strict rules. Two second-year history students observed:

> They [science students] go about it more logically . . . scientists deal in fact, while history students and artists deal in theory – we discuss theories and opinion.

> History, you can waffle, you can cover up your mistakes . . . no-one can prove you right or wrong . . . you've got to take all things into account.[14]

For history students the ability of the subject to accommodate both academic rigour and personal opinion is a great attraction. Frequently, indeed, the experience of learning history is described in highly emotional terms: as a 'love' or 'passion' for the subject. It is therefore not surprising that there is a particular emphasis upon the importance of personal engagement to interest and motivation. As one final-year student put it: 'If you're not really interested in what you're doing it's bound to affect your performance. For instance, if you're put onto a course you don't really want to do, it can be a tremendous turn-off to putting any real effort in.' What makes history particularly interesting, however, is its relevance to the present and to one's sense of identity. Explaining why things happened in the past can help students to understand the workings of the contemporary world and provide a focus from which they can try to make sense of themselves. This practical resonance of the subject is very strong. The following are common responses to the question, 'What particularly interests you about history?'

> I like the fact that history covers almost every aspect of life. It is interesting to discover our own past. It helps us to understand why and how life is as it is, and why we are like we are. It puts life in perspective. (first-year student)

> History defines what we are today. It helps us to understand what makes people act the way they do, and how their reactions in the past have created our society today. History's like a mirror on our own society. (third-year student)

The mature students in this survey were particularly interested in social history, and traditional entrants were generally more inclined towards the personality and influence of 'great political leaders', such as Peel, Bismarck, Elizabeth I and, especially, Hitler – preferences which clearly reflect different life experiences and stages of personal development. Economic history is most likely to be disliked, characterised as 'too statistical' or 'too dry', and generally too remote from the people orientation which encourages engagement with the subject.[15]

> I think what interests me is the way you can learn about people, very much like yourself, who lived and experienced life years ago. How they coped with life and problems. How wars affected them and what were their thoughts. It's the ways in which 'ordinary' people lived their lives that fascinates me. (first-year, mature student)

> What really gets me motivated is something I can relate to. For example, if we were looking at children in the age of Dickens – I grew up in a children's home. (first-year, mature student)

> Although I did political history at A-level, I found that I was less interested in legislation and institutions than in the individuals. Looking at the rise and fall of individuals, seeing why they made decisions and being able to see with the benefit of hindsight where mistakes were made, and why a truly successful ruler could lose everything in a short period of time. If you look back to the source of history and governments that's the individual. (first-year student)

Studying the motivations of key figures and vicariously experiencing ordinary lives in the past provides a lens for exploring one's own roots, values and relation to society. History is closely tied up with issues of personal identity. Joyce Cruse, reflecting upon a career of teaching the subject, notes: 'Students want to know why history matters, how it relates to their lives, if at all, and how the study of history might affect them personally.'[16] Understandably, therefore, twentieth-century topics are the most popular choice for undergraduates, for these provide the most direct route to personal and social relevance. It is clear, however, that how the subject is taught is also critical to developing and sustaining motivation. More than any other factor, students explain lack of interest in relation to teaching. One first-year spoke for many: 'Enjoyed least [at A-level] Tudor history – taught chronologically dictation style, no room for discussion – so little interest developed in the subject.'

The successful history course

For history students the key yardstick of a successful course is the quality of the tutor–student relationship. Teachers are seen as overwhelmingly the most important influence in their development, and the anonymity of the experience of studying at university is frequently compared unfavourably with the close and supportive relationships of a sixth form or Access course where students and tutors share a clear mutual goal – that of examination success.[17] In the sixth form, one student observed, 'the smaller classes and closer relationship with the teachers provided a more involved type of feeling, and thus more interest and understanding than at GCSE'.

History tutors are expected to fulfil the role of both guide and fellow traveller on what is frequently described in terms of a journey of discovery. The good tutor possesses an up-to-date, if not always complete, map of the territory, and can provide the appropriate level of inspiration and information, encouragement and support to enable student travellers to negotiate the new terrain and, ultimately, make discoveries for themselves. Among first-years, especially, and also amongst the least academically qualified students, there is often an emphasis upon the tutor *possessing* subject expertise. 'Knowing the subject thoroughly' is important to these students, and reflects a less sophisticated conception of learning. Subject expertise is less apparent as a criterion among final-year students, and when it appears the emphasis seems to be more upon the tutor *using* his or her grasp of the subject to add in pieces of information during class discussion or bring discussion back to the point.

Throughout the student responses there is an emphasis upon enthusiasm and commitment to teaching. Many go further, and 'passion' for the subject is frequently mentioned as a key attribute of successful tutoring, along with the ability to 'inspire'; expressions which again capture the emotional nature of student engagement with the subject.

A genuine love and fascination for the subject is important, and in-depth knowl-edge. A good tutor should also be sympathetic to his or her students and have the patience to explain more complex theories to those less able. (first-year student)

I think that a good history teacher has an extensive knowledge, an obvious passion for his or her subject and the ability to communicate this enthusiasm. They must be able to explain things clearly, and be willing to help or reassure students. (first-year student)

A good history tutor is someone who is enthusiastic and prepared to discuss the views of students. An enthusiastic teacher can really get you motivated. Then I become interested in the subject concerned and care about what I'm doing. (third-year student)

In some ways the notion of 'good practice' is most clearly represented in stu-dents' depiction of its opposite. Poor tutors are seen almost entirely in terms of their inability to relate to students. Many students made variations on the fol-lowing observations:

[A poor history teacher] interrogates you, so you dread getting asked a question, or has their own opinions and everything else is wrong, or enjoys showing off their own superior knowledge against the superficiality of their students, so you feel you've got nothing to say. Or just drones on unenthusiastically so you become unen-thusiastic yourself and switch off. (third-year student)

A poor history tutor is someone uninterested in teaching – only there to write books. Or someone who just passes on a great deal of facts for you to remember without any discussion or student participation. (first-year student)

One distilled his comment into the following blunt phrase: 'Treats students with low regard.'

In sum, those qualities listed below represent the key characteristics of suc-cessful tutors in the view of history undergraduates:

- Approachability: accessible and willing to help students.
- Enthusiasm for the subject matter.
- Expertise (most often mentioned by first-year students).
- Communicates ideas clearly and cogently.
- Makes the subject 'come alive'.
- Encourages and respects students' views, and open to their ideas.
- Knows how to encourage active student participation.
- Gives clear guidance on reading.
- Provides clear, constructive feedback on assignments.
- Has an obvious commitment to teaching.

The importance attached to the quality of the tutor–student relationship in this list makes the point that effective learning is felt to occur as much through interaction with others as from a one-to-one relationship between student and text. This emphasis upon the importance of the social context of learning is firmly underlined by overwhelming student preference for seminar discussion as a method for learning history. This is frequently compared to A-level, where the view that 'discussions were interesting but not held often enough' is widespread.

> Discussion is definitely the best way of learning history. It makes you really get into the subject. You have to know something about the period in question to be able to speak. It also makes you think and develop your ideas. It also leads you to being open about the ideas of others. (first-year student)

> I particularly like discussion in seminars. I love the interaction between people and the fact you realise all of you know enough to be able to talk about it. You really feel part of it. (third-year student)

Such comments also indicate a change in how students experience seminars over time. Among first-years, a general recognition that seminars are an effective means of learning history is mingled with anxiety about possessing sufficient facts to avoid exposing ignorance in a new, and sometimes frightening, social and academic context. By the third year this has given way to a much more relaxed and intellectually rewarding experience for most. Many final-year students report not only an easier relationship with other students, but also a more equal relationship with tutors.

Students clearly recognise that merely assembling a number of people together for discussion does not constitute a seminar. Rather, teaching and learning are viewed as a mutual enterprise, in which students and tutors both bear responsibility for creating the conditions for successful learning. One first-year student wrote: 'People make seminars work – tutors who encourage debate, students who get involved.' Similarly, a final-year student commented: 'Students must all have done some reading and be prepared to say something. However, most important is the tutor. If he or she just rambles on students will not do the reading, then not be able to talk. It's self-perpetuating. The tutor must encourage involvement.' Students believe that, while they have a responsibility for adequate preparation and active involvement, the tutor's task is to provide a structured and supportive environment in which discussion can thrive.

The most frequently mentioned method for encouraging student interest and involvement is debating topics, but using video ('it enables you to get a feel for the period'), primary sources, novels, maps and other artefacts are all regarded as useful aids. Variety is also often mentioned as conducive to maintaining interest, and third-years feel strongly that they should take a leading role in seminar work. Indeed, a large majority of all students feel that they should have a consultative role in all aspects of teaching and assessment. 'No involvement leads to lack of interest', said one. The least satisfying experience from the student perspective is to be deluged with information, a distaste clearly borne of previous school experience. In the words of one first-year student: 'The biggest problem is if lots of facts are thrown at you, and then you have to learn them. It's much easier to learn if you are investigating something yourself, and then reporting back and discussing what you think.' This sort of overload was most often mentioned in relation to lectures, though first-years were much more likely to feel that lectures provided a useful framework for further individual study than final-year students, and this no doubt reflects a progression in confidence. Among the latter, there is little enthusiasm for lectures unless they provide an introductory overview at the beginning of a series of seminars and, especially, engage actively with the audience. For history students human qualities are at least as important as good technical delivery.

Creating a context for learning

The above discussion suggests how an optimal climate might be created to connect teaching with student learning, and encourage students to learn effectively in history.[18] In devising such an environment, the first step is to discover, and listen to, students' own needs, beliefs and values. In a context of increasing student numbers, it is especially important that scarce resources are focused on what students themselves perceive as making a real difference in their learning. This does not mean that we, as tutors, have to accept their views uncritically, for some may be misconceptions, and encouraging students to be open to new ideas and to refine existing ones is an important part of helping them to develop more sophisticated conceptions of the subject and what it means to study it. Nonetheless, we must attempt to establish what their perceptions, expectations and perceived needs are, for these will condition how students approach their studies. Here it can be of practical benefit to acquire a working knowledge of the literature in this field.

As a second step there needs to be a commitment to review systematically and critically our own practices in terms of student learning. This involves a willingness to explore our own beliefs, habits and assumptions, and examine whether what we are doing accurately reflects what we want or say we are trying to do in terms of developing historical knowledge, skills and understanding. It also involves a sharing of ideas and experience, a critical discussion of what it means to teach history, and a positive and collaborative approach to solving those organisational and logistical constraints which hinder effective learning. Addressing the following questions can provide a useful starting point:

- What are the purposes of this history degree?
- What are our students' key characteristics with regard to prior learning and academic preparation?
- What do we want students to learn in terms of (historical) knowledge and understanding?
- What qualities or skills do we want our graduates to possess?
- Do our teaching and assessment practices reflect what we think is important for students to learn?
- Does our departmental/disciplinary culture encourage students to adopt deep approaches to learning?

The final step involves opening a supportive and developmental dialogue with students in order to find ways of bringing their values into a productive interaction with those which we, as professional historians, believe are the essential attributes of a high-quality history education. This can not only increase understanding of student perspectives in an ongoing fashion, but also ensure that students appreciate clearly what we expect, what we see as important in our subject, and how we understand teaching and learning in it. A positive exchange of experiences, views about teaching and learning, can assist students to see the relevance of their degree course at an early stage and thus adapt more easily to its demands. It can help to clear away some potentially damaging misconceptions and enable students to consider more critically their own conceptions as a means for monitoring and improving their learning.[19]

Clearly, academic learning contexts operate on several different levels, from that of the individual teaching session to that of the degree programme and beyond, and involve interactions between many elements. Each setting is unique, and there is no single method guaranteed to encourage successful learning. Rather, the blend will necessarily vary according to departmental traditions, priorities, resources and student characteristics. Success may depend as much on the ways in which issues are addressed, and changes introduced, as upon individual features of the learning environment. Nonetheless, the following constitute some core principles, based upon student experiences, which lie at the heart of creating optimal learning environments in history.

Experience, needs and confidence

Stephenson and Weil make the point that 'starting at the point students have reached is almost a first principle of teaching'.[20] Students need to reconcile and integrate new types of learning with previous experience, and developing a clear sense of progression in learning objectives and tasks is vital. This is particularly so in the transition to university, and it makes the first-year programme a particularly important point, demanding the deployment of experienced and enthusiastic staff whose expertise is particularly valued by new students.

History students at the beginning of their degree programme anticipate a high level of personal involvement and responsibility, but this does not mean that they feel prepared for active modes of learning. A-level history is based upon success in a final external examination in which students perceive thoroughness of knowledge to be at a premium.[21] The result of this assessment system can be a reliance upon recall: 'I enjoyed least at A-level learning dates. It encouraged the feeling of having to learn everything by heart. You felt you had to know a lot of facts to pass the exam, but it took a lot of the enjoyment away.' Given the need to cover a large syllabus in a relatively short space of time in preparation for a final examination, it is not surprising that when they arrive at university history students express greatest confidence in note taking, organising notes and essay writing.[22] Even with regard to essay writing, however, only just over half of the

Nottingham students felt confident or very confident, and less than a quarter of those at Bath, who possessed lower levels of confidence. Least confidence among all was expressed in giving an oral presentation, collaborative work and using primary sources. Among mature students there was also a low level of confidence in organising study time effectively and reading deeply, but more confidence in giving an oral presentation.

Encouraging students to become more effective learners, and to adopt more sophisticated approaches to their subject, is therefore a priority. This includes focusing upon a range of learning and transferable skills, including researching, reading and essay-writing skills, but with a particular emphasis upon areas of least confidence, such as monitoring one's own learning, oral presentation and group work. It also involves attention to subject-specific learning, such as history theory and methodology, and historiography, so that students are able to link prior knowledge into broader conceptual frameworks. Asking students to reflect on and share their own experiences of studying can be a powerful means of helping them to become more sophisticated learners, and help them to build the self confidence which lies behind successful learning and skills development.[23] Specific skills courses can also be useful, though they are often unpopular and require particularly clear articulation of purpose, departmental priorities and careful integration into the subject content if the skills they aim to develop are to be effectively transferred. In particular, skills teaching needs to work with the grain of student motivation and interest, and this is subject based. As Mason and Washington note: 'Without something to learn, the acquisition of skills is a barren occupation . . . What matters here is coming to grips with history, litera-ture and philosophy. The skills now appear as necessary only in so far as they advance the project of learning, not as ends in themselves.'[24]

Relevance, identity and the emotions

Interest and motivation are closely bound up with social and personal relevance, and linking topics with contemporary issues gives history a practical importance in students' eyes; connects it to the reality of their lives. As one first-year put it:

> A good history teacher will hold interest by bringing the past to life. I find that when a teacher uses actual examples from today to illustrate the past, the topic is easier to remember. Illustrations and maps shown on an overhead projector also help me to understand. In the more recent periods, videos help to stress points and make it seem more relevant and alive.

This reminds us that history provides not only a mirror on society but a lens through which students can try to make sense of themselves. For many school leavers the study of prominent politicians provides a safe (because somewhat distanced) means of exploring their own actions at a time of considerable per-sonal change. For mature students social history, and particularly topics in women's history or popular culture, often provides a strong link to, and often a conceptual framework for understanding, one's personal history.

There are many means of making history relevant to students, whether in lectures or seminars. Using visual sources, fieldwork, simulations, role play,
counterfactual exercises, case studies of personalities, debates about moral
issues, such as child labour or the Holocaust, and many other structured activities can help students to see the content of the curriculum as having meaning in
the real world – enabling them to grasp it in an imaginative as well as an intellectual sense. This emphasises that engaging with the emotions is just as important to historical understanding as developing intellectual skills. The experience
of studying history is often expressed in highly emotional language, and the
sharing of a 'love' or 'passion' for the subject is the litmus test of good tutoring
from the student perspective. Moreover, developing a personal interpretation is
an important goal, and this requires imagination and creativity as well as critical analysis and methodological rigour. It demands what one student calls 'a feel
for the time'.[25] In learning history the cognitive and emotional are inseparable.

Challenge, high expectations and support

If history provides a powerful lens for affirming one's identity, too rigid a sense
of self can be an obstacle to learning, for flexibility and openness to new ideas
are essential to becoming a more sophisticated learner in the subject. Students
expect tutors to challenge them to think critically, imaginatively and independently, and to have high expectations of them, and all the research literature suggests that this is the mark of the most effective tutors. These demands are closely
linked to motivation, and occur most obviously in the context of the Special
Subject or dissertation, where students are able to explore a topic in depth. Not
coincidentally, these are also often cited as the most enjoyable and valuable parts
of a history degree.

Equally, however, challenge is only likely to be effective within a supportive
climate if students are to develop a historical understanding which is both critical and creative. A relaxed and encouraging atmosphere, alongside clarity of
purpose and a clear sense of progression, is particularly important to students,
so that new ideas and experiences can be encountered, risks taken and mistakes
made, without excessive anxiety. In assessing the appropriate balance between
safety and challenge the individual tutor is pivotal, and regarding this role as
facilitative is essential. This does not mean abdicating all authority or rigour, but
adopting a more sophisticated view of teaching in which subject competence is
matched by an appreciation of student learning in the subject, and authority is
seen in terms of mastery of the complex interpersonal, emotional and academic
conditions in which effective learning thrives. History students look to tutors to
share their enthusiasm for, and expertise in, the subject, but also to act as
mentors who are aware of their needs and interests, and can lead them progressively towards more independent thinking in the subject. The relationship they
have with tutors determines students' perceptions of the quality of their whole
degree programme.

Support is not merely a function of teaching and tutors, however, but of the department or subject group as a whole. This is not just about providing teaching space, equipment and library resources with the needs of learners in mind, but also the concern and respect for students, and for teaching, which lie at the heart of a successful history department – and are central to student ratings of degree courses in many countries. How the department as a whole encourages a sense of personal and collective identity is therefore vital in establishing the cultural framework within which effective learning can take place – and in deciding drop-out rates. Here the need for sensitive induction and processes which actively engage students themselves, and do not merely deluge them with information, is obvious, and employing peer-support schemes can help here. A commitment to strong personal tutoring and feedback systems, and to the quality of staff–student contact generally, is also highly beneficial. All too frequently academic life at university is compared unfavourably by students with a more supportive school or college environment. In a system of expanding student numbers, including more part-timers, finding ways to help students to feel a sense of belonging, of community, is more important than ever – if also more difficult given multiple demands upon the staff. There are no easy solutions, but a commitment to open, supportive dialogue with students over the issues is certainly the best way to begin the process of finding ways to match student expectations and the realities of tutor and departmental resources.

Participation, ownership and control

A-level history is, to quote John Fines and Jon Nicol, 'teacher dominated, lecture plus notes and essays; its consequence a passive dependency culture'.[26] This conflicts with students' own belief that studying history should be akin to a journey in which individual exploration is encouraged. Students want to be engaged actively in learning the subject, and it is therefore important for them to have a sense of control over what they do – though they will almost certainly require tutors to take a more interventionist role in the early stages of the transition to university study. There is a particularly strong demand for choice (in module selection, seminar and essay topics), with a large majority of students also declaring a desire to have a strong input in teaching methods and assessment, and even in departmental decision making as a whole.

Flexible curricula and varied teaching and assessment methods are essential in providing options suited to different student needs, and might include resource-based learning packages as well as library-based options. In deciding appropriate methods it can be useful to ask staff and students to think through the following questions:

- How much control do students have over what they learn?
- Do teaching and assessment methods encourage student participation?
- What role do students play in decision making in the department?

For individual tutors, allowing students to establish 'ground rules' at the beginning of a module can be a powerful and simple means of encouraging participation and a sense of ownership and control. These rules can be typed up and circulated to all members of a seminar group as a reminder of agreed responsibilities. 'Learning contracts' are a more formal means of making expectations clear, and are particularly useful in history project work to help students to become aware of their responsibilities and the need to manage their time and task allocation.[27]

Responsibility, independence and interdependence

History students tend to believe that it is very much their own responsibility how well they do, and independent learning through project and dissertation work and open-learning materials can be very effective. They also recognise, however, that interaction with others is often a better way to get to grips with the conflicting interpretations at the core of historical issues by exposing them to a variety of viewpoints and helping them to make connections between ideas. The value placed upon collaborative work is the basis of student preference for seminar discussion, but all too often they complain that in reality the shared experience amounts to little more than a student reading out a paper followed by a dialogue with the tutor, or at most one or two of those present. Adopting an emphasis upon student-led and peer learning activity, and using more interactive teaching methods such as brainstorming, buzz groups and debates, can be useful means of developing reciprocity, but this needs to be a flexible strategy sensitive to differing levels of confidence and student numbers. Thus a more hands-on approach during year one, or at least semester one of the first year, is probably necessary. This might involve, for example, introducing debate and oral presentation work with the tutor giving more direction to discussion, whereas at a later stage students can be encouraged to become involved in peer tutoring, group projects and more autonomous learning.[28]

Reflection, assessment and feedback

Learning is not merely about doing. Rather, being able to reflect on one's experience, and what one has learned, is at the heart of developing both the critical and creative aspects of historical understanding. While reflection should align well with history students' interest in personal identity, the 'essay rush' which dominates A-level often leaves little time for reflective learning. In higher education, therefore, priority needs to be given to encouraging reflective learning, and in particular this should constitute the core of the assessment process which, as many researchers have observed, is the most powerful single influence on student learning.

Encouraging reflection in the assessment process can be achieved in many ways. Recently, records of achievement, personal learning plans, log books and portfolios have become popular, but simply ensuring that essay questions encourage critical questioning of authors' assumptions and viewpoints, as well as students' own, can be an effective reflective device.[29] So too can providing clear, constructive and prompt feedback on coursework and examination performance, with the focus on improving student learning. More adventurously, students can be encouraged to provide both formal and informal feedback to each other, and this works particularly well on oral presentations.[30] Variety can add interest, and recognises the range of skills needed to develop as well as acknowledging differing learning styles. One quick and practical method to encourage reflective learning is suggested by Angelo and Cross. The 'minute paper' takes place just before the end of a teaching session, when the tutor presents two or three questions to which students respond in writing in no more than one or two sentences. The questions are simple and straightforward: What are the most important things that you have learned? What questions or issues remain unanswered or unclear? Student responses are gathered in, and feedback given at the next session.[31] Variants on this simple audit could also provide valuable information as part of wider reviews of student experiences and understanding at the end of a whole degree programme.

Creating teaching contexts which motivate, which cultivate an intrinsic interest in learning the subject and encourage students to adopt deep approaches to learning is a task demanding considerable skill. It requires critical reflection, open dialogue, careful planning and creative design, alongside a willingness to experiment. Most important of all, however, it requires an approach whose focus of attention is always on the student as learner, and which works with the grain of student values in a spirit of open and supportive dialogue. Here teaching and learning are not seen as a duality, but rather as a single interactive process – one in which it is recognised, in Eble's words, that 'Learning and teaching are constantly interchanging activities. One learns by teaching; one cannot teach except by constantly learning.'[32] Within such a context both teaching and learning can become more rewarding, even with larger numbers, and obstacles to effective learning, whether academic, personal or organisational, can be addressed constructively. In such an environment tutors can be more confident of successfully sharing their own love of the subject and that students receive the best opportunity possible to develop fully as historians, learners and individuals.

Notes

1   B. Dobree, *Arts Faculties in Modern Universities* (Leeds, University of Leeds, 1944), p. 7.
2   D. Sylvester, 'Change and continuity in history teaching 1900–93', in H. Bourdillon (ed.), *Teaching History* (London, Open University Press, 1994), p. 9.
3   See especially, C. Argyris and D. Schon, *Theory in Practice: Increasing Professional Effectiveness* (London, Jossey-Bass, 1992).
4   There is now a huge literature on 'student centred' learning. An excellent practical

introduction is P. Ramsden, *Learning to Teach in Higher Education* (London, Routledge, 1992), ch. 7. For an American perspective, see C. Meyers and T. B. Jones, *Promoting Active Learning: Strategies for the College Classroom* (San Francisco, Jossey-Bass, 1993).

5 For an approach which emphasises the importance of student perceptions, see F. Marton, D. Hounsell & N. Entwistle (eds), *The Experience of Learning* (Edinburgh, Scottish Academic Press, 1997 edn).

6 M. Tennant, *Psychology and Adult Learning* (London, Routledge, 1997 edn), p. 3.

7 For critical reviews of the learning styles literature, see Tennant, *Psychology and Adult Learning*, ch. 7, and J. Biggs, 'What do inventories of students' learning styles really measure?', *British Journal of Educational Psychology*, 63 (1993), 3–19. For a review of the influence of personality on learning, see W. Crozier, *Individual Learners: Personality Differences in Education* (London, Routledge, 1997).

8 See P. Ramsden, 'The context of learning in academic departments', in Marton, Hounsell and Entwistle, *The Experience of Learning*, ch. 13; N. Entwistle and H. Tait, 'Approaches to learning and evaluations of teaching, and preferences for contrasting academic environments', *Higher Education*, 19 (1990), 169–94.

9 D. J. Nicol, 'Research on learning and higher education', *UCoSDA Briefing Paper*, no. 45 (1997), p. 3.

10 A 'deep' approach is characterised by an intention to understand material by looking for underlying principles and processes, relationships between elements, and relating ideas to existing knowledge and experience with the aim of transforming it into one's own interpretation. It also involves active interest in the subject. Alternatively, in adopting a surface approach the learner routinely aims to memorise or reproduce information, and makes little effort to link ideas together in a critical fashion. See G. Gibbs (ed.), *Improving the Quality of Student Learning* (Bristol, Technical and Educational Services, 1992).

11 O.-H. Ylijoki, 'Students' conceptions of teaching and learning', paper presented at the Society for Research into Higher Education Annual Conference, University of York, 1994, p. 3.

12 E. Chambers, E. Tunnicliffe and J. Close, *Report: A102 Student Survey: Studying for a Degree in the Humanities: Students' Expectations and Experiences of History* (Milton Keynes, Open University Institute for Educational Technology, 1993); J. Vaudry, 'Some sixth-formers' views of history', *Teaching History*, 57 (1989), 17–24.

13 N. Entwistle, C. Boys, J. Brennan *et al.*, *The Performance of Electrical Engineering Students in Scottish Higher Education* (Edinburgh, Teaching and Learning Advice Centre, 1989).

14 Ramsden, 'The context of learning', p. 209.

15 The same preference among school students is also noted by S. Lang, *A-level History: The Case for Change* (London, Historical Association, 1990) and O. Hallden, 'Learning history', *Oxford Review of Education*, 12 (1986), 53–66.

16 J. Cruse, 'Practising history: a high school teacher's reflections', *Journal of American History*, 81 (1994), 1066.

17 See K. Raaheim, J. Wankowski and J. Radford (eds), *Helping Students to Learn* (Buckingham, SRHE/Open University Press, 1991); J. Earwaker, *Helping and Supporting Students* (Buckingham, SRHE/Open University Press, 1992).

18 Useful discussions of ways to design learning environments are provided in A. Chickering and L. Rosser, *Education and Identity* (San Francisco, Jossey-Bass, 1993);

P. Nightingale and M. O'Neill, *Achieving Quality in Learning in Higher Education* (London, Kogan Page, 1994); G. Gibbs, 'Improving the quality of learning through course design', in R. Barnett (ed.), *Learning to Effect* (Buckingham, SRHE/Open University Press, 1992).

19 For concise practical advice on encouraging dialogue and reflection, see L. A. Stefani, 'Reflective learning in higher education', *UCOSDA Briefing Paper*, no. 42 (1997).

20 J. Stephenson and S. Weil, *Quality in Learning: A Capability Approach in Higher Education* (London, Kogan Page, 1992), p. 11.

21 For an astute analysis of A-level history, see J. Fines and J. Nicol, *Doing History 16–19* (London, Historical Association, 1994); and Lang, *A-level History*. On similar problems elsewhere, see P. Stearns, *Meaning over Memory: Recasting the Teaching of Culture and History* (Chapel Hill, University of North Carolina Press, 1993), ch. 1; G. Sheppard, 'The sense of preparation: history students and high school/university articulation', *Canadian Social Studies*, 27 (1993), 107–10; R. Lewis, 'Public relations and the public schools: barriers to academic preparation for college', *Journal of American History*, 81 (1994), 1087–92.

22 For more detail on this, see A. Booth, 'Listening to students: experiences and expectations in the transition to a history degree', *Studies in Higher Education*, 22 (1997), 205–20. See also R. Murphy, *The Key Skills of Students Entering Higher Education* (Nottingham, University of Nottingham Education Department, 1997).

23 See A. Brockbank & I. McGill, *Developing Reflective Learning* (Buckingham, Open University Press, 1998).

24 J. Mason and P. Washington, *The Future of Thinking* (London, Routledge, 1992), p. 11.

25 Quoted in D. Newton, L. Newton and I. Oberski, 'Learning and conceptions of understanding in History and science: lecturers and new graduates compared', *Studies in Higher Education*, 23 (1998), 53.

26 Fines and Nicol, *Doing History*, p. 19.

27 See G. Anderson, D. Boud & J. Sampson, *Using Learning Contracts in Higher Education* (London, Kogan Page, 1996).

28 On the wide range of possible strategies, see D. Jaques, *Learning in Groups* (London, Kogan Page, 1991).

29 On these see P. Knight and S. Brown, *Assessing Learners in Higher Education* (London, Kogan Page, 1994); G. Brown, M. Pendlebury and J. Bull, *Assessing Student Learning in Higher Education* (London, Routledge, 1997).

30 See D. Boud, *Enhancing Learning through Self Assessment* (London, Kogan Page, 1996).

31 T. Angelo and K. Cross, *Classroom Assessment Techniques* (San Francisco, Jossey-Bass, 1990). See also Stefani, 'Reflective learning', pp. 2–4.

32 K. Eble, *The Craft of Teaching* (San Francisco, Jossey-Bass, 1988), p. 8.

4 Tim Hitchcock, Robert B. Shoemaker and John Tosh

Skills and the structure of the history curriculum

In the words of one university history lecturer, 'most colleagues do not discuss the curriculum'. Nonetheless, in England debates over the curriculum have become more frequent and contentious in recent years owing to the pressures generated by the underfunded expansion in student numbers, quality assurance, modularisation and theoretical developments within the discipline. Concurrently, debates over the types of skill a history degree should inculcate have been intensified by the increasing importance accorded in academia and politics to skills development and transferability. The problems involved in history curriculum design have thus multiplied since 1988, when a survey concluded that history teaching had changed little in response to the demands of the market-place.[1]

We start our investigation by identifying the range of generic and history-specific transferable skills and aptitudes, often under-appreciated, which are inculcated in undergraduate history programmes. We then review the range of curriculum strategies to be found in English universities and colleges, with a view to identifying the practices and innovations which do most to enhance student acquisition of such skills. Throughout we have defined skills as broadly as possible, in order to include the acquisition of specific bodies of knowledge, as well as the higher levels of analytical expertise which are frequently difficult to define in terms of direct or narrow application. History is a discipline which, due to the wide range of types of thinking required, prepares its practitioners uniquely well for citizenship, employment and further learning. By adopting a wide and inclusive approach to the notion of 'skills' we hope to encourage the recognition of these aspects of a historical education and to enhance their place in curriculum design.

The skills of the history graduate

The justification for doing a degree in history needs to be related to the full life-experience of our graduates, and to the fact that the vast majority of our students will not go on to careers as professional historians. They will become teachers and civil servants, managers and entrepreneurs. More than this, we need to recognise that the lives of our graduates are not limited to their roles as workers, and that education impacts directly on an individual's perspective and behaviour throughout life.

There are personal transferable skills which a degree in any social science or humanities discipline will impart. The ability to write cogently and convincingly, to present ideas orally and to analyse information is common to most disciplines, and provides the best basic justification for doing a degree. Undergraduates are also increasingly trained to work in groups and are familiar with the use of information technology. In looking at the distinctive skills that a history student develops, we need to be careful not to undervalue the skills which they share with students from other humanities and social science subjects. History graduates, however, can claim a number of skills beyond those shared with other disciplines which relate to specific areas of historical enquiry and education, and which are, in the broadest sense, transferable.

Perhaps the most obvious set of skills that an undergraduate degree imparts are those relating to an individual's role as a citizen, as a political and social participant in the community. At its most basic, a historical education provides students with a shared body of knowledge and a shared vocabulary about how society works. While no student at the end of their degree could be familiar with more than a small proportion of the history of the world, that small proportion is in itself a valuable resource which significantly alters the relationship between the individual and the community. It gives to the citizen greater independence of mind in evaluating conflicting interpretations of politics, society and culture.

The globalisation of politics and society makes this kind of intellectual capital all the more important. While there is no longer an identifiable historical canon of important events, few history graduates can have passed through a degree without being confronted by a significant variety of perspectives. The very sense that society is changing ever more rapidly gives added weight to the understanding which graduates have of their own position in society. They are better prepared to differentiate between deep and enduring structures on the one hand, and the ephemeral trends of the media-led hothouse of daily events on the other. As a result, they are better prepared for their roles in public and private life. Moreover, comparative knowledge of societies marked by both chronological and geographical differences gives history graduates a richer perspective on the distinctive characteristics of their own and other communities.

While the division between our actions as citizens and as workers is inevitably artificial, a history degree also imparts a range of skills which are specifically relevant to the kinds of work most of our graduates do, and more generally to the constantly changing technical and intellectual environment within which we all now work. The ability to comprehend complexity and to cope with rapid change is the basic skill which new patterns of employment demand. A history degree, because it is about change and complexity, engenders a range of skills which are uniquely suited to modern employment.

As a result of the intellectual developments of the discipline itself, history undergraduates are being taught an increasingly wide range of methodological approaches. The constant dialogue between the historical profession and the other humanities and social sciences has led to the development of a self-conscious strand of methodological teaching in most history degrees which gives graduates a basic familiarity with a remarkably diverse set of approaches. Detailed documentary analysis is perhaps the core methodology upon which modern history is based, but in recent generations historians have also made profitable use of new forms of analysis drawn from literary criticism, sociology, economics and their derivatives. As a result, history graduates are broadly familiar with, and competent to use, a range of approaches which transcend disciplinary boundaries. That history students are asked, for example, to draw notions of cultural difference from sociology and of spatial organisation from geography means that, while they are seldom expert in any of these forms of analysis and frequently draw their knowledge second hand from theoretically informed historical writing, they are familiar with the strengths and weaknesses of each. The methodological eclecticism of a history degree is one of its greatest strengths, and contributes to the production of graduates who are able to cope with a tremendously wide variety of intellectual demands. This same strand of methodological teaching also entails a reflexive critique of the discipline itself, which gives students a heightened ability to criticise their own intellectual approach and, by extension, that of others. This is a particularly important skill for those who go on to work in intellectually self-contained environments such as the law and teaching.

In a similar way the building blocks of historical analysis are uniquely varied, and lead to the creation of a peculiarly open-minded and flexible approach to knowledge. Historical teaching conventionally makes only one fundamental distinction in its intellectual taxonomy: that between primary and secondary sources. And while the majority of primary sources are textual, undergraduates are also encouraged to make use of visual and artefactual sources, and to take their texts from the widest possible selection of genres. This inclusive approach to evidence encourages the same kind of intellectual flexibility which the varied methodologies of history help to create.

While the content and approach of many history degrees have changed substantially over the last couple of decades, students are still required to come to an understanding of the whole of a society or societies. Fundamentally, historical understanding is based on the assumption that, however imperfectly, we can access past experience and events. A history undergraduate is therefore challenged to deal with a uniquely messy object of study – the whole of a past society. It is not a question of limiting oneself to a single snapshot. Equally fundamental to a historical education is the ability to deal with change over time. This basic concern with change means that students discipline their understanding of events within the context of a clearly delineated set of forces. You cannot write an argument about historical change without first specifying, at least to yourself, the different levels of significance that should be given to different types of influence. Because the patterns of causation to be found in any historical transition are potentially as diverse as are the subjects of historical enquiry, a history degree gives students practice in picking out priorities from the dust heap of historical incident.

Finally, and in the same vein, it should be emphasised that history students are not asked to practise their skills on an artificial construct, whether of art or theory. They are asked to deal with the world in its entirety, to create a manageable object of study from the unimaginable whole that is history. When most people can expect to have two or three different careers through the course of their life; when the nature of graduate employment is increasingly about managing change; and when the forces at work on any given structure (whether of business or government) are growing more diverse with globalisation, it is the ability of history graduates to encompass the messy and complex, and to impose a useful order upon it, that is their greatest strength as workers and citizens. But we are not merely citizens and workers; we are also individuals struggling to make sense of our own lives. A history degree is as much about the skills we need to do this as it is about the utilitarian creation of a better or more successful society, however this may be defined. It provides us with the skills to reassess our own actions and thoughts continually, to create a context for who we are. In the process it creates individuals able to cope with the whole panoply of expectations which a rapidly changing society creates.

In summary, the skills which are specific to a historical education – as opposed to the writing and presentational skills which are common to all the humanities and social sciences – include the following:

- Familiarity with a significant body of knowledge about the past.
- Ability to make use of a wide range of methodological and theoretical approaches, and to critique their use.
- Possession of a reflexive understanding of history as an intellectual discipline, and the ability to apply this reflexivity to other disciplines, as a means of assessing one's own intellectual practice.
- Ability to assimilate and assess a wide range of evidence – both documentary and artefactual.
- Ability to understand and evaluate one society in the light of the values and history of other societies.
- Ability to describe and interpret change over time, and to cope with the 'messiness' of events.

The building blocks of the history curriculum

How does the design of history curricula promote the acquisition of these skills? In order to assess current practice we sought documentation from all higher education institutions in England which offer a single-honours undergraduate degree in history, or offer a combined degree of which history forms a substantial part. We received curriculum information from sixty-six institutions (about two-thirds of those contacted). We then looked at fifteen representative institutions in greater depth by examining selected course booklets and syllabi; and, in order to explore the relationship between curriculum design and skills development in still greater depth, we visited six institutions, where we had extended discussions with both staff and students.[2]

The building blocks of a three-year full-time undergraduate curriculum in history can be divided into eight different types of unit (sometimes labelled modules, courses or papers):

- *Methods or skills units, which teach introductory study and research skills.* These are compulsory in 39 per cent of the institutions surveyed, primarily in the first year but also in some cases in the second.
- *Information technology units, normally taught in the first year, often including little history content and taught by non-historians.* These are compulsory in 12 per cent of programmes.
- *Historiography units, surveying the 'history of history' and/or addressing various theoretical approaches to the discipline.* These are compulsory in 26 per cent of institutions, but are offered at various stages in the degree programme. These issues are also often covered in some methods units.
- *The General Paper, usually comprising an untaught exam taken in the final year which tests the student's ability to think and write conceptually about history.* This is now relatively rare and, because it is summative over the degree course as a whole, does not fit easily within the framework of modular schemes.
- *Document-based studies, usually called Special Subjects, which typically involve close study of a narrowly defined topic using primary sources.* Normally offered in the final year, often as a double unit, these units can also be found in a shorter form in the first year (sometimes within methods units).
- *Long essays or dissertations, constituting individual research projects resulting in a 5,000 to 12,000 word essay.* These are usually based on primary sources and written in the final year, though they are sometimes preceded by a shorter essay and/or a research methods unit.
- *Broad survey units, defined, for the purpose of this study, as covering more than 150 years in the period before 1800 or at least 100 years after 1800.* Such units may cover the history of more than one country, sometimes with a comparative, thematic or interdisciplinary dimension. Sixty-seven per cent of the institutions which sent us documentation require students to take such units during the first or second year.
- *Optional units.* This is typically a residual category, including all the 'content' units that cannot be categorised as surveys or Special Subjects: the length of the period studied, geographical range and extent of thematic specialisation

vary extensively, even within individual programmes. Options often cover a single country's history for several decades, frequently with a thematic dimension.

Curricula vary in the extent to which they seek to encourage explicit skills acquisition by making some of these units, or types of unit, compulsory. Table 4.1 provides a summary of information, gleaned from course brochures, concerning some of the types of unit most commonly prescribed.[3]

Table 4.1 Compulsory units by type of institution

Type of institution	Survey (%)	Method (%)	Historiography (%)	Documentary (%)	Number surveyed (no.)
Traditional university	65	29	24	76	34
'New' university (former polytechnics)	74	58	37	53	19
Colleges of higher education	67	39	15	46	13
Total	67	39	26	64	66

As in many other disciplines, teachers of history often face the dilemma of whether generic skills should be taught in separate units or whether they should be incorporated into existing units with historical 'content'. Many of the new universities (former polytechnics) offer 'history methods' units in the first (or less commonly, the second) year, where a range of generic skills (writing, compiling bibliographies, information technology, oral presentation, research and project work) is taught alongside more history-specific skills such as documentary analysis and historical methodologies; yet such units are compulsory in only 39 per cent of the institutions surveyed. Compulsory units specifically on information technology are relatively rare. Most departments continue to favour teaching generic skills within history 'content' units. In some cases, however, this aspect of first-year survey units is becoming increasingly explicit, with more time devoted to direct skills teaching. Institutions which retain individual tutorials, however, maintain that such units are unnecessary since many skills continue to be developed organically through traditional pedagogical methods.

History-specific skills are promoted in different ways in the other building blocks of the curriculum. Units on historiography (compulsory in 26 per cent of curricula and optional in many other programmes) promote disciplinary reflexivity and methodological and theoretical awareness through discussions of the history of the discipline, epistemological problems and the theoretical influences of other disciplines. Although not usually the subject of formal teaching, the questions posed on General Papers often encourage similar types of thinking. Documentary analysis, taught in separate compulsory units in almost two-thirds of degree programmes and also widely taught within survey and options units, promotes analytical skills in relation to a variety of types of evidence and encourages intellectual flexibility in relating such evidence to theoretical debates. The widely offered final-year dissertation is also highly relevant here. This exercise not only promotes skills in organisation and independent working, but also (usually) asks students to perform an intellectual high-wire act, weighing detailed evidence against broader theoretical arguments.

While documentary work promotes skills in relating the specific to the general, survey units enhance students' cultural awareness, as well as their understanding of the processes of change and continuity. In some cases a comparative element is also introduced through the study of the history of more than one country. (Explicitly comparative history is, however, only rarely required.) Although the narrowing scope of most A-level courses makes the first-year survey if anything more essential than it used to be, it now tends to receive a declining emphasis, and in a third of the institutions examined has disappeared altogether. In many other places the scope of the survey has been curtailed in deference to other claims for foundation teaching (in particular historical method, documentary analysis and study outside the discipline) and as a reaction to the increasing volume and specialisation of research. Many lecturers regard the survey as little more than irksome preparation for the more specialised (and thus more 'advanced') topics they teach in later stages of the degree.

Depending on their specific content and the approach adopted by the lecturer, 'options' units, offered in virtually every programme, promote some or all of the history skills we have discussed. All of them emphasise historical content; some teach documentary analysis; some incorporate a historiographical dimension; and others teach chronological and comparative skills through examination of a specific theme, such as gender or state formation, in more than one country over a long period.

Curriculum structure and progression

The extent to which skills are developed is also determined by where the various types of unit are placed within the overall framework of a three-year degree. By adopting different principles of progression, the current variants of curriculum design accentuate different skills. History programmes adopt one of three basic approaches in organising compulsory units, or types of unit, into a degree structure. The most common approach, and one which has been dominant for several decades, might be labelled the 'research training' model. Thirty years ago this standard pattern involved outline survey units in year one, which were meant to give a grounding in medieval, early-modern and modern history; more surveys plus options in year two; and a Special Subject in year three (often double-weighted in terms of teaching and study time), along with further options and in some cases a General Paper. Although this model continues to dominate, in recent years the number of surveys and options has been reduced and additional units have been added: study outside the discipline in year one; the occasional methods or historiography unit in years one and two; and a dissertation or (much less commonly) a comparative unit in year three. Nonetheless, the sense of progression in this type of degree structure remains clear, from the acquisition of knowledge and elementary skills in years one and two to documentary analysis in year three, with the carefully focused research of the Special Subject and dissertation seen as the culmination of undergraduate study. In essence this model provides an apprenticeship in historical method, acquired by means of a progression through a sequence of units which bears an ever-closer resemblance to the empirical source-based study usually required for research degrees in history. The impression that the degree is designed as a preparation for high-level research is strengthened by the tendency for most staff to teach Special Subjects which are closely related to their own research interests, and which in some cases generate recruits to their own specialism. With the increasingly common requirement of a research dissertation, and the growing number of Special Subjects offered in the new universities, this model of curriculum design is as popular as ever.

A second, less common but equally traditional model is much less prescriptive. This is the '*à la carte*' approach, in which staff put on units in their respective specialisms and students essentially have a free choice of the range of units offered, which are largely of the 'options' type. A historical education of this kind can be thought of as a training of the intellect which is cumulative and iterative. All components of a history degree are intended to promote a range of aptitudes (analytical, creative, communicational); the student progresses by repeatedly choosing options from a broad menu. This was the basis on which a history degree was traditionally regarded as an appropriate preparation for a career in public service. This type of degree is nowadays rarely found in its pure form, since almost all institutions require students to take some units other than options, but in some cases the level of prescription remains quite low. Since this type of degree structure allows staff maximum flexibility to offer units in their own specialisms, it is commonly found in very small departments which lack the resources to offer a distinctive programme of compulsory units at each level, and in very large departments where staff cannot reach consensus on a more prescriptive curriculum.

Both of these curriculum models introduce students to a range of generic and history-specific skills. The 'research training' model is, according to many historians, particularly good at developing skills in documentary analysis and in relating primary sources to theoretical debates, but in its early years it also introduces considerable historical 'content' and promotes comparative and chronological awareness through survey units and options. But the extent to which the latter are encouraged can be quite limited. As noted above, the traditional survey is becoming less common and a third of the institutions in our survey have no survey units at all. In those institutions which have retained the survey, comprehensive chronological coverage (through a series of units covering different time periods) is no longer held to be feasible or often even desirable. Students may be asked to choose units from a range of historical periods, but the rationale for this is often pragmatic rather than pedagogical: the need to spread teaching loads. The comparative element of such units is also often understressed. There is, moreover, no guarantee that this type of curriculum actively promotes reflexivity or methodological flexibility. Since historiography or the General Paper are required in less than a third of institutions, such issues may only be addressed at the tutor's discretion within options, surveys or documentary units. Similarly, 'à la carte' degrees can promote the development of skills in reflexivity, methodological flexibility, awareness of change, comparison and documentary analysis, but their success in doing so depends on the types of unit offered, the mix chosen by each student and the way they are taught.

A third, much less common type of curriculum places skills teaching at its very core. A few institutions which have had the opportunity in recent years to design entirely new single-honours history degrees (to replace previously offered multidisciplinary degrees) have adopted a theoretically explicit approach in which virtually the entire syllabus is organised around methodological and theoretical skills. This type of degree, offered, for example, at the University of East London, tends to rely on a much narrower range of historical subject matter (in this instance Britain, Europe and the colonial world since about 1750), studying this material from a range of approaches (methodological, thematic, philosophical, historiographical) in different units which become progressively more sophisticated. At the price of limiting historical content (and therefore the possibility of developing chronological awareness and comparative skills), this approach to curriculum design seeks to develop skills in reflexivity, theoretical and methodological awareness, and documentary analysis. Other institutions, such as the University of Northumbria and the University of the West of England, combine this approach with more conventional units in separate strands running through the curriculum.

As reflected in the relatively low level of prescription evident in Table 4.1 (the majority of institutions prescribe no more than two of the four types of unit listed), most history curricula could do more to promote the development of history-specific skills. The highest levels of prescription are found in the new universities, reflecting the more explicit 'skills' orientation of the teaching in these institutions, and especially in the entirely new approach to the curriculum adopted in places such as the University of East London. Although few institutions may wish to follow this approach in its entirety, even within the common 'research training' model we found significant innovations, both in terms of the types of unit required and their placement within the overall curriculum.

The way forward

There is, of course, no one way forward. History being the hybrid that it is, there are many ways in which the curriculum could make fuller provision for skills or could be nudged in the direction of emphasising some skills over others. The opportunity to design a curriculum from scratch happens only rarely, but the regular routine of course review can be used to make quite significant changes. Our survey has highlighted three areas which have been the focus of innovation recently and which are likely to become more important in the future.

The first of these is *reflexivity*, that is, the ability to understand the nature of history as a discipline and to be familiar with the questions which may legitimately be asked about its governing assumptions and practices. The current intellectual ferment, in which the credentials of all the humanities are the subject of theoretical appraisal by postmodernists and others, suggests that a reflexive element should feature in any training for the historical profession. But a strong case can also be made for a broader justification, on the grounds that the practitioner of any profession needs to develop the capacity for critical detachment about what he or she is doing. This is a demanding intellectual agenda, as reflected in the swelling volume of literature by both historians and critical outsiders. The fairly common 'methods course' in year one is only a beginning – and sometimes hardly that if it is confined to a descriptive 'how historians do it' approach. In many universities students are required to take a 'taster' from another discipline in their first year, and this is sometimes believed to promote methodological awareness about history. But unless the taster is itself of a reflexive kind, most history students will be little the wiser about the nature of their own discipline. In a small minority of cases the reflexive element is held back until the third year. But it is becoming increasingly clear that issues about the intellectual standing of the discipline, and its relation to other disciplines, require a cumulative process of reflection over the whole degree. Given the rising tide of interest in historiography within the profession, there may possibly be more consideration of epistemological and methodological issues in the course of content-led teaching, but this is hard to judge. The General Paper traditionally encouraged a reflexive function by requiring students to stand back and take a bird's eye view of their studies, and it still performs this function in the minority of departments where it survives (e.g. Cambridge and York Universities). But a growing number of departments are now incorporating a reflexive strand which spans two years, and in rare instances (as at Northumbria) all three. This may take the form of advanced courses in historical method, or an explicit engagement with theory (e.g. Marxism or postmodernism), or a study of the history of history writing.

The second trend concerns the emphasis given to *documentary work*. As we have seen, this was traditionally reserved for the final-year Special Subject and was regarded almost as a professional initiation that had to be earned during a two-year apprenticeship in more humdrum matters. The addition of the research dissertation only adds to that impression. But the centrality of textual interpretation to the analytical and contextual skills of the historian surely suggests a more thorough permeation. If a history degree is seen as a cumulative training in skills, it makes more sense to set about a documentary approach from the start, so that students can make the best of their opportunity for extended in-depth documentary work in year three. Moreover, the importance which historians rightly attach to the relationship between the particular and the general suggests that documentary work should be pursued *alongside* broader study, rather than as a sequel to it. The logical follow-up to a first-year course on 'the historian at work' is practical experience of reading and interpreting primary sources (in addition to the familiar pattern of reading secondary sources as the basis for an essay). In some departments (e.g. Leeds and North London Universities) first-year documentary work is a requirement. The second year may include further courses of this kind, with more intensive work on documents. This is also the point at which the conventional definition of primary sources may be critiqued and enlarged by the addition of oral sources, visual sources (including film) and computer databases. A welcome growth point is the short piece of documentary research in the second year as preparation for the final-year dissertation. The historian's claim to be a specialist in comparing and interpreting disparate forms of evidence looks much more convincing with this kind of follow-through over three years.

The third trend concerns the *comparative* mode of historical analysis. Comparing two related (but not identical) situations in order to characterise each one more precisely is commonly regarded as an asset to the informed citizen. For a history degree to provide training in this area presupposes sufficient breadth of study to generate material for comparison. One of the consequences of the globalisation of historical research over the past thirty years is that this requirement is much more likely to be met today than it was a generation ago. There are very few departments which do not offer British, European and American histories as standard fare. China, Japan, South Asia, the Middle East, Africa and Latin America are not as hard to find on the syllabus as they used to be. Most history graduates have acquired some cross-cultural awareness, with obvious topical implications.

The intellectual coherence of a geographically varied offering is greatly enhanced if the appropriate foundation is laid in year one. This is one of the reasons why survey units continue to have intellectual validity, whatever the practical difficulties in teaching them. They are the means by which most students acquire some 'period awareness' and some comparative perspective; they should be challenging in terms of breadth as well as length. If the nettle of the large-scale survey is grasped in the first year, exciting developments are possible later in the degree. Commitment to the goal of enabling students to be able to handle big historical problems spanning several societies and/or extended periods is usually signalled by the inclusion of comparative history. The label is much used in course descriptions, and it bears some relation to reality in a proportion of option-type units in year two. In these units two or more contemporaneous societies are studied together. Alternatively (and more rarely), a specific theme may be selected as a means of examining a number of societies drawn from different periods. Too often, however, any comparison is left to occur spontaneously in the student's mind rather than being incorporated into the teaching. Only a small number of departments demand a genuine demonstration of comparative insights from all their finalists. At the University of York the third year has for more than twenty years included a compulsory 'Comparative Special', on broadly defined themes such as 'peasants' and 'heroes', team-taught but with the comparative dimension kept to the fore by a unit coordinator; staff and students regard these demanding units as summative, not as an eccentric bye-way. The groundwork is provided in the first year, when all students take three units drawn from five periods of Western history from AD 400 to 1980. Sussex and Liverpool both require third-year history students to take a comparative unit alongside their Special Subject (themes include industrialisation, peasantries and national minorities in twentieth-century Europe). We also encountered some discussion in other departments of the possible enlarging of the scope of the traditional Special Subject to include a comparative dimension.

The few departments which have a substantial offering in comparative history are responding to the outside environment in a significant way. For the great majority of graduates who will find jobs outside academia, the case for large-scale analytical work is strong. The understanding of process and contrast has a particular bearing on social and political issues of the present day: the third-year student who makes a comparative study of industrialisation in Japan and the West, or who has studied the history of the family in Britain and France since the eighteenth century, has maximised one kind of historical insight which may prove at least as useful as the carefully contextualised study of original documents.

Conclusion

Historians of all people should be aware that the current debate about skills in higher education has a long pedigree. The merits of a historical education as preparation for public life have been asserted (and questioned) ever since the subject was launched as an undergraduate degree in the mid nineteenth century. As recently as 1965 some 45 per cent of all successful candidates for the administrative grade of the civil service had read history.[4] What is different now is that the ambitions of history graduates tend to be more varied, and their potential employers are much more specific about what they are looking for. Students anxious about their job prospects, and institutions keen to trim to the prevailing political wind, both have an interest in maximising the skills content of history degrees.

If the inclusion of free-standing skills units is taken to be the criterion of commitment to skills development, the degree programmes examined for our survey might be regarded as evidence of the conservatism – perhaps even outright hostility – of the history profession. This would be to misunderstand the kind of education offered in history and the other humanities. Where teaching is properly performed, the relevant skills are *embedded* in the content of the subject: both the generic skills, such as analysis, argument and presentation, and the subject-specific skills which draw on the training of historians as time specialists, such as the command of continuity, change and context. An additional argument, usually given too little weight, is that history's eclectic approach to theory and method gives students an adaptability which stands them in good stead for a life of further learning. History departments already produce graduates whose course of study equips them for employment and for citizenship, and this claim clearly needs to be asserted more vigorously in the public arena, for the enlightenment of those who regard history as an antiquarian indulgence. But an even stronger case can be made if some modification to the traditional undergraduate curriculum is considered. In planning improvements there will be scope for adding an explicit skills element, such as a unit dedicated to historical method, or information technology or study skills. But our survey suggests that the skills agenda will be addressed more fruitfully through the promotion of *academic* developments with a significant dividend in high-level skills. We have pointed to three such developments: reflexivity, documentary study and comparative work. The range of current historical study and the creativeness of those who teach it are the best guarantees of the discipline's continuing responsiveness to the demands of the world outside academia.

Notes

1 Maurice Kogan, 'History', in C. J. Boys, *et al.* (eds), *Higher Education and the Preparation for Work* (London, Jessica Kingsley, 1988), pp. 21–38. For a more recent survey of some of the issues faced by curriculum planners, see Alex Cowan, 'Planning a history curriculum', in A. Booth and P. Hyland (eds), *History in Higher Education: New Directions in Teaching and Learning* (Oxford, Blackwell, 1996), pp. 21–38.
2 The institutions visited were Cambridge University and the Universities of East London, Leeds, Northumbria at Newcastle, West of England and York. We would like to take this opportunity to thank the staff and students of all these departments for their generous assistance.
3 We would like to thank Tony Murray for assembling this information from the course brochures. The figures should only be considered approximate since the documentation was occasionally incomplete or difficult to interpret.
4 Evidence to the Fulton Committee (1968), quoted in G. Connell-Smith and H. A. Lloyd, *The Relevance of History* (London, Heinemann, 1972), p. 29.

5 Hannah Barker, Monica McLean and Mark Roseman

Re-thinking the history curriculum: enhancing students' communication and group-work skills

Picture the scene: ten students are sitting around a table. One of them has just delivered a poorly structured paper in a hung-over monotone and now it is time for the others to pose questions. The tutor anticipates the usual dead silence. To her surprise, there *are* questions. Then she realises why: the questioner is Volker, an exchange student from Germany. Volker does not share the diffidence, the individualistic approach or the reluctance to take oral contributions seriously, of his English counterparts. Instead, he assumes that questions are for asking, and that the interactions between the student paper-giver and the other students will be an important part of the learning experience.

The point of this example is not to sing the praises of the German educational system (though it undoubtedly does have many virtues). It is often *our* best students who go abroad, and perhaps they too are shining examples in France or Germany. But the frequently positive experiences which many British teachers have had with exchange students over recent years have helped to crystallise the frustrations that gave rise to the present project: above all, the feeling that in terms of skills and attitudes to learning, most of our students are not equipped to get the best out of seminar teaching. This perception derives not just from the frequently made comparisons between 'home' students and exchange students. It is borne also from the sense of many older colleagues that undergraduates arriving at university today lack basic skills which could be taken for granted among their predecessors, and from the view of many younger colleagues that the traditional history seminar, based on a model that is at least thirty years old (if not more), is often frustrating and unproductive.

In response to this problem, we set out to redesign part of the history curriculum at the University of Keele in a way that would integrate students' acquisition of learning skills with the teaching of history. In particular, we sought to enhance students' ability to work and communicate in groups. In so doing, we sought to enhance not only the quality of teaching which undergraduates receive and their learning experience, but also the quality of the teaching experience of history tutors: an area all too often overlooked.

Skills and history in higher education

Despite what we perceive to be a common desire among those who teach history to improve students' skills, there is also a widespread feeling of unease about labelling and quantifying what it is that students are supposed to learn, aside from the formal demands of the curriculum. More specifically, historians do not like to talk about 'skills'. In Britain, as elsewhere, the issue of skills is of course clearly at the forefront of much educational thinking in the late 1990s, particularly in light of the Dearing Committee's report,[1] but also as a result of the Higher Education Funding Councils' Teaching Quality Assessment exercise and the Graduate Standards Programme. Historians, in common with teachers of other academic disciplines, are now under pressure to be explicit about the kinds of skill which they think a history degree develops and, in particular, they are being asked to identify those 'transferable' skills which will make students more employable when they graduate. Using the language of skills, we are encouraged to formulate a notion of 'graduateness' and to identify the 'value added' nature of a degree.

The desire of government agencies, employers' groups and others to make the benefits of a history degree more explicit has attracted much criticism. Most recently, the working party of the History at Universities Defence Group (HUDG) published a report addressed to the Quality Assurance Agency which stated bluntly that

> historians have become used to expressing an approach to the discipline in a language of skills more because they believe that this is now what is expected of them than because they are in any way comfortable with this approach. They are unhappy with the crude and simplistic accounts of academic standards which emerge from any attempt to focus on aspects of the discipline rather than judging the whole. They reject the description of intellectual activities through single word concepts which fragment learning experience.[2]

The conclusion of the report is corroborated by educationalists, who point out that the notion of 'skills' has its origins in behaviourist theories and is associated with training in vocational areas.[3] They argue that skills or 'competency' approaches to education assume that expert behaviour can be atomised into pre-specified parts, each observed and measured. These approaches held sway in vocational courses in the United States in the early part of the century, and at the time John Dewey argued vigorously against them: 'When educators conceive vocational guidance as something which leads to definitive, irretrievable and complete choice both education and the chosen vocation are likely to be rigid, hampering further growth.'[4] The entrenched view of skills implicitly devalued such capacities as creativity and intuition.[5] It is clearly not appropriate for the study of history, which requires the 'intelligent effort of the learner to integrate the parts into a whole that is greater than the sum of its parts,'[6] as well as a tolerance of the uncertainty of knowledge.

Yet the impulse to formulate a model of objectives towards which history students are being educated does not come just from institutions associated with government bodies and employers, or indeed from the higher echelons of university management. It is also clear that concern about standards from inside university history departments, and a desire to improve the quality of students and their work, has led to discussions about subject-specific skills, and the teaching of these skills, which necessarily involve making explicit what historians think these should be, even if they avoid using the language of skills, graduateness and value-added education. While the definition of 'skill' discussed above can be termed 'quantitative', it is also possible to conceptualise 'skill' as qualitative: as a cognitive and social development which hones the ability to behave expertly. From this perspective, skills contribute to the ability to make judgements about, for example, what questions to ask or which is the better of several arguments. Some of these skills can be made explicit in learning tasks, but with no guaranteed outcomes. In this way education remains fundamentally unpredictable but, we believe, of ultimately greater value.

Along with many historians and teachers in other disciplines, we feel that developing students' skills works best when it is embedded within the curriculum. Stand-alone skills teaching, in our experience, generally fails because students do not appreciate its academic value when apparently isolated from the subject which they are studying. As the Dearing Report recorded, an Open University project which used both an 'embedded' and a 'bolt on' method of skills development in its programmes found considerable advantages in the embedded model.[7] In other words, skills are better acquired in a context which is relevant to the learner.[8] But despite the educational benefits of such an approach, the initially high costs of embedding skills, often requiring courses to be completely redesigned, must also be borne in mind.

We found that developing integrated skills courses was no easy task at Keele or anywhere else. This was not least because at the same time that universities are being pressurised to modify their teaching and introduce other initiatives implicit in the desire to identify and promote 'value added' education, cuts in resources, the prioritisation of research brought about by the Research Assessment Exercise and modularisation are all acting to make such innovations more difficult. Added to this, of course, are the problems of institutional inertia and the reluctance or inability, due to a lack of expertise on the part of individuals or departments, to introduce new approaches to teaching.[9] While these factors present difficulties and constraints, they also indicate the desirability of universities coming to grips with their own educational dilemmas and challenges. In a climate in which there are increasing demands for accounts to be made about the quality of teaching,[10] and in which particular ideas about what constitutes 'good practice' are in danger of being imposed, it is important for academics in each discipline to work out and articulate solutions and improvements.

In order to improve the quality of teaching and learning in history using innovative techniques, and focusing specifically on areas which we have highlighted as particularly important in terms of students' transferable skills (namely communication and group working), we have drawn heavily on the experiences of other universities (in particular, Hull, Newcastle, Nottingham, Teeside and York) and on the work of educational theorists working in this field, David Jaques in particular.[11] We proceeded on the premise that while it is important to avoid reductionist interpretations of 'skill', there is a strong educational case for the explicit incorporation of communication and group work in undergraduate history. Academic disciplines involve students in constructing knowledge and understanding for themselves. This is achieved by their active involvement in manipulating subject matter through the use of written and spoken language. The more opportunities students have to discuss challenging questions informally and formally, the more likely they are to learn effectively. This has always been the aim of the traditional seminar. There is also evidence that working in groups motivates students because it can provide the experience of 'relatedness' which enhances an experience of learning.[12] Furthermore, group work emphasises the potential of collaborative thinking about history, and there is convincing research to show that working together raises the expected standard of the quality of learning.[13] It can also enhance the work of knowledge construction. As Polyani argues, 'Knowledge and organisation are properties of groups',[14] while Collins connects skill to social interaction: 'The problem of skill comes partly from treating expertise as a property of the individual, rather than interaction of the social collectivity. It is in the collectivity that novel responses become legitimate displays of expertise.'[15] Highlighting communication and group work reinstates and reconfigures the central part that language and interaction play in learning undergraduate history. Our intention is to make them more explicit and to guide students in how to improve them. The aim is more confident and skilled historians.

Choosing to concentrate on communication and group-working skills does not mean that we aim to down-play the importance of other skills associated with studying for a history degree. Indeed, we endorse the way in which the HUDG working party has outlined the general abilities which the study of history encourages and develops under the headings 'analytical thinking', 'creative thinking' and 'communication and presentation'.[16] Although the working party spoke in terms of 'enhancement of abilities' and specifically avoided mentioning skills, it provided a useful outline of the intellectual objectives to which historians are currently educated. It is clear from our course planning that many of the 'abilities' listed by the HUDG report under separate headings – organising and synthesising evidence, understanding conceptual frameworks and problem solving, for example – will be incorporated into our scheme. Indeed, communication skills and group work can be seen as the basis for the development of critical abilities. Learning to debate informally with others; to pursue and complete demanding academic tasks collaboratively; and to select and present ideas formally with clarity and cogency will all contribute to the development of the high-order cognitive skills necessary for undergraduate study of history. It may be, too, that if this aim is achieved, the employers consulted by the National Committee of Enquiry into Higher Education who complained about the inadequate communication skills of graduates will be satisfied.[17]

Considerations in course planning

Once we had decided to focus on the development of students' capacities to think collectively and to be active, critical and independent learners, we needed to address the question of how these aims could be made concrete in course design. This involved consideration of goals; the selection, organisation and sequence of content, teaching methods and learning activities; and assessment and evaluation. We were strongly influenced at the same time by three main principles. One of the most important of these was that all aspects of course design should attempt to be congruent.[18] It follows from this, that if we want students to work collectively and to understand complex ideas and arguments, we must ensure that learning activities are designed to require this and that the assessment rewards it. Pursuing this principle led naturally to the second principle: finding ways of teaching which encourage a spirit of enquiry and the construction of understanding and knowledge. Here we followed Bruner's suggestion for arranging the 'practice of inquiry' by setting 'difficulties, puzzles and problems to be solved'.[19] The third principle which informed our planning was to encourage a 'deep' approach to learning characterised by the intention on the part of the student to understand the subject matter by, for example, relating and distinguishing evidence and argument. [20] The features we intended to pursue were: good teaching (associated with helpful feedback, clear explanations, attempts to make the subject interesting and an interest in student progress); clear goals; appropriate workload (since too much content leads to 'surface approaches'); appropriate assessment (i.e. congruent with aims); and opportunities for students to make choices.[21]

While these principles and aims have informed our thinking about an innovative course, our planning has been undertaken against a background of constraints which have necessarily affected the outcome of that planning. Constraints reside in individuals, departments, universities and the higher education system as a whole. In the following account we describe how we have attempted to pursue theoretical principles while taking account of everyday constraints in a research-led university. First, making the course appear as transparent as possible – both to students and teachers – is clearly very important to avoid initial confusion and possible hostility. With the aid of teaching examples and explanatory notes we hope to enhance staff and student awareness of the roles and processes taking place within their seminars. Although at Keele we have found the reaction of our colleagues to our proposals to be very positive, we know from the experiences of others that this is not always the case, and that in other places the greatest battle in trying to introduce innovative methods of teaching has been fought not with students, but with other members of staff. While such issues did not arise for us, the unfamiliarity of colleagues with educational research and current thinking was still a problem, and this needs to be combated with special staff seminars in addition to the provision of printed material.

Such difficulties with staff and students were, however, small compared with others we faced in course planning. Allowing students to enhance and apply their skills within the framework of a 'substantive' history course is not straightforward. Above all, although as the literature and practical experience of educational experts makes clear, an emphasis on skills development may enhance learning in the longer term, it necessarily entails a reduction in the amount of history material that can be covered within a given time. At Keele, this is particularly critical and challenging, because in the first-year programme (when this course will be taught), history accounts for only a third of students' learning time. We chose to replace two existing courses on the modern era, one covering the nineteenth century and one on twentieth-century history. In common with other universities, Keele's philosophy has been to give a reasonably broad grounding in the first year, introducing students to a range of periods which they may well not have studied prior to coming to university, and giving a relatively seamless coverage from the medieval to the modern period. While we understand and appreciate this philosophy and want to retain a reasonably broad grounding in the first year, we also recognised that the new course could not cover the same breadth as the two pre-existing modules. This situation was exacerbated because we were committed to building into the course some student-directed small-group project work. The result was that we decided to limit the substantive coverage to about half the ground covered in the previous two modules, and to restrict the course to the period 1850–1945.

The issue of how to structure the course was also very involved. While wanting to introduce innovative methods of teaching and learning, we were reluctant to place this within the context of a very traditional and conservative historical framework in terms of the subjects covered and the way in which we asked the students to explore them. For this reason we constructed a thematic approach which centred around the following topics: the challenge of modernisation; class, gender, race and the birth of mass society; imperialism and war; the European civil war; the failure of diplomacy; and World War II and the Holocaust in post-war memory. Being so prescriptive in terms of what was covered by students during the course and when, although vital to its success, also created a serious problem with library resources which could only be addressed by using special funds to allow for the bulk buying of certain texts.

Other limits on course planning were set by a desire not to increase staff contact hours nor to increase the number of seminar room bookings. These constraints have undoubtedly limited the flexibility and innovativeness in our choice of teaching formats, but probably secured the support of our colleagues. Moreover, they are, of course, constraints that apply to many other institutions.

They mean that we have had to have recourse to far more lecture sessions than we felt desirable measured against the goals of the skills course itself. However, learning from the approaches developed elsewhere and in educational literature, we incorporated into the course design suggestions, models and guidelines to encourage lecturers to develop interactive elements and sub-sessions within the large-lecture format.[22]

Lectures, therefore, still remain a prominent element of the course, comprising 50 per cent of staff/student contact. Even with the introduction of innovative teaching methods within lectures, they will still take place in a largely traditional form. Seminar teaching, on the other hand, is far more conducive to the adoption of new approaches. In planning the types of teaching method used on the course in seminars, and placing communication and presentation skills centre-stage, we decided to use a variety of techniques. Successive seminars set different kinds of group task, which include: small groups commenting on a text and reporting back to the whole class; small groups creating texts, for example propaganda texts or position papers; 'brief for the minister', in which small groups work to produce a brief for a third party to deliver; formal debate, in which teams seek to assert a particular position; and, most importantly, a group project conducted over several weeks on a specific topic of research, culminating in a formal, assessed presentation. Seminars also experiment with different patterns of group formation/communication, including: individuals making formal presentations to the group; sub-groups reporting to/arguing with one another; 'syndicates', in which sub-groups are entrusted with specific tasks and findings are summarised by the tutor; small groups 'snowballing' (culminating in groups crossing over and disseminating findings); and 'fish bowling', where the outer group observes an inner group discussing an issue. All of these approaches are supported both by educational literature and by the experience of teachers in history and other disciplines.[23]

As Ramsden has argued, 'assessment plays a key role in determining the quality of student learning'.[24] We have, therefore, considered seriously the form it should take. The project will be assessed by a mix of tutor, self and peer assessment, with the project presentation being given a group mark. Literature about assessment has alerted us to a number of issues, in particular introducing innovative forms of assessment extremely carefully;[25] establishing clear and helpful criteria;[26] and encouraging students to make judgements about, and be responsible for, their own progress by the well-planned use of self and peer assessment.[27] We decided that the first semester's assessment should be based on a mixture of seminar contribution (20 per cent), gobbets paper (40 per cent) and essay (40 per cent); while the second semester assessment comprises general seminar performance (20 per cent), essay (40 per cent) and group project work (40 per cent).

Finally, in such an experimental course evaluation is essential. There is a particular need to collect systematically and interpret information about the course that will help in the making of judgements about changes, modifications or fine tuning in subsequent years. In this respect, formal student evaluation at the end of the course can be supplemented by other sources of information. These include the quality of student learning evinced in teaching sessions as well as in formal assessments; informal feedback about the students' experience of learning; and teaching staffs' experience of teaching in ways which may be new to them.

Conclusion

We remain convinced that the incorporation of skills teaching is of great importance to the future progress of history students, even if we share others' caution about the way in which skills are interpreted and the political overtones of much of the language surrounding them. In addition, it seems clear that skills can only be usefully and meaningfully introduced into the history curriculum if they are embedded in history courses: that is, courses which deal substantively with matters of historical content and do not just cover skills in an isolated context. As with the introduction of any new module or course, and particularly those which utilise less traditional forms of teaching, practical problems of implementation arise which are impossible to ignore. However, with sufficient staff interest, the willingness to compromise and preferably some form of extra funding, our experience is that such courses are possible, as well as desirable.

Notes

1 The National Committee of Inquiry into Higher Education, *Higher Education in the Learning Society: Report of the National Committee* (London, HMSO, 1997).
2 HUDG, *Standards in History: Final Report of a Working Party of the History at the Universities Defence Group to the Quality Assurance Agency* (London, HUDG, 1998), pp. 5–6.
3 P. Hodkinson and M. Issitt, *The Challenge of Competence* (London, Cassell, 1995); T. Hyland, *Competence, Education and NVQs* (London, Cassell, 1994).
4 J. Dewey, *Democracy and Education* (New York, Free Press [1916], 1966), p. 364.
5 P. Ainley, *Class and Skill: Changing Divisions of Knowledge and Labour* (London, Cassell, 1993).
6 *Ibid.*, pp. 12–13.
7 L. Hodginson, *Changing the Higher Education Curriculum Towards a Systematic Approach to Skills Development* (Milton Keynes, Open University Vocational Qualifications Centre, 1996).
8 J. Arnett, *Training for Transferable Skills* (Manpower Services Commission, Sheffield, 1989); G. Gibbs, *Study Guide for Certificate in Higher Education* (Oxford, Oxford Centre for Staff Development, undated).
9 See L. Hodginson, *Personal Transferable Skills in Higher Education* (Milton Keynes, The Open University Vocational Qualifications Centre, 1996).
10 In Britain, the Institute for Learning and Teaching, launched in June 1999, will be responsible for an accreditation framework for teachers in higher education.

11 D. Jaques, *Learning in Groups* (London, Croom Helm, 1992, 2nd edn). See also J. McLeish, W. Matheson and J. Park (eds), *The Psychology of the Learning Group* (London, Hutchinson, 1973); J. Rudduck, *Learning Through Group Discussion* (Guildford, SHRE, 1978); A. Wilson, 'Structuring seminars: a technique to allow students to participate in the structuring of small group discussion', *Studies in Higher Education*, 5:1 (1980); M. Miles, *Learning to Work in Groups: A Program Guide for Educational Leaders* (New York, Teacher's College Press, 1981, 2nd edn); D. Jaques, *Independent Learning and Project Work* (Oxford, Oxford Centre for Staff Development, 1989); G. Gibbs, S. Habeshaw and T. Habeshaw, *53 Interesting Things to Do in Your Seminars and Tutorials* (Bristol, Technical and Educational Services Ltd, 1989).

12 R. M. Ryan and C. L. Powelson, 'Autonomy and relatedness as fundamental to motivation and education', *Journal of Experimental Education*, 60:1 (1991), 49–56.

13 D. W. Johnson and R. T. Johnson, *Learning Together and Alone* (London, Prentice-Hall, 1987); M. Reynolds, *Groupwork in Education and Training* (London, Kogan Page, 1994).

14 M. Polyani, quoted in S. Washburn, 'Human behaviour and behaviour in other animals', *American Psychology*, 33 (1978), 405–18.

15 H. Collins, *Artificial Experts, Social Knowledge and Intelligent Machines* (Cambridge, MA, MIT Press, 1989).

16 HUDG, *Standards in History*.

17 National Committee of Inquiry into Higher Education, *Higher Education in the Learning Society*, p. 133.

18 P. Ramsden, *Learning to Teach in Higher Education* (London, Routledge, 1992); D. Rowntree, *Developing Courses for Students* (London, McGraw-Hill, 1981).

19 J. S. Bruner, 'Beyond the information given', in N. Entwistle and D. Hounsell (eds), *How Students Learn* (Lancaster, Institute for Research and Development in Post-Compulsory Education, 1975), pp. 105–16.

20 N. Entwistle and F. Marton, 'Contrasting perspectives on learning', in F. Marton *et al* (eds), *The Experience of Learning* (Edinburgh, Scottish Academic Press, 1984); F. Marton and R. Saljo, 'On qualitative differences in learning', *British Journal of Educational Psychology*, 46 (1976), 115–27.

21 P. Ramsden, 'A performance indicator of teaching quality in higher education: the Course Experience Questionnaire', *Studies in Higher Education*, 16 (1991), 129–50.

22 G. Gibbs, S. Habeshaw and T. Habeshaw, *53 Interesting Things to Do in Your Lectures* (Bristol, Technical and Educational Services Ltd, 1984); A. Jenkins, 'Encouraging active learning in structured lectures', in G. Gibbs, *Improving the Quality of Student Learning* (Bristol, Technical and Educational Services Ltd, 1992).

23 Jaques, *Independent Learning*; G. Preston, 'Seminars for active learning', in A. Booth and P. Hyland (eds), *History in Higher Education* (Blackwell, Oxford, 1996), pp. 111–27; D. Baume and C. Baume, *Running Tutorials and Seminars* (Oxford, Oxford Centre for Staff Development, 1996).

24 Ramsden, *Learning to Teach*, p. 182.

25 A. Booth, 'Changing assessment', in Booth and Hyland (eds), *History in Higher Education*.

26 A. Booth, 'Assessing group work', in Booth and Hyland (eds), *History in Higher Education*; S. Brown, C. Rust and G. Gibbs, *Strategies for Diversifying Assessment*, (Oxford, Oxford Centre for Staff Development, 1994).

27 *Ibid.*; G. Gibbs, *Assessing Student Centred Learning* (Oxford, Oxford Centre for Staff Development, 1995); L. Andresen, P. Nightingale, D. Boud and D. Magin, *Strategies for Assessing Students* (Birmingham, SCED, 1993); D. Boud, *Implementing Student Self-Assessment* (Sydney, HERDSA, 1991); S. Brown and P. Dove, *Self and Peer Assessment* (Newcastle, MARCET, 1991).

Integrating information technology into the history curriculum

Recognition of the value of information technology (IT) to innovations in teaching and learning in higher education has gained ground in recent years. As Donald Spaeth puts it, the developments in IT have produced a 'challenge for academics . . . to find new ways to take advantage of the vast sets of resources in order to enrich their teaching and student learning'.[1] In some ways this challenge has been met, and few academics and students today are untouched by the advancement of IT. There is now 'scarcely a history degree . . . in the UK that does not contain some element of computation'.[2] Few academics are now without a PC on their desk, and the 'humble' word-processor has become an essential part of the historian's tool kit for the production of scholarly work. Most academics are familiar with e-mail, and the majority of students are now introduced to this in the first year of their course. The 'magic box' which attracts the highest expectations is the World Wide Web, with its opportunities for searching for historical information, ranging from bibliographical sources and on-line journals to teaching resources such as historical databases. As one commentator puts it: 'we are witnessing the most revolutionary change to have occurred in the fundamental pattern of scholarly communication since the invention of the printed journal in the seventeenth century.'[3] Academics can now access a range of information sources in a machine-readable form, and these include statistical data, text, images and moving pictures with audio. Although there is still concern over the availability and accessibility of such resources, there is a growing realisation of the need to disseminate information and to develop initiatives for the promotion of electronic sources.

Developments in history and computing since the 1980s have also seen an increasing use of spreadsheets and database applications as tools for organising and analysing historical information. Both these programs can be profitably used as a teaching resource, and they are a means of allowing students greater access to primary sources. Spreadsheets allow students to use, process and present historical statistics, and gain an understanding of quantification in historical investigation. A database management system is a program used to construct and operate a historical database, which consists of a table of structured historical records; for example, a list compiled from the census returns. In the past, these applications have been associated with the use of computers to develop subject-specific skills relating to quantification, and it is most likely that they are still most heavily used by economic and social historians. However, a number of instructional packages are coming to fruition which take the possibilities of using computers in the classroom a step further. Electronic history seminars, for example, use hypermedia applications. Students can gain access to instructional software which incorporates photographic images, maps and diagrams, video and audio, and data handlers. These are often distributed on CD ROM and are a classic demonstration of the increasing versatility of modern computer programs. It is now 'easier than ever to move data and results between database management systems, statistical analysis programs, spreadsheets, and word processors'.[4]

The increasing flexibility of computer software is evident in recent initiatives in the production of electronic lectures which cover a range of historical subjects. For example, in Britain the Teaching and Learning Technology Programme (TLTP) has developed source-based tutorials on a variety of issues, including Women's History, The Coming of Mass Politics and the Industrial Revolution, using what is called an 'enriched lecture' format. A 'subject expert', who is not necessarily an expert in computers, produces one or more lectures which are 'enriched' by introducing supporting examples to the basic text drawn from a variety of 'core resources'. Such initiatives are important to the diffusion of instructional learning systems using computer technology. They will form part of the material that lecturers can use for computer-assisted learning. They help to integrate historical research with teaching, and the tutorials have a wide appeal across the history curriculum, covering a range of subjects and chronological periods. The tutorials use multimedia applications to integrate a variety of historical sources: secondary historical texts, historical documents, statistical data sets and graphics, visual images, film clips, maps and diagrams, and bibliographical references and glossaries. They are designed to be user friendly, and to be used in the history curriculum either as a special study, a key teaching resource for project work, or for independent study and archival reference.[5]

Despite this new technological horizon there remain, however, considerable barriers to the diffusion of IT in history departments. Our own experience shows that tutors can be frustrated by the lack of technological advice available on problem solving and, once a project is underway, there is often then a sudden realisation of the time-consuming nature of producing material for computing-based history courses. These observations are confirmed by a recent report on IT in the History of Art which recognises the problems of enhancing subject-specific capabilities in computer usage, the need to persuade staff of the advantages of acquiring new skills, and the need for 'institutional support'.[6] Similarly, a recent analysis of the advantages of the World Wide Web on the Internet concludes that, despite institutional initiatives and technological developments in this area, there are still problems concerning the participation of historians on the Web, the standardisation of good practice, the problem of copyright, and the need for 'training and awareness'.[7] The computer is clearly not a 'magic box' which can simply provide a cost-free medium for developing new methods of teaching. Indeed, there is still considerable debate over the contribution that computing can make to the teaching and understanding of history.

The outcome of these factors is that, as yet, the use of computers in British universities and colleges is limited to individual courses which largely tend to focus on computer-based methods. This suggests that there are still barriers to entry in terms of integrating a history and computing dimension into the curriculum. Indeed, if it is to be more widely integrated, then a clear case must be made for its inclusion. It is not enough to appeal to the notion of the 'magic box', a form of technological determinism, nor is it sufficient to suggest that IT is necessarily good for students in terms of developing transferable skills. What is required is to make explicit the particular capabilities and attributes relevant to the historian which can be advanced through the use of computer-aided teaching. As Everett argues, the advent of new computer software does not come without costs, but historians might also focus more on the benefits that these more sophisticated programs can bring to the teaching of future generations of historians.[8] After teaching students IT since the late 1980s, there still seems to us to be an element of salesmanship in the process, not only in the need to confront student resistance to the wider application of computers in history, but also to persuade our own colleagues of its potential benefits.[9]

Developing the historian's subject-specific capabilities

Part of the resistance to IT in history is related to the wider debate concerning the tensions between the accumulation of transferable skills as against subject-specific knowledge and scholarly practice. The nature of this general debate is articulated at the professional level by concerns over the infringement of intellectual property rights by a perceived need to introduce a higher vocational element into humanities-based courses. As Marshall Gregory puts it: 'There is a constant new pressure to move education towards a skills-based curriculum . . . to treat students as if they are mere mechanisms for getting the skills needed to run a post-industrial society out into the market place.'[10] Such a critical perspective has not been lost on practitioners of history and computing. For example, Tim Hitchcock is highly critical of skills-driven IT for historians, and somewhat caustically remarks that, 'the teaching of IT to history students at the undergraduate level is currently being driven by two things, pedagogic economy and skills training.' The trend seems to be to use historical computing to present large amounts of information more effectively to students, or to pacify employers who are increasingly demanding that graduates are computer literate.[11] This type of agenda will do little to generate critical awareness and the capability for a wider appreciation of the material being used.

Our own perspective on the relation between history and computing is that skills-driven courses in history have inherent dangers relating to the swamping of the subject by an emphasis on technology for technology's sake, but that it would be a mistake to dismiss the vocational aspects of IT for, in a world where information is of growing importance to organisations, IT skills are a key attribute of the modern graduate and, whether we like it or not, cannot be ignored. Rather, we should find ways to integrate IT within a teaching strategy which genuinely probes the tension between technical capabilities on the one hand and the enhancement of subject knowledge and understanding on the other, and works with the grain of student motivation in history which, as Booth points out in chapter 3, is subject focused. Thus Middleton's account of a first-year economic history course at Bristol University emphasises the importance of the computer in developing both an understanding of key theoretical concepts and a greater understanding of change over time. Using spreadsheets, students could test a range of hypotheses, considering the limitations of the historical material used as well as its potential, and integrate theoretical models with a variety of data. Yet students at Bristol were also keenly aware that the computer skills they acquired were marketable, both in terms of short-term and vacation opportunities and for their longer-term career prospects.[12] In this example, transferable skills are an important spin-off from the process of teaching economic history with a computer. Nevertheless, transferable skills, such as critical analysis, effective communication of new ideas and their construction and presentation, numerical skills, and the organisation and evaluation of information, have always been acquired as part of the process of teaching and learning history in general, and are not simply confined to the field of economic history. Thus an advantage of a history and computing input into the degree structure is that it allows the student to appreciate the computer as a device for aiding historical enquiry, while at the same time making 'a positive contribution to a student's career development'. In this sense, transferable and subject-specific skills are reciprocal.[13] As Hopkins argues, the study of history is not an exercise in training historians, but rather it has a dual function, to 'educate minds' and to equip them with the capabilities they will need in the future. Further, computing is not age specific, and the more mature student returning to education can find the experience rewarding,[14] especially as he/she often has basic IT skills accrued from work experience. This has obvious implications for the development of history courses which use computer technology.

The main question facing the teacher of history is how far the computer should become the focus of historical investigation. Middleton was aware of this question back in 1989, when he asked whether the computer was to form part of the existing way that history is taught, or whether it was to transform completely the teaching of the subject, and thus the subject itself.[15] In answer to this question, we would certainly not claim that the use of computers has, as yet, fundamentally reshaped the subject of history itself; after all, the study of history is not dependent upon the use of computers. For example, researchers often apply computing only when they have a particular problem to solve which cannot be advanced by using manual procedures alone. Nevertheless, the increasing flow of information now made possible by the computer, and in particular through computer-aided research, offers students a greater access to the raw material of the historian, historical primary sources.[16] In this sense, the computer can be seen as a tool which can be used to good effect to augment existing teaching methods.

The use of the computer as a tool for use with historical sources can be illustrated by the example of the use of databases by historians. A historical database is a collection of historical records which are organised in a machine-readable form into fields, or categories of information. The program used to build and operate a database is the Database Management System, of which commercial examples are DBase IV and Microsoft Access. With historical information now becoming increasingly available to historians, for example via the World Wide Web, and with researchers producing more sources in machine-readable form, it is almost inevitable that there will be a demand by historians for the technology to utilise it effectively. As Spaeth notes, historical research requires the historian 'to read, transcribe, organise and evaluate large quantities of data', and data-handling software is ideal for facilitating this process.[17] An example of a database that we use with our own students, customised from our own historical research, is shown in Table 6.1. It is used to explore the business structure of the cotton industry during the industrial revolution. The data were extracted from a primary source, a factory inspector's survey for 1833. The fields of the database table contain information on the attributes of cotton firms, their name and location, the processes they were engaged in and their total employment. Using these data, students can examine the structure of the industry, the size distribution of firms, the type of productive activity they were engaged in and the distribution by locality. Students can also be made aware of the limitations of this information, and of the need to acquire additional facts and to ask additional questions of the data.[18] This is only one illustration, and historians are now using computerised data sources in their teaching which cover a wide range of historical themes. For example, Mawdsley and Munck demonstrate the potential of using databases drawn from census data to explore household patterns, and they also use a spreadsheet to examine data on political parties and voting patterns. 'Text handling' software, which provides a tool for examining primary sources such as 'letters, depositions, charters and treaties' is also now available. As yet, this is not commonly used by historians in teaching, although '[it has] considerable potential, especially for cultural and intellectual historians'.[19]

Unlike manual procedures, the use of a Database Management System allows students to process large quantities of data quickly, and quite complex groupings of records can be achieved in seconds. Historians, of course, use a wide range of source material, and the storage and analysis of these sources is essential to their work. Often the sources are large and complex, and present a considerable challenge in terms of analysis and interpretation. A Database Management System can provide a valuable aid to facilitate this process, but

Table 6.1 A business history database

Firm	Location	Process	TEMPLOY
Birley & Kirk	Manchester	I	1692
Ormrod & Hardcastle	Bolton	I	1576
McConnel & Co.	Manchester	S	1545
Bolling E & W	Bolton	S	1356
Houldsworth T	Manchester	S	1201
Horsefield Joseph	DHS	I	1183
Ashton Thomas	DHS	I	1149
Marsland T	Stockport	I	947
Taylor Hindle & Co.	Bolton	I	924
Collinge & Lancashire	Oldham	I	853
Murray A & G	Manchester	S	841
Stirling & Beckton	Manchester	I	873
Lees J & Sons	Stockport	I	796
Oxford Road Twist Co.	Manchester	I	774
Smith William	Stockport	I	761
Lambert Hoole & Co.	Manchester	S	752
Ogden T R & T	Manchester	S	712
Guest James	Manchester	I	712
Howard C & T	DHS	I	648
Sampson Lloyd & Co.	Stockport	I	632

Notes:
DHS = Duckinfield, Hyde and Staleybricke.
S = Spinning firms only.
I = Integrated firms.

does not preclude the intellectual judgement of the historian. The software cannot determine the strengths and weaknesses of the sources, or provide the final interpretation of the results. It does, however, permit academic rigour by allowing the easier processing of large amounts of information, the testing of alternative interpretations, and a degree of speed and accuracy which cannot be attained by manual processes. Indeed, the computer as a tool for historians allows a greater awareness 'of the nature and implications of their source material'.[20] By viewing the computer as a means of enhancing the use of historical sources by our students, we can provide a clear rationale for introducing history and computing into the curriculum. But computer-aided learning is also being influenced by the development of instructional software, which is also valuable for the history teacher. We have already referred to interactive teaching tutorials, such as those produced by the History Courseware Consortium, but there are also important developments at the University of Southampton with its Historical Document Expert System. By developing specialist multimedia software, the aim is to disseminate core teaching material for academic use.[21] A number of commercial multimedia packages are also now available on CD

ROM; for example, the *Who Built America?* project.[22] Developments in instructional software may well transform the way history is presented in the future, and they certainly offer the prospect of developing independent learning among students. However, the work is still in its experimental stage, and its reception by students and by the historical profession is still an open-ended issue.

In this section we have raised questions concerning the validity of introducing IT into the history curriculum. In our view, computing can make a valuable contribution to the teaching of history and, at the same time, make more explicit to students the need to acquire key transferable skills. The latter, however, is a spin-off from the development of history and computing courses which directly engage with the specific subject of history. The computer is a tool which historians can profitably use to facilitate the study of history, and it also has the potential to be profitably employed as an instructional medium. Given this, we now turn our attention to some practical suggestions for the integration of IT into history courses at an undergraduate level, and offer some basic principles, based upon our own experience and that of our students, which are fundamental to creating an environment for the dissemination of IT within the history curriculum.

Integrating IT into the history curriculum: basic principles

In the approach outlined above, there is a clear emphasis on what Spaeth calls 'teaching history with a computer rather than computing as a subject in its own right'. In this, there are two common approaches currently in use in the teaching of computing to history undergraduates. The first is the 'workshop' approach. In this, 'students learn to use general-purpose programs to explore and analyse historical data derived from primary sources'. The computer is therefore viewed as a tool which can introduce students to the advantages of studying primary sources, whether statistical, textual or visual. Thus this approach 'may also be termed "tools-based" or "source-based"'.[23] The second approach is to view the computer as the medium for providing instruction on a particular historical theme, an approach we have already referred to above. The important work of historians through the History Courseware Consortium (TLTP projects) is an example of this approach, and the electronic lectures, using interactive multimedia capabilities, which have been developed will provide a valuable stock of material for instructional teaching.

Both of these approaches can be profitably used within the context of an overall commitment to integrating IT into the history curriculum. In both approaches there is a focus on enhancing the student's capabilities as a historian: an appreciation of the structure of historical sources and an understanding of historical issues. The fundamental aim is to teach history with a computer and not computer science. Such courses should not be seen as appendages to existing modules, but rather should be presented to students as an integral part of doing history and enhancing subject-specific understanding and knowledge.

Such an approach is reinforced by a study, conducted by the Department of Computer Science at the University of York in 1996, into developments of computing provision for a wide range of students, in terms of the needs of subject-specific areas. A key finding of the study was that 'computing is best taught within courses in which it is used'.[24] The scope for introducing computing to history students is widened by such an approach, and it further justifies the time that both teachers and students can devote to such courses.[25]

A key feature of course development is to provide discipline-based material which stimulates the student's interest in the subject. Students should use computers in 'historically meaningful ways'. On the other hand, by focusing on the specific discipline the student is pursuing for a degree, there is an attempt to enthuse students with an appreciation of computer technology and data analysis. If this is accepted as a basic principle, then it obviously leads to questions concerning the processes by which this can be achieved. What structures can be established which allow students to progress through the degree and enhance their confidence in using the computer as a historical tool? The answer to this question is conditioned by three factors. First, the institutional context in which curriculum development is set; what is the support for history and computing, and how is it viewed within the aims of the institution? Second, the nature of the material used and the type of software applied are dependent upon the nature of the subject being taught. For example, does the course provide for a wide range of historical disciplines, or is it more narrowly focused? And third, what are the capabilities of the student cohort; is there a mixed ability in terms of IT capability, and is there a large percentage of mature students?

The above factors will determine the way that IT is integrated into the degree structure. At Sheffield Hallam University we provide History and Computing modules in all three years of the degree in Historical Studies (see Table 6.2). However, we believe that a key to the success of integrating IT into the curriculum is the experience of students in year one. At the beginning of the degree all students should be given basic instruction in using computer software, and also introduced to its potential in the study of history. An example is provided by our first-year modules in Computing within the history degree at Sheffield Hallam. The institutional context, set by the university, is very much pedagogic in that there is a clear emphasis on driving vocational skills across the various subject disciplines. In history this is accepted, but tempered by the development of IT elements which are based on enhancing these skills through the subject base. Thus students are introduced to IT in two modules during their first year of study. In the first semester they participate in a six-week series of computer workshops as part of a general history-studies methodology unit, Skills for Historians. Here, they are introduced to word processing, the World Wide Web, the use of e-mail, and so on. A key factor in ensuring a successful reception by students is to integrate their learning of the software with a clearly defined set of outcomes for assessment. For example, students are set projects which have a specific problem-solving basis to them, such as performing searches on the Web

Table 6.2 History and Computing modules in the curriculum at Sheffield Hallam University, 1997–98

Stage	Module	Technique	Software	No. students
Level 1 Semester 1	Skills for Historians	Part of this devoted to IT skills – word processing, internet, e-mail, etc.	Microsoft based	90
Level 1 Semester 2	Introduction to History and Computing (compulsory)	Word processing and Use of Spreadsheets	Microsoft Word 6/ Microsoft Excel V	90
Level 2	History and Computing (optional)	Spreadsheets and basic introduction to database	Microsoft Excel V and Microsoft Access 2	40
Level 3	Historyand Computing: Approaches to Business History (optional)	Spreadsheets and databases	Microsoft Excel V and Microsoft Access 2	15–20

for information on historical topics and undertaking bibliographical searches on the Internet. Similarly, word processing is adapted within the framework of learning basic scholarly practices, such as the writing of historical essays and referencing by automatic footnoting. Future students will also be introduced to electronic conferencing, which they will be invited to use in small-group projects on another first-year history module, Continuity and Change. The intention of the initial provision of computing for our students is to engage with subject-based problems and issues, while at the same time ensuring that they acquire experience and confidence in using IT for future progression. On the latter point, we have a mixed cohort of students in terms of their technical capabilities. We are finding increasingly that computer skills learnt in previous education are more advanced, but we still have a significant number of students who have only a limited experience, if any, of using computer software.

This introductory experience is followed in semester two by a specific module: Introduction to History and Computing. This is compulsory for all history students, and aims to develop history and computing following the format of the workshop approach outlined earlier; namely, to provide students with an 'understanding of how historians work, by enabling them to explore and form their own interpretations of historical source material'.[26] The choice of source material is determined by the nature of the history degree itself. We offer a specifically Modern History degree course which covers a wide range of historical fields:

economic and business history, political history, social and cultural history, social history of medicine, women's history and the history of imperialism. In this respect the aim is to demonstrate the use of computing across the discipline by basing the module on a range of historical themes or topics. For example, students examine structural change during the industrial revolution; the standard of living of workers, 1850–1914; and emigration from Britain during the nineteenth century. At present, we use, in particular, spreadsheets (Microsoft Excel V) as the main software for this module. We are keenly aware of the need to develop among our students an understanding of basic quantification, and how the historian can organise, calculate, present and interpret the patterns of historical statistics. The data sets used can also be constructed from primary sources fairly easily, and presented to students in a machine-readable form.

The delivery of this module is via workshops and seminar discussions. The former are concerned with the hands-on use of computers by the students. A series of technical tasks is set (see the example in Figure 6.1), which is backed up by an instruction guide to allow the student to proceed step by step. Further, the data to be used are fully explained to students, and they have access to instructional lectures on the Internet which provide a discussion of the historical theme to be explored, as well as the historiography surrounding it. A set of historical questions is also provided for the students, to facilitate the process of interpretation. This is important at the first-year level for, as Spaeth points out, 'Although the computer allows students to explore source materials independently', the task of looking for patterns is not always easy for students at the beginning, and especially for those who are new to using computers.[27] Further, our experience shows that students gain confidence in constructing interpretations if they have a platform for discussing their findings. Thus seminar discussions are used to prompt students to develop confidence in oral communication and to present their version of the findings. Nevertheless, our aim is to use computing to project the value of student-centred learning within the overall teaching and learning philosophy of the degree.

The student is at the centre of the process, teaching and learning are interactive and the lecturer acts as a facilitator, employing methods of delivery which prompt students to engage with task-based activities. Such an approach to teaching and learning is now well recognised as an important element of the student experience. Computer technology offers an additional means for the student to develop an appreciation of the need to learn independently, and 'we need to give students the ability to control the process, rather than seeking to control it ourselves'.[28] As Morgan and Trainor argue:

> The computer enables students to approach and interrogate types and amounts of information about the past that would, without new technology, be unavailable to them. In the process their work becomes less passive, more participatory and, potentially, more imaginative. Likewise instructors can free themselves from the necessity to rely overwhelmingly in their teaching on lectures and tutorials based on secondary works.[29]

Figure 6.1: Example of first-year exercise sheet: emigration in the nineteenth century

In the workshop complete the following tasks:

1 Open the spreadsheet EMIG.XLS, which contains data for emigration by country of origin, 1820–99.

2 Enhance the table by centring the main heading across columns, centring text and numbers in cells; expand the width of columns and provide borders for the table.

3 Produce a pie chart for 1820 which shows the proportion of emigrants going to each destination.

4 Produce a pie chart for 1899 which shows the proportion of emigrants going to each destination.

5 Produce a line chart which shows the pattern of emigration to the USA between 1820 and 1899.

6 Produce a line chart which shows the pattern of emigration to the North American colonies and to Australia/New Zealand between 1820 and 1899.

7 Create a new column with the heading Total Emigration. Now calculate the total emigration for all destinations annually between 1820 and 1899.

8 At the bottom of the table calculate the total number of emigrants for each destination between 1820 and 1899.

9 Create five new columns so that you can calculate the proportion of emigrants going to each destination between 1820 and 1899. Title the column headings: % USA; % North American colonies, etc. Now calculate the proportion of emigrants annually between 1820 and 1899:

   a) to the USA
   b) to the North American colonies
   c) to Australia/New Zealand
   d) to the Cape and Natal
   e) to other destinations.

An important issue here concerns the type of assessment which is set for a module of this type. Our practice is to base assessment on project-based activity, setting clear tasks for students to attain, and requiring a finished article in the form of a word-processed report. In the report students demonstrate their understanding of the historical theme, the presentation of data using tables and charts, and the interpretation of the information provided. It may be added that group work forms as a key role in the learning and assessment process. In the workshops students work in groups and group interaction is encouraged. Again, this fits in with established teaching and assessment strategies of our history degree which recognise the value of group work both in terms of the teaching of history and of the development of important transferable skills.

We believe that getting it right at the beginning is important, and there is a need to enthuse students with the advantages that computers offer to historical study. At the same time, the process of learning-by-doing equips students with IT capabilities which are transferable in character. Through the use of computers in history, transferable skills are made more explicit, and they provide valuable attributes for future graduates. It also provides an important learning curve for those students who wish to explore the use of computers as they progress through the degree. Thus an optional History and Computing module is offered to second-years, and this recruits around forty students out of a cohort of about eighty. This module enhances the student learning curve by introducing methods of basic database design and operation, as well as using now-familiar software such as spreadsheets. We base the module on a specific historical topic, which incorporates some of the main strands of British history taught on the second year of the degree; economic, social and political. For example, we have been using the theme of Edwardian Britain over the last two years, examining topics relating to an important turning point in British history. Students thus gain an understanding of key events in economic, social and political history, as well as becoming more aware of the debates over Britain's role as an imperial nation. Computer-based workshops, which focus on task-based exercises relating to the historical sources provided, are integrated with more conventional methods such as lectures and seminar discussions. The latter are used for providing both the empirical content of the module and for exploring the interpretation of the source material. Assessment is geared towards enhancing independent learning through group-based project work.

The aim at Sheffield Hallam University is to use IT as one of the ways to develop an appreciation of the value of independent learning by students, but also to equip them with the technical capability to pursue more specialist modules in history and computing in their final year of study. Thus in the third year of the degree students can choose to do a special topic in business history which uses a historical database to explore the changing pattern of business structure between 1880 and 1940. Again, the assessment criteria are based upon students developing independent project work, with the lecturer acting in a supervisory capacity. We are also increasingly aware that final-year students are employing the skills they have acquired by using computer software, mainly spreadsheets and Database Management Systems, for the collection and processing of information for their dissertation topics. This is a rewarding trend, and a justification of the value of IT in the curriculum. Although we have travelled a considerable distance in developing IT within the curriculum at Sheffield Hallam since the late 1980s, there are nevertheless a number of problems and issues which still need to be confronted, and which, we believe, are endemic within the history profession itself. In conclusion, we will examine these issues and also reflect on the present state and future development of computing within the history curriculum.

Conclusion

There have been rapid developments in computer hardware and software over the last ten years, and the future looks increasingly promising. However, our own perception is that the diffusion of IT in the history curriculum is, at present, incremental and certainly not revolutionary. There is a paradox between the diffusion of the technical capabilities of IT and the level of its diffusion as a teaching medium. History and Computing still tends to be confined to one or two enthusiasts who carry out the bulk of the teaching and are largely responsible for the developmental aspects of the modules. We may, of course, have set a false paradox, in the sense that it is unreasonable to assume that history and computing should necessarily be diffused across all subject fields within history. After all, we would not expect that all members of a history department would be expert in every branch of history; historians tend to be specialists in their own area of study. Seen from this perspective, history and computing as a new branch/field of historical research and teaching has made considerable advances in terms of becoming embedded into the history curriculum.

This view also helps in confronting the issue of the form of integration in the curriculum: for example, should history and computing be optional or compulsory? There are obviously problems with forcing an element of compulsion either on staff or students in this area, but we strongly believe that there is a case to be made for providing a solid foundation at the beginning of a student's studies. This provides a platform for all students to acquire a basic understanding of computer applications, but also allows them to pursue optional modules as they progress through later stages of a degree. These modules often reflect the subject specialisms of those who are engaged in the teaching and development of IT as a teaching medium. Certainly, in the example we have given of Sheffield Hallam University, the final year of the degree is associated with the use of computers in economic and business history, reflecting the subject specialism of those who teach it. In this situation, and given the labour-intensive nature of setting up such courses and the need for expenditure on equipment, optionality would seem the best approach at present.

It may be, however, that history and computing will in the future attract more adherents as software with a wider appeal, such as textual databases, becomes more widely disseminated. Further, the expanding World Wide Web and developments in instructional software, such as TLTP initiatives, offer a medium for the application of computers to the study of a range of historical topics.[30] This software should help to broaden the use of computing across a wider spectrum of the history curriculum, although we must be careful about evoking a simple technological determinism. The experience of the last decade has shown that the diffusion of IT in subject areas such as history is not shaped simply by technological developments. Rather, the spread of history and computing has been shaped by a consideration of the trade-off between a set of internal and a set of external factors. The former is related to the role of staff enthusiasts who are driven by intellectual interests and the potential of history and computing for enriching the student learning experience, while the latter is related to institutional imperatives which increasingly centre on student outcomes and 'employability'. We do not believe that the success of history and computing in the future will be dependent upon some form of reconciliation between the internal and external forces; they will remain. Rather, we believe that it is the relative balance of these forces which will determine the pace and extent of integrating IT into the history curriculum. The challenges of the next decade will prove as interesting as the last, and as advocates of using computers in the teaching of history we look forward to the next millennium with considerable optimism.

Notes

1 D. A. Spaeth, 'Computer assisted teaching and learning', in A. Booth and P. Hyland (eds), *History in Higher Education* (London, Routledge, 1996), pp. 172–3.

2 W. A. Speck, 'History and computing: some reflections on the past decade', *History and Computing*, 6 (1994), 28–9.

3 R. Heseltine, 'A policy framework for networked information: history and the humanities', *History and Computing*, 7 (1995), 22, 24, 28.

4 J. E. Everett, 'Annual review of information technology developments for economic and social historians, 1997', *Economic History Review*, 51 (1998), 387.

5 A. M. Wissenburg, 'TLTP history courseware consortium: a project report', *History and Computing*, 8 (1996), 46–7 and 'TLTP updates: the history courseware consortium: core resources for historians', *Craft*, 18 (1998), 2.

6 W. Vaughan and T. Cashen, 'Training', p. 2: part of a *Report of the Working Group on Computing in History of Art, Architecture and Design* (1997), Internet address: http://www.hart.bbk.ac.uk/AcoHum/training.htm.

7 A. Gibson, 'WWW and the internet: new opportunities for historical discourse', *History and Computing*, 7 (1995), 81–9. For a further discussion of the potential of the Web, see G. Price, 'The World Wide Web and the historian', *History and Computing*, 7 (1995), 104–8.

8 Everett, 'Annual review', p. 396.

9 See, for example, R. Lloyd-Jones and M. J. Lewis, 'Consumer resistance: selling computer skills to history first-time buyers', *Craft*, 2 (1990), 12–13.

10 M. Gregory, 'Skills versus scholarship (or liberal education knows a hawk from a handsaw)', in A. Heath, C. Rowland and E. Chambers (eds), *Skills Versus Scholarship in Arts and Humanities Higher Education, Proceedings of a Conference Hosted by the Humanities and Arts Higher Education Network* (Milton Keynes, Open University, 1997), pp. 5, 15.

11 T. Hitchcock, 'She's gotta have I.T.: teaching information technology to undergraduate history students', *History and Computing*, 5 (1993), 194.

12 R. Middleton, 'Computer techniques and economic theory in historical analysis', *History and Computing*, 1 (1989), 23, 35.

13 M. J. Lewis and R. Lloyd-Jones, *Using Computers in History: A Practical Guide* (London, Routledge, 1996), p. 6.

14 D. Hopkins, 'The politics of historical computing', *History and Computing*, 1 (1989), 47.
15 Middleton, 'Computer techniques and economic theory', p. 36.
16 For example, a number of historians have used historical databases to generate and interpret large volumes of historical information. See, for example, E. Mawdsley, N. Morgan, L. Richmond and R. Trainor (eds), *History and Computing III: Historians, Computers and Data* (Manchester, Manchester University Press, 1990). For an excellent example of computer-aided research see R. J. Morris, *Class, Sect and Party: The Making of the Middle Class, 1800–1850* (Cambridge, Cambridge University Press, 1991), especially ch. 1. For a review of computing and research see Everett, 'Annual review', pp. 383–4.
17 Spaeth, 'Computer assisted teaching', p. 56. For an examination of the practicalities of using database-generated research in the classroom see R. Lloyd-Jones and M. J. Lewis, 'What can we do with historical databases? Applications in teaching and research', *History Microcomputer Review*, 10 (1994), 42–54.
18 See Lewis and Lloyd-Jones, *Using Computers in History*, pp. 126, 130.
19 See E. Mawdsley and T. Munck, *Computing for Historians. An Introductory Guide* (Manchester, Manchester University Press, 1993), chs 4 and 9. For the discussion on text-handling software see Spaeth, 'Computer assisted teaching', p. 158.
20 Mawdsley and Munck, *Computing for Historians*, pp. 185–6, 187–8.
21 For a discussion of developments in multimedia applications in history, see Spaeth, 'Computer assisted teaching', pp. 169–72.
22 R. Rosenzweig, *Who Built America? From the Centennial Celebration of 1876 to the Great War of 1914* (CD ROM) (New York, Voyager Company, 1993).
23 Spaeth, 'Computer assisted teaching', p. 156.
24 P. H. Cribb, *Report of Computer Science Department* (York, University of York, 1996), p. 3.
25 P. Denley, 'The computer revolution and redefining the humanities', in D.S. Miall (ed.), *Humanities and the Computer: New Directions* (Oxford, Clarendon Press, 1990), p. 15.
26 Spaeth, 'Computer assisted teaching', pp. 159–60.
27 *Ibid*, p. 165.
28 Hitchcock, 'She's gotta have I.T.', p. 197.
29 N. J. Morgan and R. H. Trainor, 'Liberator or libertine? The computer in the history classroom', in Miall (ed.), *Humanities and the Computer*, p. 64.
30 See Spaeth, 'Computer assisted teaching', pp. 167–71.

History in cyberspace: challenges and opportunities of Internet-based teaching and learning

Over the past decade computers have become integrated within, and even an integral part of, academic work and research practice. Although information communications technology (ICT) is increasingly on political, commercial and research agenda, use by academics to develop or support teaching and learning is often the exception rather than the norm. This chapter traces the history of the Internet and its use within higher education (especially in Britain), and discusses some of the problems, as well as the potential, of Internet-based teaching and learning. We describe Lancaster University's History Internet Project (HIP) and conclude with suggestions for incorporating the Internet within history teaching programmes, along with some of the potential pitfalls that lie in wait.

We are standing, according to some accounts, on the verge of a great scholarly revolution, whereby the resources of all libraries, museums and archives will be integrated and available to all, irrespective of locality; connecting academics and students with each other and breaking down barriers of time and space.[1] This scholarly revolution is being enabled by the application of communications technology to information technology, which makes possible the conversion of paper documents and books, as well as photographic images, pictures, video and sound, into electronic format which can then be transmitted between computer networks as a digitised signal using modem technology; by electric or fibre-optic cables, or via satellites. The staggering and potentially limitless growth of the Internet is prompting questions about how academics and students work, research, teach and learn in this rapidly evolving, protean Web of networked information and connectivity, described by Jerome McGann as a 'fabulous circle whose centre is everywhere and whose circumference is nowhere'.[2]

Over the past five years, research has tended to focus on the culture of the Internet and the nature of its virtual communities and identities;[3] or explorations of the shifting relationship or interaction between reader, writer and text, and between self and knowledge.[4] Within this literature the bias is from, and towards, experience in the USA.[5] There are rather fewer published studies which consider Internet-based teaching and learning within higher education in the UK.[6] Furthermore, within this discourse the humanities are almost entirely absent,[7] with history contributing one rather small part.[8] To some extent the nature and scope of the literature may be explained by the newness of the technologies themselves. Yet, post-Dearing,[9] part of the explanation is undoubtedly because the role or function of ICT in teaching and learning has yet to be identified by many academic institutions, and academics, as being relevant and meaningful, or a necessary adjunct to their work. At the time of writing, there are few examples of pan-campus initiatives to support, develop and enable the adoption and adaptation of the Internet specifically for teaching and learning. Within such contexts, it is usually the departmental Web-o-phile who is alone in maintaining the departmental Web site, developing online courses or electronic seminars, sorting out e-mail glitches or forwarding interesting Web sites to colleagues.

The making of the Internet

Over the past decade it is estimated that the Internet grew by some 6,000 per cent, rising from 5,000 to 30 million users by 1994.[10] By 1995 the Internet was well and truly in the public and, significantly, in the commercial domain.[11] As of November 1998, it was calculated that numbers online globally had reached over 150 million, with the overwhelming majority concentrated within the Western world.[12]

The growth and expansion of the Internet from the US military network, ARPANET, in the 1960s, to academic networks and, in the last three years, into the global market place, is largely attributable to the development in the early 1990s of the World Wide Web. In the last two years the expansion of affordable home computing and cheap telephony has enabled the Internet to move out of its rather esoteric ghetto to a mass 'point and click', 'plug and play' audience. Researchers working in computing and communication sciences predict profound changes over the next decade, enabled by developments in digital and satellite communication technologies, which will connect more and more to ubiquitous and increasingly localised networks, including: Vehicle Area Networks, Desk Area Networks and Body Area Networks.[13]

Stephen Heppell, Director of ULTRALAB, a learning technology research centre at Anglia Polytechnic University, has argued that the Internet 'is more about communication than the dissemination of information'.[14] As important as the Internet has been to enable communication – and H-Net, the American discussion list available at Michigan State University, and *Electronic Seminars in History* from the Institute of Historical Research[15] are two examples of how it may be used by historians as a forum for discussion – the proliferation of virtual universities and museums, and digitised archives and libraries illustrates the ways in which the Internet is being used not just as a communications tool but to provide content-based resources.[16] Of particular note are projects which make rare, valuable texts available online.[17]

As a resource, the Internet should be of particular interest to historians for two main reasons: first, there are a number of Web sites which have been, or are in the process of being, developed by libraries and archives, which offer an *additional* point of access to information; and second, there are several Web sites which are in themselves new archives, often developed by enthusiasts or which have been funded by outside organisations. Among the former is the virtual Public Record Office,[18] which will enable all readers to gain access to some publications electronically, either at the Record Office or from around the world. The Scottish Cultural Resources Access Network is a good example of the latter. Aimed primarily at secondary schools, it aims to make available one and a half million text records derived from existing museum, gallery and archive records by the millennium, plus '100,000 related multimedia resources . . . [and] 100 multimedia essays, based on these resources, for educational use'.[19] As digitised reference material becomes more readily available online, it is exerting a powerful dynamic on other institutions to digitise key holdings, and to review current archival practice[20] and access and copyright issues in the light of new technologies.[21]

Networks of power and control

While the opening up of online resources to academics and students, and to a wider networked audience, by libraries, archives and institutions is generally welcomed, opinion about the quantity and quality of online information, and its impact upon academic work, is sharply polarised. From doomsday scenarios[22] to millenarian proclamations issued with almost evangelical zeal, the Internet could portend the 'death of the book', even of text itself,[23] or herald a 'brave new world' of information availability.[24] Writing in 1995, R. J. Morris argued that historians, whom he described as only just having stabilised in the age of the database, would need new technical and intellectual skills to manage the looming, and somewhat threatening, information-rich world.[25] The implicit, sometimes explicit, concern in such a 'never mind the quality, feel the bandwidth' world, where most may publish (and plagiarise) freely, is the basic untrustworthiness or 'instability' of much of the material being published online, being outside the norms, values, and to some extent *control*, of the academic establishment.[26] Although the Internet may be lauded when used to open up archival material which may otherwise be difficult to access, it exists in an academic culture where learning from, and with, books predominates. There are deeply embedded academic protocols and rules which govern the shape of the output of much scholarly work and creativity, and to this the Internet is startlingly subversive. Jaded surfers are, perhaps unsurprisingly, particularly wary of, and frustrated by, the Internet's shifting 'now you see it, now you don't', will-o'-the-wisp nature of the error message: 'Error 404, file not found'.

It is not only the fluidity of information availability that seems to pose a problem. At the heart of the matter are concerns about how the role of the academic, as teacher and researcher, is being shaped by the networked society. John Unsworth notes concern in the USA:

the electronification of scholarly communication has become the occasion of more
than a little anxiety over the past five or six years. This gradual but apparently inevitable change in the way we go about our business is affecting scholars and students
in many different disciplines of the humanities and the sciences . . . The change that
is taking place has profound implications, implications that are ethical and philosophical, economic, formal and generic, legal, and – sometimes overwhelmingly –
practical and procedural.[27]

Unsworth describes fears of obsolescence, disorientation and of losing the 'ines-
timable value' of a lecturer's presence in the classroom. The very sanctity of
scholarship seems to be at stake. He adds:

the same fears surface, often in strenuous arguments against the perceived technological threats of depersonalization, of inauthenticity, of subjugation to the
mechanical, and perhaps most centrally, of the substitution of quantity for quality
. . . In a word, the common element is a fear that, as scholars, teachers and human
beings, we stand to lose our mysterious uniqueness – or, what comes to the same
thing, that this uniqueness will no longer be honored – in the new technological
landscape.[28]

These are concerns with which UK academics may certainly identify. But are we
really powerless before the relentless 'independent and inexorable march of new
technology' or should we reject explanations which are rooted in technological
determinism?[29] Perhaps it is not the technology, or the information it carries *per
se*, that is the problem, but the context within which it is located. Thus the availability, application and use of technology in an information age, or information
in an increasingly technological age, exposes issues of access, control and cen-
sorship, of inclusion and exclusion by class or gender. At the same time as the
Internet enables potentially greater access to global resources, in the present
global context it is perhaps the most high-tech means of excluding the majority,
creating a chasm between information 'haves' and 'have-nots'.

But are the 'haves' being overloaded with an unmanageable amount of information? Mass publishing, from magazines, paperback books and digital televi-
sion to multimedia, has never provided us with so many choices or so much
information of vastly varying quality to filter. But, as experienced information
users, consumers and producers we, quite simply, consider, accept or reject what
we experience. And what if we do not read everything (did we ever expect to)?
Then, as we always have done, so we will continue to make the most of that
which we have. And then disagree. The problem is not the Internet *per se*, not
that there is too much technology, but that there is too little, not that there is too
much information, but that perhaps there is too little.

Hypertext and learning

In a posting to an Internet newsgroup three years ago, a subscriber asked the
question, Has anyone written research in hypertext format, or would anyone

accept a dissertation in hypertext format?[30] We suspect that the answer from many historians would not have been 'yes'/'no'/'let's discuss this', but 'what's hypertext?'

The term 'hypertext', first coined by Theodore H. Nelson in the 1960s, describes 'nonsequential writing – text that branches and allows choices to the reader, best read at an interactive screen. As popularly conceived, this is a series of text chunks connected by links which offer the reader different pathways.'[31] Applying hypertext authoring to the Internet has brought to life the possibilities of this as a *global* resource, weaving texts together into a protean Web of connections to a myriad of other sites, which could incorporate a variety of media: video clips, photographic images or audio. Hypertext links, usually contained in highlighted text or images, are activated with the click of a mouse button, a simple action which has the power to break down barriers of time and space, and blur the boundaries between disciplines and even, arguably, between cultures.[32] In such an environment, texts cease to be isolated or contained objects with clearly defined parameters, but can be linked together in potentially novel, variable and challenging ways. Used effectively, hypertext enables Web authors to create texts with links to libraries, museums, archives or private collections in several disparate locations, and provides the reader or browser with a choice of pathways through a Web site, enabling her/him to progress as independent and active learners.[33]

Unfortunately, some of the material which is currently published online does not take advantage of this medium. Rather, it seeks to replicate the format and style of printed texts and/or the structure of existing courses: the format is linear and difficult to navigate, making for a pretty wretched online learning experience. Moving existing lectures, course bibliographies, handouts and timetables on to the Web will not enhance student learning *per se*, only enable the student to access (and print out) course materials when he/she wishes; the only value to this being the saving by departments of some photocopying costs. Course tutors need, therefore, to consider and explore the qualitatively different teaching and learning 'space' which is possible via hypertext and the Internet. For example, the ways in which the Internet may be used to:

- encourage active and independent learning (online hypertext lectures with a range of choices and pathways through the content, also offering opportunities for students to contribute to the content; Uniform Resource Locators (URLs) within course reading lists);
- test ideas and encourage critical reasoning (Web of interpretation, evaluation of online resources);
- enable communication within and beyond the seminar room (open and distance learning; discussion groups);
- encourage subject exploration, information retrieval and network literacy (effective searching of networked information);
- develop student creativity with text, pictures and sound (creation of student Web sites);

- develop presentational skills via online publishing (considering how to communicate information via the Internet);
- provide pools of understanding between subject areas to link knowledge (provide links between disciplines);
- enable differentiation (e.g. use of hypertext within Web pages to provide different pathways through a particular topic for students of differing abilities and/or with different learning styles);
- open up learning opportunities to students in under-represented sectors.

Pilot study

The HIP[34] in the Department of History at Lancaster University was established in 1997 with the intention of enabling staff and students to appreciate and critically assess the impact of the Internet and the globalisation of information within an existing academic programme. It had two specific objectives. First, it sought to enhance staff and students' powers of critical evaluation in relation to the structure, purpose and content of online historical information. Second, it hoped to explore the potential of hypertext as a learning experience in itself by introducing students to Hypertext Markup Language (HTML) authoring and Web site construction. HIP employed two strategies. It surveyed the quality of existing Web-based historical material with a view to incorporating it within existing courses. It also built upon a project course, History in the Community, which involved a small group of students who conducted research and acquired the technical and presentational skills necessary to construct a Web page on an aspect of local history for an outside organisation.[35] This element of the project involved the cooperation of staff at Lancaster University – Information Systems Services and WebTeach – and other external institutions, most notably Lancaster City Museums.

Embedding Internet resources within seminar preparation, course bibliographies and through Web page design and creation proved to be difficult for a number of reasons. Most staff and students who participated in HIP, though enthusiastic, had varying experience of Internet use, and were generally inexperienced users. Their concerns were by no means unique or unusual, but mirrored those expressed by other groups of academics.[36] Most did not know how to conduct effective searches for Web-based information, or how to create, edit and save a list of bookmarks/favourites.[37] None knew how to cite electronic sources within footnotes. At the outset, therefore, time needed to be allocated both to develop appropriate and focused worksheets and supporting online course materials, and for basic 'hands-on' Web surfing sessions to introduce the main features of online searching, information retrieval and copyright issues, and e-mail communication. The wider provision of such training to academic staff and students would need to be supported by suitable and sufficient access to networked computers, without impacting upon or inhibiting open access to these resources by other users. Practical concerns also dominated, particularly obtaining access to machines in the university open-access computer labs, although this was a problem for all students and not just for those wishing to access the Internet. Students generally found that searching for suitable material (which, incidentally, was available online) was often excessively time consuming and frustrating, and they were happier when provided with a list of gateway Web sites to browse, rather than themselves having to find a suitable starting point from which to progress. Students often argued that course tutors should identify and provide a list of Web resources, in much the same way as they already recommended texts and/or articles, and wanted clear guidelines on how to cite electronic sources, as well as reassurances that they would not be penalised by baffled or sceptical course tutors for the inclusion of electronic source material.

More significantly, however, as might be expected from an open-access medium with often undeveloped (or absent) peer review mechanisms, the quality and purposes of Web-based historical materials proved to be very variable. Many sites are still the product of personal enthusiasms or developed for purposes far removed from academic learning. Most of the providers are individuals and groups, many with specific axes to grind or causes to promote. Some fail to provide details of authors. Commercial organisations and local and national government frequently incorporate historical material in sites, but this is invariably incidental to the purpose of the site. Only a few provide references for their information. Dedicated educational sites containing verifiable historical material are the exception rather than the rule; most of these contain predominantly introductory material and are frequently targeted at school audiences. The fact that the majority of the major educational providers online, as well as Internet users, are American is reflected in the preponderance of sites dealing with American history. The number of sites concerned with specific places, people, subject areas and periods therefore varies enormously, and without any obvious rationale. Overall, and justifiably, students were highly critical of the quality and range of historical information and the levels of analysis and debate which are currently available on the Web. There is plenty of traffic on the Internet, but not much of it is heading in the historian's direction.

The other aspect of the project, involving the construction of a Web site, proved to be more rewarding, although it was also a time-consuming experience for students and staff. Rather than being a disadvantage, the diversity and variable quality of material on the Web provided students with the opportunity to enhance their critical awareness of the nature of historical material and the ways in which hypertext was being, or could be, used to present it. They successfully developed their own lists of criteria when evaluating the quality of sites. These included historical accuracy (bias, nature of authorship, source references), presentation (visual appearance, structure, ease of navigation) and suitability for purpose in relation to intended audiences. In addition to this, the research skills involved in the project and the contacts made with organisations outside the university, students felt that the active process of constructing Web sites for the presentation of their findings was particularly valuable. First, it increased students' technical abilities and confidence. All students felt that the information technology skills they had acquired would be valuable and that they had enhanced their attractiveness to employers. Second, it forced them to devise a set of criteria to evaluate the purpose and presentation of information and ideas through an entirely different medium from that to which they were accustomed. Finally, and rather more unexpectedly, it confronted them with copyright, ethical and legal issues. Copyright was identified as a major problem, as the 1988 Copyright Act, which covers electronic or digitised work, is considerably more prohibitive than the regulations which govern photocopying. When the students came together to work on the group project 'Historic Lancaster',[38] they spent considerable time contacting authors, museums and galleries to request the necessary permission to reproduce images online.

At the end of the year, the students submitted a group report reflecting on their own learning and their contribution to the project. It is clear from this that they felt that the project had given them the opportunity to gain a variety of valuable and transferable skills, and the creation of a Web site, published to a global audience through the department's Web pages, had been a deeply satisfying experience. The work was largely examined through the medium of the Web, with reference to their own criteria for the presentation of historical material on the Web. In addition to the content itself, these included ease of navigation, appropriate use of images, full referencing of sources, copyright clearance for images, relevant external links, bibliography of other resources, details of authorship and date of original publication (and subsequent revisions).

Future developments

HIP was an experimental project that was primarily confined to the integration of existing Web resources within existing courses and the possibility of using the medium to develop student critical evaluation and technical abilities. We are conscious of the dangers of generalising from it, and of any 'warm glow' that could be imparted by the 'novelty' factor. Such is the speed of change in Web technology, design, content and accessibility, that many of our conclusions are also necessarily tentative. It is to be hoped, for example, that practical problems associated with speed of access are likely to diminish in the near future, and that students are likely to need less persuasion to use, and less instruction on how to search, the Web, or to exploit it for communication. Indeed, the need for instruction may be greater among staff.

Earlier technical innovations in education suggest that we need to be aware of being overly enthusiastic about the prospects for dramatic change, despite the hype. Experiences with video and audio cassettes, specifically designed software packages and CD ROMs suggest that while these have a capacity to enhance delivery of courses, they have not replaced text-based materials or 'traditional' modes of learning. It is clear that historical data on the Web are of variable coverage and quality, and although it is highly likely that the quantity will increase in coming years, it is difficult to envisage anything which has a potential commercial value being made freely available. It is obvious that, however much the Internet expands, the printed source will for some time retain considerable advantages in terms of accessibility, flexibility and quality control. Some of the key skills which the Web clearly facilitates – the ability to search for information; evaluate its authenticity, validity and importance; and to communicate views effectively within a specific environment – are also those we would wish students to develop in more 'traditional' courses.

The novelty of what the Internet offers is not more of the same, but a qualitatively different learning space. HIP has suggested one possible avenue, notably the potential to incorporate hypertext, and the skills associated with it, into student learning portfolios. But the communication revolution which the Internet represents is much more than this. It has the potential for video conferencing, asynchronous seminars and discussion groups which offer the opportunity to expand the spatial and temporal boundaries of communication, and for the design and delivery of online courses which offer students a genuine interactive experience and scope to develop their own learning trajectories. Neither is unproblematic. Electronic communication lacks the intensity of interaction possible through personal contact and face-to-face debate, and early research suggests that it may only be effective when supported with collaborative learning activities.[39] Internet discussion groups have yet to be enthusiastically embraced by the majority of the academic community, and for teaching purposes they may be better viewed as a supplement rather than replacement for face-to-face discussion, even on courses which involve a considerable element of distance learning. The evolution and adoption of interactive Web-based courses raise serious pedagogic and practical issues. Whose responsibility should online course development be? Do academics have the appropriate skills, indeed time, to design and produce *effective* online learning environments, or should this be left to instructional design professionals? Just how many Web-based or Web-authoring courses would students be happy to enrol in? How many would tutors be happy to develop and assess? Who *owns* the work which is subsequently published online? Should such materials have unrestricted access, or will entry inevitably be controlled by passwords or subscription, or limited in other ways such as by Intranets? As yet, there are no clear answers to these questions. Progress will depend upon the extent to which academic institutions and individuals are willing to devote time and resources to working with the rapidly changing technologies; a process which is likely to have opportunity costs as well as presenting dangers of technological obsolescence. Exploitation of the Internet is not, and will not be, cost free; it will demand considerable investment in hardware and time which may ultimately prove prohibitive. We may, however, learn from experience in the USA:

University administrators need to look seriously at the economics of implementing WBI [Web-based instruction]. If instructors are given the time that is actually
required to work using this form of delivering education, then it can be [an] . . .
educationally effective and cost-effective method of instruction. However, if
instructors are expected to develop, maintain, and support this type of instruction
with the same time expectations of F2F [face to face] delivery, the quality of education will be in jeopardy and instructors will run the risk of burn out.[40]

The major challenges, however, are those which are already familiar to any tutor
who has worked with, or promoted the use of, computers for history learning: a
lack of adequate resources and/or problems associated with open access to those
resources. Although approximately £1 billion, or 8–10 per cent of total turnover,
has recently been spent on information tenhnology by higher education institutions in the UK each year, it was estimated in 1997 that an additional £1 billion
would be needed by 1999 to upgrade existing facilities and implement staff and
student training programmes.[41] At the same time, public funding of higher education fell by 30 per cent between 1989 and 1997. The Dearing Report made a
number of recommendations to enable the full exploitation of ICT by higher
education institutions in the future. We cannot afford to ignore them.

Over the next three or four years, there will be an increasing number of ICT-
aware and -literate young adults enrolling for undergraduate courses. These students are currently attending schools, which are, or are in the process of being,
connected to the National Grid for Learning (NGfL).[42] By 2002, all UK schools
should be connected to the Internet via the NGfL, and all existing primary and
secondary teachers and school librarians will have been trained in the use of ICT
across the curriculum.[43] However, it should not simply be this context which
makes the need for comprehensive ICT strategies and supporting staff development across higher education an urgent one. The Internet, as our work for the
HIP suggests, offers an alternative means of developing and supporting teaching
and learning, possibly to supplement existing courses but, more excitingly, also
to develop new ones. Cutting through the hype, we should take time to explore
the Internet, to take the best of it, and to make it part and parcel of the learning
experience.

Notes

All URL links were active at the time of writing: February 1999.
1 J. McGann, 'Radiant textuality', <http://www.iath.virginia.edu/public/jjm2f/
   radiant.html>.
2 J. McGann, 'The rationale of hypertext', <http://www.iath.virginia.edu/public/
   jjm2f/rationale.html>.
3 On cyberculture see D. Silver, 'Teaching cyberculture, readings and fieldwork for an
   emerging topic of study', *Computers and Texts* (Computers in Teaching Initiative
   (CTI) in Textual Studies Newsletter, July 1996); D. Porter (ed.), *Internet Culture*
   (London, Routledge, 1997); A. Smith, 'New communication technology and chang-

ing political boundaries, <http://www.mediastudies.org/CTR/Publications/smith/smith.html>.

4 J. Unsworth, 'Electronic scholarship, or, scholarly publishing and the public', <http://www.iath.edu/public/~jmu2m/mla-94.html>; W. McCarty, 'A potency of life: scholarship in an electronic age', <http://www.kcl.ac.uk/humanities/cch/wlm/essays/Potens>.

5 C. Bellamy, 'The author of history in the age of electronic reproduction: hypertext and the historian', unpublished MA thesis, University of Melbourne, 1998; Silver, 'Teaching cyberculture' Unsworth, 'Electronic scholarship'; G. P. Landow, *Hypertext: The Convergence of Contemporary Critical Theory and Technology* (Baltimore, Johns Hopkins University Press, 1992); H-Net, 'Humanities and Social Sciences online' <http://h-net2.msu.edu>.

6 For online sources of information, see CTI 'Changing the face of university teaching' <http://www.cti.ac.uk/> and Teaching and Learning Technology Programme 'TLTP central web' <http://www.tltp.ac.uk/tltp/>; for international papers discussing the pedagogical uses of the Internet, see H. Maurer and R. G. Olson (eds), *Proceedings of WebNet 98 – World Conference of the WWW, Internet & Intranet*, 2 vols, (Charlottesville, Association for the Advancement of Computing in Education, 1998); T. W. Bynum and J. H. Moor (eds), *The Digital Phoenix: How Computers are Changing Philosophy* (Oxford, Blackwell, 1998); S. Stein, *Learning, Teaching and Researching on the Internet* (Harlow, Longman, 1999).

7 J. Martin and H. Beetham (eds), 'C&IT: learning outcomes evaluated', *Active Learning*, 8 (July 1998); edited highlights of a one-day colloquium organised by the Humanities Computing Unit, Oxford University, April 1998 at <http://www.thesis.co.uk:80/tp/1/PRN/OPEN/EVENTS/BEYONDHYPE/hype.html>.

8 See CTI Centre for History Archaeology and Art History <http://www.arts.gla.ac.uk/www/ctich/>; compare H-Net, 'Envisioning the future, creating the humanities classroom of the 21st century <http://www.h-net.msu.edu/~envision/> with Humanities Computing Unit, Oxford University, G. Glasfurd, 'Connecting with the past? Some reflections on using the Internet for history', paper given at the International Association for History and Computing conference, Toledo, 1998, for scant, and rather dated outline of e-mail, JANET (Joint Academic Network) see, D. I. Greenstein, *A Historian's Guide to Computing* (Oxford, Oxford University Press, 1994) ch. 2; brief discussion of the future possibilities of the Internet, see P. Hudson, 'A new history from below: computers and the maturing of local and regional history', *The Local Historian*, 25:4 (November 1995), 209–22; R. J. Morris, 'Computers and the subversion of British history', *Journal of British Studies*, 34 (October 1995), 503–28. Non-historians: B. Campbell and I. Davies, 'History student-teachers on the information highway', *Teaching History*, 88 (July 1997) 33–6.

9 The National Committee of Inquiry into Higher Education, *Higher Education in the Learning Society: Report of the National Committee* (London, HMSO, 1997).

10 *.net* (December 1994), p. 40.

11 A. J. Kennedy, *The Internet & World Wide Web, The Rough Guide 1998* (London, Rough Guides, 1998), p. 392.

12 NUA Internet Surveys, <http://www.nua.ie/surveys/how_many_online/index.html>.

13 G. Q. Maguire, 'Personal computing and communication, the near future' <http://www.it.kth.se/~maguire/Talks/webnet98–981108a.pdf>.

14 Quoted in A. Dabbs, 'Wired for learning', *Education Direct* (February 1998), p. 76.

15 <http://h-net2.msu.edu/> and <http://ihr.sas.ac.uk/ihr/esh/eshmnu.html>.
16 See especially, International Federation of Library Associations and Institutions, Digital Libraries <http://www.ifla.org/II/diglib.htm>; Electronic Journal and Text Archives <http://www.ifla.org/II/etext.htm>; eLib Electronic Libraries Programme <http://www.ukoln.ac.uk/services/elib/>; Online Education <http://www.newprom-ise.com/>; Virtual Museum Tours <http://www.dreamscape.com/frankvad/museums.museums.html>.
17 See especially, The Bodleian Library <http://www.bodley.ox.ac.uk/welcome.html>; Royal Commission on Historical Manuscripts <http://www.hmc.gov.uk/>; National Archives of Ireland <http://www.nationalarchives.ie/>; Repositories of Primary Sources <http://www.uidaho.edu/special-collections/Other.Repositories.html>; Historical Text Archive <http://www.geocities.com/Athens/Forum/9061/index.html>; Data and Program Library Service <http://dpls.dacc.wisc.edu/archive.html>; The Internet Classics Archive <http://classics.mit.edu/>.
18 The AD2001 Programme <http://www.pro.gov.uk/ad2001/>.
19 Scottish Cultural Resources Access Network, <http://www.scran.ac.uk/faq/quest1.htm#how>.
20 Encoded Archival Description, 'Making finding aids available online', <http://www.pro.gov.uk/ad2001/ead.htm>.
21 McGann, 'Radiant textuality' For a thoughtful critique of this, see N. Baker, 'Discards', in *The Size of Thoughts, Essays and other Lumber* (London, Vintage, 1997), pp. 125–81.
22 See especially, S. Birkets, *The Gutenberg Elegies: The Fate of Reading in an Electronic Age* (Boston, Faber and Faber, 1994), and compare with the 'end of the world' predictions consequent upon the development of the Gutenberg press in the fifteenth century: A. Manguel, *A History of Reading* (London, Flamingo, 1997), pp. 134–5.
23 ULTRALAB, 'Children of the information age and the death of text', <http://www.ultralab.anglia.ac.uk/Pages/ULTRALAB/A_Good_Read/Death_of_text.html>; see also K. Dave, 'The future of publishing', Project Gutenberg <http://promo.net/pg/kushal.html>.
24 J. E. Everett, 'Annual review of information technology developments for economic and social historians, 1996', *Economic History Review*, 3 (1997), p. 543–55.
25 Morris, 'Computers and the subversion of British history', p. 528.
26 W. McCarty, 'A potency of life: scholarship in an electronic age', <http://www.kcl.ac.uk/humanities/cch/wlm/essays/potency1.html>. The Electronics Libraries Programme, funded by the Joint Information Systems Committee, is currently working on projects which seek to overcome problems associated with resource discovery and verification (see Everett, 'Annual review', p. 549).
27 Unsworth, 'Electronic scholarship'.
28 *Ibid*. See also Palinurus, 'The academy and the corporation: teaching the humanities in a restructured world', <http://humanitas.ucsb.edu/liu/palinurus/index2.html>.
29 A. L. Friedman, *Computer Systems Development: History, Organization and Implementation* (Chichester and New York, Wiley, 1989), p. 6.
30 See J. McGann, 'Radiant textuality' <http://www.iath.virginia.edu/public/jjm2f/radiant.html>.
31 Landow, *Hypertext*, p. 4.
32 For a discussion of cultural imperialism and the 'New world information order', see E. W. Said, *Culture and Imperialism* (London, Vintage, 1994), pp. 352–3. For rival

interpretations of the Internet as new imperialism or globalising force, see especially: N. Barrett, *The State of Cybernation: Cultural, Political and Economic Implications of the Internet* (London, Kogan Page, 1997); C. Keep *et al.*, 'Marshall McLuhan and the Gutenberg galaxy', The Electronic Labyrinth <http://jefferson.village .virginia.edu/elab/>; M. Geyer and C. Bright, 'World history in a global age', *American Historical Review,* 100:4 (October 1995), 1037, 1041; B. Mazlish, 'Comparing global history to world history', *Journal of Interdisciplinary History,* 18:3 (Winter 1998), 385–95.

33 Particularly good examples of this are the Institute for Advanced Technology in the Humanities: Research Reports <http://jefferson.village.virginia.edu/reports.html>; the Victorian Web <http://landow.stg.brown.edu/victorian/ victov.html>; the Great Chicago Fire and the Web of Memory <http://www.chicagohs z.org/fire/intro/>.

34 HIP, <http://www.lancs.ac.uk/users/history/hip_dep1.htm>.

35 M. Winstanley, 'History and the community', in A. Booth and P. Hyland (eds), *History in Higher Education* (Oxford, Blackwell, 1996), pp. 207–23.

36 A. Littlejohn and N. Sclater, 'Overcoming conceptual barriers to the use of Internet technology in university education', in Maurer and Olson (eds), *Proceedings of WebNet 98,* pp. 586–90.

37 Bookmarks (Netscape) and favourites (Explorer) are lists of Web sites which a user wishes to make note of for future reference. (Netscape and Explorer are browsers; that is, the interface which enables a user to access the Web.)

38 <http://www.lancs.ac.uk/users/history/Lanchistory/index.htm>.

39 S. R. Hiltz, 'Collaborative learning in asynchronous networks: building learning communities', in Maurer and Olson (eds), *Proceedings of WebNet 98,* pp. 433–9.

40 D. Harapnuik, T. Craig Montgomerie and C. Torgerson, 'Costs of developing and delivering a Web-based instruction course', in Maurer and Olson (eds), *Proceedings of WebNet98,* p. 394.

41 The Joint DfEE/HE Sector Working Group, *Information Technology in Higher Education, Report to the Secretary of State* (DfEE, July 1997), p. 5.

42 NGfL <http://www.ngfl.gov.uk/>.

43 New Opportunities Fund, <http://www.nof.org.uk/>.

Part II

Enhancing teaching and learning

Motivating students by active learning in the history classroom

Halfway through the first day of a history course, as the class is discussing the purposes and significant issues of studying history, two (prearranged) intruders burst into the class, shout some angry words at the teacher and students, and then storm out of the room. After a brief discussion, the teacher asks the students to describe the incident in writing and redistributes their accounts. In small groups students read these primary historical accounts from different eyewitnesses and develop a short history based on these written sources. Obviously, several different versions emerge, which leads to a lively discussion of the validity of historical sources and the inevitability of differing interpretations of the same event. The discussion could also include the analysis of some physical evidence left by the intruders, such as their graded essay from taking the course two years earlier, or an underlined book on human rights. This idea, adapted from an exercise first described by Barbara Norton and Jim Oberly, is active, engaging and immerses students immediately in various theoretical issues involved in 'doing history'.

This one teaching strategy is among hundreds that one can find in the History Teaching list service (<H-TEACH@H-NET.msu.edu>). The list's participants suggest ways of motivating students to love history, as we do, and to be joyously involved with the texts, themes and questions of history that interest and excite us. Many professors complain that students are not as motivated and prepared as they used to be (meaning, as *we* were). To whatever extent this is true, the responsibility for their motivation rests primarily with us. The purpose of this chapter is to suggest several practical strategies for involving students more actively in our history classrooms as a way of motivating them to accept more responsibility for their own learning.

Despite the distressing reality of larger classes, advocates for change in higher education urge moving away from large lectures and towards the active learning that happens in small groups and tutorials. Studies of effective educational practices in recent years cite active and small-group cooperative learning, high expectations combined with frequent feedback, 'hands on' experiences practising the skills of the discipline and enthusiastic teachers as key elements in motivating students to learn.[1] History education is no different in pursuing these active learning and inclusive pedagogical directions.[2]

The teaching strategies that follow are divided into five sections: brainstorming, visual representations, student questions and small groups, debates and role playing, and thinking historically by immersing students in the interpretation of primary sources and detection of interpretive points of view. The intent of this chapter is to describe several specific historical teaching strategies in each section that can easily be translated into one's own classroom practice. They are applicable to lecture auditoriums with 200–300 students in fixed seats, to seminars with 6–20 students and to tutorials. This is not a theoretical chapter or even a report on the literature, but rather a 'tried and tested' set of practical suggestions for history instructors.

Fundamental to these teaching approaches are two goals of conventional wisdom. The first is the importance of teaching students to think historically as they are actively engaged in the skills of 'doing history'. The second is that this fundamental goal occurs in the process of acquiring the basic factual and conceptual knowledge of a particular course. Although I have sought to include examples from all fields, as an American historian my examples will often reflect both my teaching context in a liberal arts college and the content of American history. I am confident that readers will easily adapt these suggestions to their own contexts and specialised fields.

Brainstorming

Brainstorming is an effective way to accomplish several teaching/learning goals at the same time, especially on the first day of a new term or at the beginning of a new unit, and in both large classes and small. Students bring to most courses both a degree of familiarity and considerable misinformation. To honour their prior knowledge (and to discover their misconceptions), walk into class the first day and write the title of the course on the board: 'The Afro-American Experience', 'Women in the Middle Ages', 'Cultural Life in Ancient Athens', 'Race, Class and Gender in Nineteenth-Century England', or whatever. Take each key word in the title and invite students to free associate, saying whatever comes into their minds about that word.

For example, walk into the room on the first day and write 'American History' on the board. Then invite students to call out all the words and images that they can think of for 'American', for 'history' and for the two together, writing them all on the board (or on a transparency) exactly as students say them. The words associated with 'American' inevitably lead to issues of national identity, as well as to a listing of popular conceptions of national traits. The words associated with 'history' will reveal student ideas and misconceptions about the nature of history, as well as leading to a discussion of issues of historical truth, interpretation and purpose. The response to 'American history' provides a kind of pretest of the quality of knowledge a group of students has, including a sense of the extent to which the class focuses on political, social, cultural or other kinds of historical category.

In facilitating a brainstorming exercise, I often need to prompt a group by suggesting that they respond in 'words, images or feelings' or by challenging them to 'double the list'. The point of brainstorming as a public activity is that hearing ideas, concepts and words generates others. When the board (or a transparency) has been filled, ask: 'What patterns, themes and issues do you see?' This lifts the discussion to the level of analysis; themes, categories and even metaphors or catchy phrases emerge which can create student ownership by becoming the operative organising concepts of the course. The only rules for brainstorming are that 'anything goes' and that the teacher should acknowledge *every* comment by writing it down, honouring student wording. To change the language or to ask students to explain what they mean will interrupt the process and can kill the energy and intimidate shy students. Only rarely (in brainstorming) would I ask a student to clarify or explain a comment, making sure I checked with him or her for permission to change the language. Within a few minutes at the start of a course, then, brainstorming provides the teacher with a sense of what a new class of students knows (and does not know) about a topic. Numerous students get to speak, and a tone of involvement and mutual responsibility has been set. Students share ownership of the course right at the start, including the language that frames the course.

Brainstorming is also useful when beginning a new topic. Ask students to call out 'everything you know about World War I' (or Darwinism, China, slavery, the Renaissance, or whatever). As recorded on an overhead transparency or chalkboard, a list will unfold of a mixture of specific names, dates and events, feelings and prejudices, and implicit interpretive judgements. To ask students to call out what they know about slavery, for example, elicits many images about the politics of the Civil War and the physical horrors of slavery, but very little about slave culture and community. That tells us something right away. Another use of brainstorming is to create a cognitive map of historical interconnections. For example, in the middle of the blackboard write an important but ill-defined term such as 'romanticism', 'liberalism' or 'feminism', or specific events such as the Magna Carta, Opium Wars or Corn Laws, and invite words, images and specific historical facts associated with that word or event. As students call out words and images, the teacher does some categorising, drawing tentative lines showing the various ways the suggestions might be interconnected. To follow up, assign students to revise the map, either as individuals or in small groups, suggesting other ways of organising relationships. This activity involves both analytic and synthetic thinking skills, and gives students practice in working with issues of comparative history and causation, as well as learning specific knowledge as part of the process.

Another way to introduce a new topic with brainstorming – as well as to get feedback on how well students are learning – is to ask students to make statements they believe to be true about an issue. 'We know it to be true that the Middle Ages were . . .', 'We agree that it is true about the New Deal that . . .', 'It is true that the causes of World War I were . . .'. Generate a list and analyse each claim, with some students presenting their truth statements and others raising questions about them. By examining each truth claim interactively, the class models a collaborative process of analytic thinking. This is especially useful for dealing with emotional or romanticised topics, such as race, gender or native peoples, where demythologising may be necessary. This strategy reveals the complexity of knowledge and generates questions and issues requiring further study, perhaps in a research paper or examination question.

Visual representations

Brainstorming is effective not only because lists are collaboratively generated and subjected to analysis, but also because it is a visual activity. Many students are motivated by visuals because they can more easily understand and remember a concept if they see it. But in utilising visual learning we need to teach students how to 'read' a visual text as rigorously as printed ones. The process is both cognitive and affective.

Consider the evocative power of slides as a way of involving students actively in the interpretation of a single visual image. For example, show an emotionally powerful slide of a Thomas Nast cartoon, or a photograph of a family or famous scene such as Pearl Harbor, Kent State, Amritsar or Tiananmen Square, or a political campaign poster, or a painting (Hogarth or Hopper for English and American social history). Ask students first to 'describe what you see' and then to analyse what it means. 'Facts' precede analysis, and the learning moves from seemingly lower-order 'what is happening?' and 'what do you see?' questions to higher-order 'why?' and 'what do you think about it?' questions. Working with visual imagery at the beginning of a class (or in the middle of a lecture) activates student energy and enhances the vividness of the content for the day. Imagery is fun, motivating and teaches a cognitive skill.

Or, invite students to call out one visual image that stands out from a particular reading or topic. 'From your reading about Columbus [or Frederick Douglass, the Pullman Strike, the Spanish Armada, women's lives during the French revolution, etc.], what one specific scene, event or moment stands out in your mind? What do you see?' The recall of imagined scenes prompts further recollections, and a flood of images flows from the students. Listing the images on the chalkboard provides a visual backdrop to the lecture or deeper discussion that follows. The class collaboratively creates a collage of images, followed by the analysis of patterns, themes, tensions, paradoxes and other generalisations drawn from the list.

Students can create their own visual representations as well as interpret well-known ones, even for complex concepts. In a Philosophy of History course I ask students, in small groups, to draw an image or logo (either literal or symbolic) to represent the ideas of historians such as Van Ranke, Macaulay, Marx, Michelet, Trevelyan and Carlyle. The task takes students into the text (Fritz Stern's *Varieties of History*[3]) to find significant passages that suggest an appropriate visual representation. The danger, of course, is reducing sophisticated philosophical positions to a caricature. Working with visual images, however, is a highly motivating way to lead students gently to engage with difficult theories and ideas.

Student questions and small groups

The writer James Baldwin observed that the purpose of education is to create in a person the ability to look at the world for him- or herself, to ask questions of the universe and then to learn to live with these questions. This, he believed, is how a young person achieves his or her own identity. How, then, can we help students to develop this ability and then to take their questions seriously? To generate questions, ask students before a class to prepare questions about their reading or a topic and bring them to class – there is no better way to ensure their preparation for the discussion. In small classes ask a student to read all the questions aloud first, and invite the group to listen for reiterated themes and patterns. With larger groups I collect and collate the questions, or randomly select a few before discussing responses with the class.

Another way to generate questions is to ask: 'A question I still have about the immigrant experience [feudalism, Puritanism, the sexuality of slavery, or whatever] but have been afraid to ask, is. . .' Another variation is to ask students, as they enter the classroom, to call out questions about the text or topic that they hope will be answered that day. At some point halfway through a period divide the students into pairs or small groups and ask them to 'take five minutes and agree on *one* question that you would like to explore further'. This will sort out fewer, more thoughtful questions, and will lead to some peer teaching and learning as one member of a group answers another's query in the course of the search for a consensus question.

Questions work well in small groups. No matter the size, a large class can always be divided into pairs or small groups of between three and eight, thus serving many purposes. The first is to provide energy shifts from lecturing to allow students to practise their understanding of key course concepts. The second is to empower more students to test how well they are learning by writing and talking about their ideas in a safe context. Third, teachers have an opportunity to assess learning as well as to establish personal contact with students as they move around listening to a sampling of the small-group discussions. The quality and substance of student questions is an excellent way for an instructor to get feedback on what students do and do not understand.

There are three crucial points to consider in helping small groups to work efficiently. First, the instructions should be clear, simple and task oriented. Examples: 'Which character in *The Iliad* best represents the qualities of a Greek hero?', 'What was the crucial turning point in Malcolm X's life?', 'Which example defines imperialism best, and why?', 'Identify three positive and three negative features of the reign of Queen Victoria', 'Generate a list of restrictions on women's freedom in the nineteenth century', 'If you were Lincoln, what would you have done about Fort Sumter?', 'Find what you think is the key paragraph in Macaulay's essay'. Second, give the groups a sense of how much time they have to do their work. And third, it is crucial to make time for public reporting (debriefing) before class time is over. Groups are interested in what other groups have decided; moreover, by hearing a wide range of different – or confirming – perspectives, student historical understanding is enhanced.

Teachers can energise even large auditorium lecture classes by separating students into small groups, first by asking them to write for a couple of minutes on a question and then by having them talk with two or three others. 'What's the most important point I've been making for the past ten minutes?', 'Which explanation of the causes of the Thirty Years' War makes the most sense to you?', 'How would you, as a woman, have asserted your autonomy in a Victorian marriage?', 'Which aspect of Puritan theology bothers you the most, and why?' After a few minutes invite volunteers to call out their conclusions and concerns. One need only hear a sampling of responses to get a sense of the class. This active learning strategy not only provides feedback on learning to the teacher but also prepares students for the lecture or assignment that follows.

Debates and role playing

Although debates are an energising way to motivate students, it is important to note that we must be sensitive to the aversion of some students to what they may perceive as confrontational learning, and that neither one of two polar sides of a historical argument obviously contains the whole truth. Nevertheless, it is sometimes pedagogically desirable to force students to choose one or the other side of a dichotomous question and to defend their choice. Consider, even in a large lecture setting, a debate on such questions as the following: 'Was Burke or Paine more right about the French Revolution?', 'Was Nat Turner's revolt justified?', 'Did the English Civil War increase or decrease the liberties of the people?', 'Should the United States have annexed the Philippines or not in 1898?' By taking advantage of the central aisle dividing a large lecture hall, the logistics for structuring debates become quite simple. Students can either support the side of an issue assigned to the half of the hall where they happen to be sitting or, as prearranged in conjunction with a video or reading assignment, they could come to class prepared to take a seat on one side or another. In an auditorium with two doors, post signs over the doors marked 'Burke' and 'Paine'. In a seminar, assign students to opposite sides of the table. Once students have physically, as it were, put their bodies on the line, they are receptive to answering a simple question: 'Why are you sitting where you are?' That is usually enough to spark a rather lively debate.

Sometimes more structure is necessary: 'From the right side of the room let's hear five statements on behalf of the "Hawk" side of US involvement in Vietnam, after which we will hear five statements from the left on the "Dove" side.' The process can be repeated, including rebuttals, before concluding by asking for two or three volunteers to make summary arguments for each side, and perhaps taking a final vote. Important questions, however, do not divide neatly into halves. Students would never settle for forced dichotomous choices. When some students (quite rightly) refuse to choose one side or the other, create a middle ground and literal space: 'Those who repudiate both sides, sit in the middle.' Now three groups are invited to state their positions, and the complexities of historical learning increase. Students in the middle, for example, might learn how difficult it is to try to remain neutral on heated emotional issues; those on the fringes might learn how complex truth is.

Role playing is another highly motivating active learning strategy, and is useful to illuminate the experiences and difficult choices of ordinary people and of economic, religious and racial groups. The process is not as complicated as one might think. First, a mini-lecture establishes the context and setting for the role playing. Second, the class is divided into a number of small groups, each assigned a clearly delineated social role. Third, each group is given a specific task – usually to propose a position and course of action. And fourth, the proposals offered by different groups will inevitably conflict with each other in some way – racially, regionally, ideologically, tactically, or over scarce funds, land, jobs, power or resources. Given these conflicts, harmonious closure is as difficult to achieve in a role-play as in history itself.

The following examples will suggest others. Create a New England town meeting in 1779 in which a variety of groups (landed elite, yeoman farmers, Tory loyalists, militiamen and soldiers, riff-raff, tradesmen, lawyers and ministers) are charged with drafting instructions for delegates to a state constitutional convention. Or, challenge several groups in the summer of 1865 – defeated Confederates, southern Unionists, victorious northern Republicans and freedmen – to develop lists of their goals and the strategies for accomplishing them. Or put a whole class into the same situation. Ask students how they would achieve their goals as emancipated slaves on a Georgia plantation in 1865, or unskilled workers in a Sheffield steel mill in the 1870s, or immigrant miners facing a lockout in Pennsylvania in 1892, or suffragists in the 1910s or civil-rights activists in the 1960s. A political history variation is to make yourself a national leader in crisis; say, Napoleon in 1800, Lincoln in 1861 or Churchill in 1945, and create groups of advisers on different issues to suggest policy. Extend the exercise by adding a meeting whose purpose is to consider different proposals. Students could prepare speeches and caucus to develop strategies, coalitions and tactics for achieving their goals, and to see the deliberations through to some conclusion.

Because role playing, especially with conflicting groups, can get heated and potentially out of control, it is necessary to direct the process forcefully. If necessary, restore order by shifting to the discussion of what was learned. The cardinal rule of role playing in order to ensure cognitive reinforcement of an emotional experience is that more time should be spent in debriefing than was taken in the exercise itself. Given careful planning, clear directions, assertive leadership, thoughtful debriefing and a lot of luck, role playing is an effective strategy involving enormous energy and learning.

Thinking historically

I hope it has become clear that in all of these active learning approaches students are practising the skills of thinking historically. This phrase, of course, has several meanings, from learning how to decode and interpret a primary source, to appreciating the complexity of change and continuity over time and in different cultures, to an awareness of the inevitability of differing historical interpretations of a particular event or phenomenon. To help students think historically also means to immerse them as far as possible in the moral and cultural ethos of the past. Students learn to think historically by getting out of their present time and into the kinds of real choice people faced in the past. The role-playing situations described above do just that. Other examples are to put students in the courtroom trial of Anne Hutchinson, where they must decide whether to banish her to Rhode Island. Or situate them in a Powhatan or Pequot village faced with the establishment of an English settlement on the edge of a game-bearing forest ten miles away. Or assign half the students as British regulars on the road to Concord to find smuggled goods, and the other half as colonial Minutemen in the tavern on Lexington Green in the early April morning of 1775 wondering what to do when the redcoats arrive. Or invite students to complete a compelling unfinished human story: 'What will happen to the confident Athenians in Sicily?', 'What should Napoleon do about Russia?', 'What options does the young Pakistani immigrant woman have as she arrives in London?' Student answers, no doubt complicated ones involving both historical narrative and some flights of fancy, unfold in a mixture of interactive brainstorming, mini-lectures for necessary context and reasoning from evidence. Immersing students in the past dealing with human decisions and their consequences teaches them complex historical realities.

A second major form of historical thinking is by interpreting primary sources, the bedrock of our craft. We have already seen how both to motivate and teach interpretive skills to students with evocative visual sources. The most important historical skill our students need, however, is how to do close reading of primary documents by using an old-fashioned but woefully ignored technique, *explication du texte*. Although we would choose a variety of public sources, we would balance the political history with the social and cultural history found in diaries, autobiographies, novels and other literary sources. Depending on the level and size of the class, the instructor might first demonstrate how to read a passage, with students following along with handouts or an overhead. But soon it is their turn to practise the craft. There are many ways to select appropriate passages and to structure such a class. Invite students, either ahead of time or at the start of class, to 'find one or two sentences from the reading you found particularly significant and be prepared to justify your choice'. Or, 'find one passage you especially liked and one you disliked'. Students are then ready to read these aloud and discuss them. Lively interaction is likely because all students will not select the same passages or interpret them in the same way. For an especially difficult passage, small groups could be asked to struggle with the meaning and determine the main point of the passage. Invite a few groups to report their reflections, thus providing the class with an opportunity to react to differing interpretations.

This process of how to read analytically can be applied to many different kinds of text. We introduce students to a variety of different sources used in recovering the past: maps, census data, graphs and charts, personal writing, political documents, broadsides, material culture, quantitative data, songs, paintings and other visual sources. Think of such class sessions as 'history labs'. Distribute historical sources in class – a tax record, a household inventory, a diary entry, a folk tale, a will, an old tool, a family photograph – and ask: 'What do you see? What does the source say?' After teasing out the content of the source, ask higher-order questions of significance: 'What does it mean or tell us? What implications do you draw from the source on how people lived?' Thus students get practice not only in interpreting primary sources of various kinds but also in discovering and exploring differing interpretations.

I actually start teaching historical interpretation with a textbook. Good texts, like monographs, have both a thesis and informing conceptual themes, as well as a social, political, economic or cultural orientation. As good as my students are, I still find they do not know how to 'read' a textbook, much less a monograph or journal article, so I spend time early in the term doing that in class. Whatever the reading, we look at the preface and introductory material to detect point of view and approach, as well as at the opening page or two of an early chapter. Ask students, perhaps in groups, to 'identify a passage which you think best illustrates the major thesis of the chapter [or book], and why'. This exercise needs frequent repetition for students to become adept at identifying thesis statements; when they do, they are better able to frame them in their own writing.

At some point students are ready to deal with different schools of interpreting historical phenomena. 'Slavery' works well, for there are three distinct interpretive schools: traditional white southern apologists, revisionist northern neo-abolitionists and black-perspective autobiographers. I associate each of the schools with three places and times on the plantation: morning in the Big House, hot afternoon in the fields and 'from sun down to sun up' in the slave quarters. This imagery imprints the three schools for students and reinforces their awareness that history – in this case, slavery – is constructed over time by people with contextual reasons for the sources they use and the particular view of slavery they present. We look at illustrative examples of each school, matching primary source material with passages from historical monographs. Another assignment to teach historiographical understanding is to have students write a comparative book review of two works on slavery (or on any topic) written at least 30–40 years apart.

Final reflections

This chapter began with teaching strategies immediately engaging students in 'doing history' on the first day of class. Here is another, more elaborate and founded on the principle of connecting student lives with the essential questions and craft of historical thinking. On an early day in the term I tell students that they are going simultaneously to write a mini-biography (of another student) and experience what it is like to think as a historian. The activity is in four steps, done in pairs, each involving individual reflection and writing, followed by talking in pairs, and concluding with the whole class identifying and discussing the historical issues in the exercise. First, I ask students to think back and begin the process of writing notes on their own life history about ten years ago. The choice enables them to avoid what might be a particularly painful period. I then ask them to give the notes to a partner (their 'biographer') and talk in pairs about what they learned from the process: How would they go about recovering the past? What written, oral and material sources might they use? What is the role and danger of relying upon memory in retrieving the past? Debrief the whole class on these kinds of question.

The second step is to ask them to write the history of their life during the month of September (or August or October) two or three years ago. The follow-up is similar. Third, I ask them to write the history of their life – yesterday. Unlike the first two parts, where issues of sources, retrieval and judgement were primary concerns, here the problem is selection, presentation and point of view (i.e. Should I move chronologically through the day or pick a representative incident that illustrates a theme, or some combination of the two?). The fourth step is to turn over all the notes to the partner, who then writes a mini-biography, making sure to include a thesis that connects the three disparate periods of the life. This personalised activity raises many significant issues in the researching and writing of history: making sense of fragmentary sources, the inevitability of selection and interpretation, and continuity and change over time.

Indeed, these active learning strategies take time, at the cost of 'covering the material'. So, what to do? There is no tougher teaching/learning question. Two thoughts: it is inherent in being a historian to make content and interpretive selections in looking at the past, choices based on what we think are the essential questions and most significant facts and concepts of our field. Similarly, we make pedagogical choices; these depend on our goals, who our students are and what we know about student learning. Second, active learning is not necessarily incompatible with coverage. For example, one day I decided that my students needed to learn the skill of reading a textbook chapter by looking in depth in an interactive way at just three key paragraphs. When class was over, I realised that in the process of discussing those paragraphs in depth we had in fact dealt with the major factual and conceptual issues of the entire chapter.

As a teacher, the choices I make assume that student motivation is enhanced by successes. It is crucial that students have a sense that they are acquiring historical knowledge, concepts and skills, and that they value the habits of mind and heart involved in the study of history. Moreover, students need to claim ownership and responsibility for their own learning as a result of having been actively involved in it. As an early advocate of active learning, Ralph Waldo Emerson, once wrote in his journal: a wise person 'must feel and teach that the best wisdom cannot be communicated [but] must be acquired by every soul for itself'.[4]

Notes

1 The following are only five of the many recent sources on active and other forms of student-centred learning: C. Bonwell and J. Eison, *Active Learning: Creating Excitement in the Classroom*, ASHE-ERIC Higher Education Report No. 1 (Washington, DC, The George Washington University School of Education, 1991); C. Meyers and T. B. Jones, *Promoting Active Learning: Strategies for the Classroom* (San Francisco, Jossey-Bass, 1993); W. Campbell and K. Smith (eds), *New Paradigms for College Teaching* (Edina, Minnesota, Interaction Book Co., 1997); D. F. Halpern and Associates, *Changing College Classrooms: New Teaching and Learning Strategies for an Increasingly Complex World* (San Francisco, Jossey-Bass, 1994); A. Chickering and Z. Gamson, 'Seven principles for good practice in undergraduate education', *AAHE Bulletin* (March 1987).
2 See, for example, R. Blackey (ed.), *History Anew: Innovations in the Teaching of History* (Long Beach, CSU Long Beach Press, 1992), drawn from the 'Teaching innovations' feature of the *AHA Perspectives* magazine (Washington, DC, AHA).
3 F. Stern, *Varieties of History* (New York, Vintage Books, 1972).
4 *Journals of Ralph Waldo Emerson*, III (Boston, Houghton Mifflin, 1910) p. 280.

9 Peter Davies, Janet Conneely, Rhys Davies and Derek Lynch

Imaginative ideas for teaching and learning

'It seemed to me that the main difference between lectures and seminars was that in seminars the tutor sat down.' It could be postulated that this quotation is representative of what many students feel about teaching and learning in the university context; the belief that somehow lectures and seminars are often far too similar, and that seminars – the focus of this study – often suffer from the over-dominance of the 'expert' tutors.[1] So, too, many tutors feel frustrated by the level of student participation in university seminars, the ability of students to think through issues, and the quality of undergraduates' oral communication and group-work skills. Large class sizes and the growing diversity of the student population exacerbate problems of motivation and preparation.[2] It therefore seemed important to us to facilitate seminars that were more student centred and participatory, and which utilised a greater variety of methods in the ways that small-group classroom sessions were organised, in order to make seminars more 'active', interesting, imaginative and challenging. As Frederick has pointed out:

> The highest challenge we face as classroom teachers is to motivate our students to love history as we do, and to be joyously involved with the texts, themes, issues, and questions of history that interest and excite us. Although our students may seem less well motivated or prepared these days, ultimately the responsibility for their motivation rests with us.[3]

In addition, it is clear that there is a growing interest in attempts to improve the learning experience of students. The Higher Education Funding Council for England, for example, is particularly aware of such efforts,[4] and as Fisher and Taithe note: 'There is now an apparent consensus of opinion regarding the need for issues surrounding the quality of teaching in higher education to be addressed.'[5] But a key question remains: Are universities responding adequately to the demands of students and their different learning needs? On the whole, it is assumed that the university learning experience is about individual and independent learning, facilitated by tutors who will help and encourage student participation in the learning process. However, there is no consensus about the best way to do this. The contention of our work is that history seminars must become more practical and activity based. As Frederick states: 'Every study of effective educational practices in recent years cites active and small-group cooperative learning, high expectations combined with frequent feedback, "hands-on" experiences practicing the skills of the discipline and caring teachers as key elements in motivating students to learn.'[6]

In practical terms, the aim of our work was to prepare and produce a handbook of forty teaching methods suitable for seminar use.[7] Four particular areas of interest and importance for the historian were identified: numerical data, visuals, abstract ideas and primary sources. All were felt to be important to the teaching of history, yet in need of some fresh thinking and impetus. We asked key questions: With numerical data, why not introduce a puzzle element? With visuals, why not challenge students to represent a pictorial source in another form? With abstract ideas, why not put a concept 'on trial'? And with primary sources, why not role play a text?

The process of research

There were several phases or dimensions to our research. These can be summarised as follows:

1 *Research and preparation.* In this first 'planning' phase, group members focused on devising and creating seminar activities in their chosen area (whether numerical data, visuals, abstract ideas or primary sources). This entailed talking with other teachers and tutors, with group-work specialists in other fields and with students. It also involved building upon the work of a wide range of educational writers and developers.[8] The result of this was that each researcher developed ten new seminar activities with which to experiment and to test.

2 *Testing.* Here we had to think about the following questions: How were we going to plan and deliver our activities? Were the activities to be employed in 'quarantine', so to speak, or as part of a wider lesson or seminar? Were we going to present the outline of the activity as we would present a standard lesson plan? And how were we to evaluate and assess the teaching and learning outcomes? In the end we decided to be flexible, but thorough. A variety of approaches would be employed: activities might be tested in class or in the focus-group context; they might run for different lengths of time; and we would think clearly about the specific aims and objectives of each technique and its prospective learning outcomes. The use of 'aims' and 'objectives' was particularly helpful, supplying us with a valuable yardstick against which to measure the success of the overall teaching and learning experience.

3 *Focus groups.* For those of us teaching in higher education, small focus-groups (the size of these groups varied from three to eight students) were con-

sidered the most appropriate for testing our ideas. The fourth member of the team felt that, in a secondary school, a whole-class teaching strategy for the activities would work best. Consequently, in this environment the activities were tested on students with a wide range of ability across a range of ages – though mostly fourteen-, sixteen- and seventeen-year-olds. There are, clearly, merits and drawbacks to each of these two types of approach. The focus groups worked well and were helpful in creating a sense of staff–student 'partnership' and facilitating a two-way exchange of ideas. It was particularly encouraging to learn that students wanted to be involved in discussion about the advantages and disadvantages of certain seminar activities. However, the focus groups largely consisted of well-motivated students, and those participating were lively, honest, critical and provocative in their feedback. 'Whole class' testing was, obviously, more authentic as it involved all students, but it too was not without its difficulties, not least the management problems associated with class sizes of thirty-plus and the lack of close personal contact between tutor and student.

4 *Content.* The subject matter used in the classes varied according to the tutor. Those team members teaching in higher education tended to use the field of modern British and international politics, while the tutor in secondary education used British and European history as the medium. Another difference, and one which raises a number of important issues, was the teaching context in which the activities were set. Whereas the university team delivered their activities in classes that were separate from their main teaching, the secondary school teacher used activities in lessons that originated in a predetermined scheme of work. As such, the university students were taking part in self-contained sessions that they could not prepare for, although care was taken to choose subject matter on which the students would be fairly well informed. But, rather than being a problem, this turned out to be very useful in the sense that students were often very spontaneous in their comments and were not influenced by previous ideas.

5 *Evaluation techniques.* The research team employed a series of strategies in the evaluation process. In both arenas – focus-group and whole-class testing – the development work involved the use of several key tools: student questionnaires, 'observer' questionnaires, one-to-one interviews with students and group discussion.

These five aspects of our work can be illustrated here by some examples of particular activities. One of these activities is introduced in full (Example 1), while the two others are presented more selectively.

Example 1, numerical data: recognition tests

Description

Setting and context
This method – in essence, a provocative puzzle-cum-challenge – is a particularly novel teaching and learning device. It would be especially useful where students are studying the particular characteristics of, say, a political party or a national economy. It challenges students to identify hidden axes or hidden statistics on the basis of other details on display in a table.

Learning aims and objectives
Aims: To improve students' understanding of the subject matter and to enhance their confidence in dealing with numerical data.
Objectives: To challenge students via a puzzle-style exercise, and to promote improved learning through structured and supported competition.

Programme of activities
5 mins Teacher introduces session – and its aims.
5 mins Background – general big-group discussion about party electorates.
15 mins Handout is given to small student mini-groups and, via a series of 'comprehension' questions attached to the table, each group is challenged to identify the missing figures and the blanked-out axes; small-group discussion ensues.
10 mins Teacher reveals answers – more discussion in big-group (or small-group) context.

Example test
See Table 9.1 on following page.

Learning outcomes
Students will have developed their understanding of how statistics can be used and manipulated; gained insights into the nature of party politics; and discussed the meaning of key statistics in small- and large-group contexts.

Evaluation

- This was the first 'numerical data' exercise to be tested; it worked well and provoked good debate. It was, according to individual students in the testing group, 'fun', 'useful', 'something new which is encouraging', and an original teaching method that resulted in both group bonding and an increase in knowledge.
- It is essential that the tabular data presented to students are accurate – for example, all rows must add up to 100 – there must be no areas of ambiguity and the whole exercise must be made as student friendly as possible. There

Table 9.1 How Britain voted in 1992 (market research categories)

| | Class | | | Sex | | [Age (years)] | | | | |
	ABC1	C2	DE	a	b	18–24	25–34	35–54	55+	All
All	43	27	30			14	19	33	34	100
Con	54	39	31	44	41	39	40	43	f	43
Lab	c	d	e	34	37	35	38	34	g	35
Alliance	21	17	19	18	18	19	18	19	h	18
Others	3	4	1	4	4	7	4	4	3	4
Total					100					

Table taken from D. Butler, *British General Elections since 1945* (Oxford, Blackwell, 1995).
Source: Mori.
Overall results: Con, 42; Lab, 35; Lib Dem, 18; Nats, 2; Other, 3.

Exercise:
1 Discuss the gender basis of the parties' votes. Identify the axis categories a and b. Which column relates to which gender?
2 The Labour vote, by class, has been erased. Discuss the likely spread of the Labour vote across class categories ABC1, C2 and DE. Insert figures for c, d and e on the basis of your knowledge of the Labour Party and its specific electorate.
3 In the 55+ column, what do f, g and h stand for? How would the 55+ generation vote? Discuss this matter and insert figures for f, g and h.
4 There are two 'bogus' figures in this table (i.e. two numbers which I have switched round). Identify which they are and explain how you deduced that it was these two figures which were 'bogus' (n.b. I have not altered anything in the 'Others' row).

are always eagle-eyed students who will be looking for errors and inaccuracies. One student, for example, claimed that the table was 'slightly unclear' and 'a little confusing'. Another talked about 'problems with the documentation'. The bottom line, obviously, is that an exercise can be adversely affected or founder, almost fatally, if the data presented to students are flawed.
• The questions accompanying the table should not be the sole forms of the exercise; there should be other discussion elements, both before and after the table-based exercise (whether big-group or small-group). In general, the feeling seemed to be that the students needed more time to give depth to their discussion and extra questions to spark debate.
• Is the competition involved in this method good or bad? The consensus among the students seemed to be that with competition one had to be careful; some students might worry about it, and the ultimate danger was that the 'competition' element could outweigh or minimise the 'learning' element. It was felt that group competition was probably a better idea than individual competition. Some students said that by nature they just did not like competitive exercises such as puzzles and crosswords – but this, naturally, applied to

some and not to others. One student argued that the puzzle element of the exercise was 'a bit dubious' and that it would have been far better just to analyse 'complete and correct tables'. Another said that pure discussion – without competition – enabled all opinions to be aired and to be recognised as 'right'; but that in the specific context of Recognition Tests the merit of competition was that it focused students on the data in hand. Overall, the view seemed to be that competition was healthy because it put 'pressure' on the groups and they performed better as a result.

- In terms of participation it was clear that the use of student mini-groups (with two or three students per group) produced some quite intensive discussion. Students seemed to feel that this was a productive way of organising the session, if also slightly time consuming (e.g. breaking up and coming back together quite regularly). The student view was that enhanced participation was a natural effect of the method: participants were 'comfortable' and 'relaxed' and everyone with opinions was able to contribute. Healthy discussion was encouraged, even though, it was argued, raw statistics still had the potential to make students clam up instinctively! The feedback also suggested that students had learnt from other students' comments and took them on board – and that it was these views, and not just the data, which were significant in enhancing learning. Indeed, one student said that he had learnt more than he expected to, because of the input of other students.
- Students were satisfied with the role of the tutor: as a 'guide' – setting up the discussion, encouraging participation and keeping the debate flowing. They appreciated the tutor's 'briefing' role, and approved of the way in which he initiated, rather than controlled, discussion.

Summary

Merits

- A significant, and popular, puzzle-cum-challenge element.
- Competition – can provoke students into productive classroom activity.
- Inquisitive and motivated students!

Possible problems

- Pre-class preparation – slightly messy and tricky!
- Competition – can have negative effects on some students.

Fine tuning: improvements to be made

- An additional role-play element (post-puzzle) to bring out further aspects of the data.
- Tables must always be clear (and add up!).

Verdict

• Provocative – and can be a stepping-stone to effective learning and further discussion.

Example 2, visuals: propaganda posters

Description

Setting and context
This is a particularly useful activity for analysing the doctrine of a political movement and assessing the mood of a particular audience from the past. Posters can be devised after looking at a number of written sources which outline a movement's ideas, whether in the form of speeches, radio broadcasts or news-sheets. In this particular case, a class of GCSE students devised a Nazi propaganda poster, after analysing a range of written sources dealing with the party's programme and its appeal to the discontented elements of German society in the early 1930s.

Learning aims and objectives
Aim: Students are to convert Nazi ideas taken from written documents into a visual medium, and so enhance their understanding of the main tenets of the party's ideology and the appeal of the Nazis to a discontented German people during the 1930s.
Objectives: To enable students to analyse and discuss a political movement's ideology and appeal; produce a visual image illustrating the appeal of the party to a particular social group; develop an empathetic awareness of what it was like to produce propaganda (in this case, in 1930s Germany); and present their ideas to the rest of the class and share findings.

Programme of activities
10 mins The teacher leads a discussion of the appeal of the Nazis in 1933, explains the activity and places students into small groups. One group is asked to devise a poster which would appeal to the working classes; the other groups are asked to create posters to appeal to the middle class, to the Junker class, to women and to the German population as a whole (i.e. a poster with cross-sectional appeal).
30 mins The groups then produce their own particular posters.
20 mins The students display and present their posters to the class as a whole, which takes notes on the Nazi party's main ideas and how it attempted to achieve cross-sectional mass support.

Learning outcomes
Students will have acquired an important understanding of propaganda, its nature and purpose; been given the opportunity to express themselves, and their

ideas, in a non-standard manner; and been encouraged to become aware of the mindset of a key movement in modern history.

Example 3, abstract ideas: cognitive mapping exercise

Description

This activity involves students delineating politically or culturally significant regions by drawing new boundaries on blank or partially labelled maps. The aim is to provoke students into thinking about the relativity of boundaries and other related geopolitical issues.

Evaluation

- The exercise was undertaken with two groups of students. It was incorporated into mainstream teaching with foundation-level classes on International Relations (several classes of twelve students). Feedback was through verbal discussion. The map used was of Asia, a region relatively unfamiliar to the class. However, students had time to read texts in cultural geography, which helped them to address the questions. In the second instance, four advanced-level students were given maps of Europe and surveyed by questionnaire. These students also gave more systematic verbal feedback.
- In both cases, the exercise generated considerable class discussion. There were significant disagreements about where boundaries should be drawn and why, and students pointed to their increasing awareness of how individual countries could see things from quite different perspectives. Students also felt that the use of maps and visual images added life to a discussion of concepts such as 'regions' or 'identities' which might otherwise appear to be somewhat abstract. A minority of weaker students, however, tended to see the exercise as a test of geographical knowledge. Country labels and a greater emphasis on the discussion of concepts at the end would be particularly helpful in overcoming this perception.
- There were no adverse comments on the role of the tutor or of other students: the attention was focused on the maps and on the arguments they evoked. This teaching method is also quite flexible. For instance, the subjectivity of boundaries or identities could be highlighted by asking students to play the role of official cartographer or negotiator for particular countries. In some cases, for example in foundation-level courses, the tutor might also want to encourage the learning of some political geography, as well as a general discussion of identity. Thus the exercise could be tailored to specific needs by increasing or decreasing the amount of labelling on the maps. But, on the whole, students felt that more labelling was better, especially if the focus was to be on ideas and concepts.

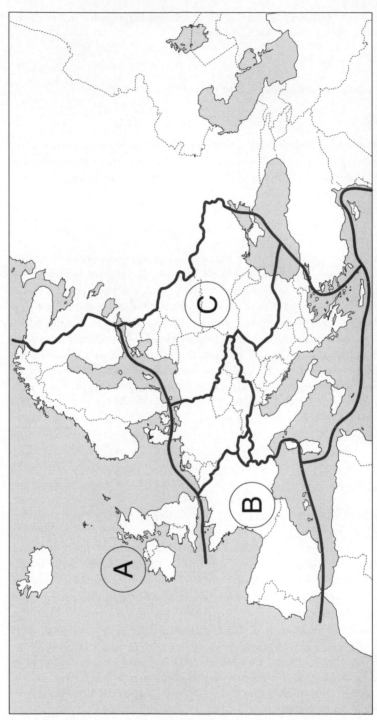

Figure 9.1: In this unlabelled map, the student has emphasised three main points: (A) the distinction between continental Europe and the northwest European periphery; (B) a southwest European area incorporating France and the Iberian peninsula; and (C) an East European region (although there is some ambiguity over the boundaries of the latter). Interestingly, the student included the Czech Republic in the central European area, despite its status as a Slavic country, and was able to identify German influence and the sophistication of Czech political and economic ambitions as a basis for his decision. Attitudes to the EU enlargement process were clearly at work in this effort, and this led to a discussion of other criteria for the definition of regions on the continent.

The above examples convey the essence of three particular teaching and learning methods. As well as explaining the 'mechanics' of the activity, each summary tries to explain the role of tutor and students in the class session, and gives some indication of the dynamics inherent in the exercise. The opinions of the participants are, obviously, crucial, and these are assessed in the 'Evaluation' section. These were the key pillars of our action-research method.

Outcomes

On the practical level, the key outcome of our work was a handbook of seminar ideas for tutors. On the theoretical level, what emerged was an in-depth discussion about teaching, learning, and the most effective way to format seminars and facilitate substantive classroom discussion. This discussion had an array of important outcomes.

First, it became obvious that students were both supportive of our work and genuinely wanted to be involved in it. They enabled us to refine our classroom methods and to think about our general approach; this 'student's-eye-view' of the world was central to the process and directed us to participant reactions which might normally be overlooked by busy teachers. The students also pointed out that the informality characteristic of many of the classes helped them to acclimatise to what was actually required, and encouraged them to contribute. As one put it: 'We were being treated as adults.'[9] Indeed, many students expressed appreciation for our genuine interest in the question of how they felt about, and what they needed from, the teaching and learning experience. They also went away with a greater sensitivity to 'how' they learn, as well as to the content of their learning.

Second, our research provoked debate about seminar and group teaching among staff. Some colleagues were initially concerned that we were attempting to establish a dichotomy between our 'better' methods and their 'stale' approaches, but once our objectives were explained this problem was easily resolved. Indeed, they subsequently provided useful inputs into our work and participated in, or observed, our focus-group classes. The open-mindedness about the relative value of various approaches to small-group teaching was fully vindicated, as our investigation showed that each approach had its merits in a particular context. This observation even applies to approaches that some would consider 'traditional'.

Third, we were left with the feeling that the 'debriefing' phase of classroom sessions was, possibly, the most important. If the students recall the class, but fail to recall the substantive points about the historical phenomena behind it, it cannot be said to have been a success. We found that, at the end of each and every session, the debriefing exercise both deepened students' awareness of important connections between the method and the subject matter, and provided tutors with important feedback on what was learnt and how well it was learnt.

Needless to say, discussion of the limitations of a teaching method can be as instructive as discussion about the content.

Finally, it would be fair to say that one common set of concerns which arose during the exercise was the issue of tutor control over the learning environment. This, of course, is a perennial issue in all areas of educational research, especially in the primary and secondary sectors.[10] It raised two important questions in our work: (1) to what extent should the tutor shape and control the flow of discussion; and (2) how do we respond to unintended and undesirable outcomes?

Since we aimed to produce free-flowing discussion and to maximise student participation in seminars, we did have an interest in limiting tutors' control inside the classroom. On the other hand, each lesson has a purpose and there is usually some conception of relevant and irrelevant learning. A balance must therefore be struck between spontaneity and direction. Spontaneity is useful for what educationalists call 'discovery learning', in which students generate and internalise their own way of understanding concepts and principles. It is a reaction against the didactic method in which facts are administered by the tutor and largely memorised by the student without much internal processing. But our search for balance between direction and spontaneity leads us to suggest that 'guided discovery' learning (i.e. discovery learning within parameters which assist the overall process) and 'structured discovery' (discovery learning deliberately geared to serve lesson, module or course objectives set out by the tutor) are more useful concepts. We have already stressed our eagerness to avoid the suggestion that one approach is 'correct' and others of little value. Indeed, those more familiar with traditional approaches may choose to vary the amount of structured guidance in their classes as they begin to experiment with discovery approaches. The relationship between didactic teaching and these methods is essentially scalar rather than crudely dichotomous. Perhaps Petty sums things up best when he says that students generally enjoy any kind of group work, 'so long as the teacher is able to direct activities meaningfully'.[11]

This chapter has discussed the origins of our research work, the process we followed and the ultimate outcomes. To conclude though, it is worth focusing on the most significant points to emerge out of the project. First, it is clear that the idea of 'joint' staff–student development work can be extremely productive. It is apparent that students are interested in the potential of active group work – just like their tutors – and feel that their opinions and ideas need to be taken on board in the fine tuning of practical classroom techniques. It should also be said that the findings of this project are, in many senses, only preliminary. They are testimony to the undoubted potential of this kind of research, and also perhaps a stepping-stone to further development work. While the teaching methods outlined in the handbook are, as it were, practicable and 'fully formed' (notwithstanding the possible need for future amendments), the insights into student opinion are in essence just a snapshot of the prevailing attitude 'on the ground'. As such, we feel that there are valuable lessons to be learnt from the exercise and important ideas to be built upon.

We should also acknowledge that the project encountered its problems and had its obvious limitations. The testing process in particular was fraught with difficulties: How authentic was the focus-group environment? Were the students behaving 'naturally'? Were the groups representative? Were the results valid? All these questions were raised at one point or another. In the end, the reality was that the testing sessions – whatever their imperfections – were productive and stimulating. The tutors involved used their professional judgement to inform their commentaries, and throughout, the sessions were fundamental to the project – to learning about student attitudes and to refining the teaching methods designed by the research group.

It should also be said that the individuals involved in the project could not help but be sensitive to the attitude of colleagues. In the university setting (but far less so in the school context), this attitude ranged from the overtly hostile to the indifferent and the very positive. In our dealings with other staff, the message we were trying to get across was that 'new' methods are not a substitute for 'established' techniques. Rather, we argued, they should be viewed as complementary; as forming, if you like, an alternative 'menu' to utilise selectively. Throughout, we wanted to stress two main points: first, the merits of tutors reflecting on their small-group teaching methods, analysing them and ultimately refining them;[12] and second, the practical, transferable nature of the 'active' methods being developed. Clearly, there are some constraints – the techniques are most suitable for seminars in discussion-based subjects – but we believe that with some fine tuning and adjustment, and with the necessary discretion, all the methods could be used not only quite widely in the university context, but also beyond higher education.

The fundamental message to emerge out of our work is this: small-group work in history has considerable potential, and teachers and tutors should not be afraid to experiment with new methods. Students will be supportive if actively involved in the process, and the history classroom can become more productive and enjoyable for both tutors and students.

Notes

1 'Seminars', in the specific context of this project, are defined as small-group learning sessions (as against tutorials, which are defined as individual or one-to-one events involving a tutor and a student). On the subject of interactive lectures, see J. Hart, 'Innovative lecturing: rising to the challenge', in J. Hart (ed.), *Innovations in Computing Teaching*, SEDA Paper 88 (March 1995); and also L. W. Andresen, *Lecturing to Large Groups*, SEDA Paper 81 (April 1994).

2 See History 2000 Project Newsletter, January 1997, p. 2.

3 P. Frederick, 'Motivating students by active learning in the history classroom', *Perspectives* (October 1993).

4 Higher Education Funding Council for England, subject overview report: 'History/quality assessment of history 1993–4' <http://www.niss.ac.uk/education/hefce/pub95qo-3-95>.

5 R. Fisher and B. Taithe, 'Developing university teachers: an account of a scheme designed for the postgraduate researcher on a lecturing career plan', *Teaching in Higher Education*, 3:1 (1998).

6 Frederick, 'Motivating students'.

7 The handbook is called *Catalysing Discussion: 40 Classroom Ideas for Teachers and Tutors*. It is available through History 2000.

8 Throughout our research, we were greatly indebted to previous research in the same area carried out by, among others, G. Gibbs, *Discussion with More Students* (Oxford, PCFC, 1992); G. Gibbs and T. Habeshaw, *253 Ideas for Your Teaching* (Worcester, TES, 1990); S. Habeshaw, G. Gibbs and T. Habeshaw, *53 Problems with Large Classes* (Worcester, TES, 1992); S. Habeshaw, T. Habeshaw and G. Gibbs, *53 Interesting Things to Do in your Seminars and Tutorials* (Exeter, TES, 1992); D. Baume and C. Baume, *Learning to Teach, Running Tutorials and Seminars: Training Materials for Research Students* (Oxford, The Oxford Centre for Staff Development, n.d.); R. Hubbard, *53 Interesting Ways to Teach Mathematics* (Bristol, TES, 1990); D. Bligh, D. Jacques and D. Warren Piper, *Seven Decisions when Teaching Students* (Exeter, EUTS, 1981); R. Macdonald, 'Teaching and learning in small groups', *SEDA Special Paper*, No. 2 (July 1997); P. Davies, *Catalysing Discussion* (Huddersfield, University of Huddersfield, 1997).

9 Comment from Linda Lawton, a student in one of the focus-group sessions. She also argued that seminars 'bridge the gap between school and industry'. This ties in with L. McDowell's comment to the effect that 'students felt that their wider experience was unacknowledged and considered irrelevant to their studies'; see 'University-wide change: staff and curriculum development', in P. T. Knight (ed.), *Staff and Educational Development Paper*, SEDA Paper 83 (May 1994), p. 32. See also History 2000 Project Newsletter, January 1997, p. 3.

10 For a discussion of discovery learning, see G. Petty, *Teaching Today: A Practical Guide* (Cheltenham, Stanley Thormes, 1993), pp. 221–9; and L. Cohen, L. Manion and K. Morrison, *A Guide to Teaching Practice*, (London, Routledge, 1996, 4th edn).

11 Petty, *Teaching Today*, p. 168.

12 For more on reflective practice, see L. Beaty, 'Developing your teaching through reflective practice', *SEDA Special No. 5*; L. A. J. Stefani, 'Reflective learning in higher education: issues and approaches', *UCoSDA Briefing Paper Forty-Two* (January 1997).

'Deep learning' and the large seminar in history teaching

Over the last ten years, student numbers in higher education have increased enormously, while financial resources have remained limited. This has presented history departments throughout Britain with a dilemma: whether to maintain traditional teaching methods in the face of quite different demands, or whether to explore new avenues. Nowhere, it seems, has this situation affected history teaching more acutely than in the realm of group work. Lectures do not change their internal dynamics markedly when numbers are increased. Seminars, on the other hand, become quite different animals when the number of students is raised from what is often believed to be the 'normal' size of between five and ten students, to what is becoming the reality at many institutions: groups of between fifteen and thirty students.[1] Such numbers present a challenge, and many history teachers have experimented over the years with different teaching methods.[2] Experimentation has, however, tended to take place within conventional frameworks and has not usually been sustained or systematically evaluated. With the onset of greater numbers, staff have been under pressure to innovate to a far greater extent, yet they have tended to do so on their own, as individuals and without much expert advice. Even if they had time to look for it, moreover, they would often find that the practical educational literature on seminars deals largely with groups below the size of fifteen.[3] What happens above that figure is all too often left to the imagination, practical experience and intuition of the tutor.

A project undertaken at Kingston and Newcastle Universities sought to address this situation in two ways. First, it aimed to contribute to the literature on the subject of teaching increased class numbers, based on the analysis of data gathered from a national survey and discussions between staff and students on their experiences.[4] Second, the project aimed, following an action-research method, to encourage staff and students to experiment with a range of techniques to improve learning in seminars, to define what they think group work should be achieving, and to encourage students to adopt 'deep approaches' to their learning. In this sense our work was an exercise in collaborative reflective practice with students.[5] We used the distinction between 'deep' and 'surface' approaches to learning to inform our discussions.[6] 'Surface' approaches to learning are characterised by students completing assigned tasks and memorising information. Typically, students fail to distinguish between principles and examples, treat tasks as external impositions, focus on discrete elements of work without attempting to integrate them, and do not reflect on the purposes or strategies of their work. 'Deep' approaches to learning, on the other hand, are characterised by students vigorously interacting with their subject, exploring underlying principles, reflecting on the logic of arguments, and relating new ideas to previous knowledge, concepts to everyday experience and evidence to conclusions. According to most educational literature, 'deep learning' is best achieved through action-based techniques; that is, through participation, discussion, reflection and personal interaction with a subject. The seminar, therefore, has been viewed as far more likely to facilitate 'deep learning' than the passive, informational lecture. History tutors at both Kingston and Newcastle were presented with the concept of 'deep learning' at the outset and asked to discuss whether it accorded with what they thought seminars ought to be achieving. This enabled us to identify the differences, if any, between the aims of seminars at the two institutions and those encapsulated in the term 'deep learning'. Tutors were asked to identify what seminars ought to achieve and, where possible, to redefine 'deep learning' according to their own aims and considerations.

Context and method

Newcastle University's history department is a traditional one, offering a range of courses in medieval, early-modern and modern history, with distinctive strengths in British, American and European history. The annual intake into its single-honours degree programme rose from around thirty in the late 1980s to seventy-five some ten years later, with another twenty taking the joint degree in politics and history. History courses are also taken by many Combined Arts students. Staff numbers, meanwhile, have remained largely static at around twelve to fourteen. The department's teaching methods rely mainly on lectures, seminars and one-to-one tutorials – the latter having survived longer than at many other UK universities. Though large student numbers for particular courses are not a novelty at Newcastle, efforts in the 1980s to maintain similar-sized student cohorts for various courses have tended to break down in the 1990s, leaving both increased numbers and increased inequalities. Rather than increasing seminar-group sizes in response to larger numbers, there has been a tendency to cut down on seminars and tutorials, sometimes putting little or nothing in their place.

Kingston University has a history degree programme as well as a history of ideas degree programme within a School of Humanities, together with a social and economic history programme in a School of Economics. The number of full-time staff teaching in the history field is six, and in history of ideas three, while the main body of history students now comes increasingly as a result of two-subject degree combinations through a modular scheme, as well as from part-time students. While Newcastle has been able to rely to some extent on postgraduates for teaching support, at Kingston, with a relatively small postgraduate community, a crucial reaction to increased numbers has been to raise seminar sizes.

In order to take account of differences in the traditions and practices of the two departments, it was felt that discussions ought to proceed at each university independently, so as to allow issues and solutions to be discussed with reference to the particular educational context and conditions of each place. This would mean that differences in the way the project was pursued at each institution would themselves be an important feature of our work. On the other hand, it was agreed at the outset that the methods of evaluation – questionnaires asking staff and students to reflect on the way seminars had operated – should be the same in the two departments so that direct comparisons could be made and general conclusions reached. It was also agreed that staff from Kingston's Teaching and Learning Support Service (TLSS) and Newcastle's Academic Quality Enhancement Unit (AQEU) should be closely involved in discussions, in order to inject ideas and expertise in educational development. In addition, a national questionnaire was sent out to history departments throughout the country in order to acquire some basic information about seminar practices elsewhere, against which the findings of the project could be compared. In our evaluations we ended up with 1,116 student questionnaires, reflecting the experience of eighty-six separate seminars.

At Kingston the project began with three meetings between the six participating historians and representatives of the TLSS. At these meetings staff were asked to define what a seminar was, and what they felt it ought to achieve. This allowed them to define 'deep learning' as it was applied at Kingston. They were also asked to talk about the way in which student numbers had changed, and how they had coped with these changes. Staff were then introduced to techniques drawn from a range of educational literature, and asked to add others which they felt had been useful in dealing with large numbers. In this way there emerged a list of suggested solutions to the challenge posed by large numbers, representing an amalgam of expert knowledge and individual tutor experience. They included:

- pyramiding/'buzz groups' (two or three students discuss and then share their ideas with others);
- fish-bowls (small groups discuss while the rest of the class observes);
- student-led seminars;
- brainstorming;
- role play;
- workshops (students undertake a collaborative project);
- informal group and one-to one peer-assessment;
- demonstration by tutor followed by tasking by students;

- division of group into explicit factual and conceptual task forces;
- tutorless groups;
- case discussions (groups devise case studies for other students);
- cross-over groups (where members move from one group to another and are interviewed);
- syndicates (students work in groups in parallel);
- synectics (either through brainstorming with primed groups of students or use of analogy whereby students are encouraged to think of new ways of perceiving a subject);
- creative exercises (e.g. posters, reports);
- presentations by groups/individuals with tutor involvement;
- court enquiry (formal, with witnesses);
- silent classes (with all communication done on paper);
- essay writing and peer marking (with prior discussion).

Staff were each asked to select six techniques which they would like to try, and to write a short report saying why they had chosen these techniques.

In the second semester, the project team at Kingston applied the new techniques they had chosen for their seminars at all levels of the history degree, and in courses on the French Revolution, the Contemporary World, Early-Modern Europe, Patterns of Irish Nationalism, Philosophies of Nature, Orientalism, Italian Renaissance, Britain and Germany since 1848, and the USA in the Nineteenth Century. Extra staff were called in to create smaller seminars in certain cases. As staff tried various techniques, their own responses and comments on the seminar, as well as those of their students, were recorded on proforma questionnaires. The questions asked students to say whether the group was too big, too small or just right; whether they felt more informed and, more confident about the underlying arguments; and whether the seminar had encouraged them to wish to learn more about the subject. The staff, meanwhile, were also asked to comment on the size of the group, and were encouraged to analyse the way the session had gone and how it might be improved. Half-way through the project it was decided that the original multiple-choice student questionnaires should be replaced at both Kingston and Newcastle by text-based ones: Newcastle had started earlier than Kingston and 'questionnaire fatigue' had already started to manifest itself. The new questionnaires simply asked students to comment as much as possible on the seminar, and staff were asked to prime students first through a general discussion on the way things had gone. During this semester it was also agreed to hold semi-structured group interviews with students to find out more about their experience of seminars. These were answered by two panels of students selected to form a cross-section of student types and abilities, and their responses were recorded on tape.

At Newcastle, the project team consisted of seven of the department's lecturers and a number of postgraduate tutors. Staff, tutors and students were all involved through lunch-time meetings, where their experiences and proposals were discussed together informally. Here, ideas about seminar teaching were disseminated, staff were able to compare notes, staff not involved could find out what was going on, and advice was brought in from the AQEU. One of the main differences between Newcastle and Kingston was that, rather than having a relatively small number of teachers, each experimenting with a variety of teaching methods, Newcastle chose to work with a larger number of teachers, each starting with only one main approach. In some cases, one teaching method was maintained throughout the semester; in others, teachers tried different methods as they went along. Apart, therefore, from the understanding that seminar groups would be large, lecturers and support tutors at Newcastle were free to run their seminars as they thought appropriate – resulting in diversity of approach, as well as experimentation and adaptation throughout the year. This meant that Newcastle's team was making comparisons *across* but also *within* courses. Student and staff responses were monitored by means of the questionnaires described above, with the format changing, for the reasons indicated, between the first and second semesters. The lunch-time meetings proved to be another, and perhaps even more valuable, means of gauging student and staff responses. Although the discussions were structured, the informal context encouraged free expression of opinion and also, perhaps, a sense of joint ownership of the project. This was certainly something which the department and the AQEU were hoping to achieve.

At the end of the year, the results from Kingston and Newcastle were brought together. Computing staff were employed to carry out a statistical analysis of the questionnaires, while an attempt was made to analyse the findings of the text-based responses.

Key findings

Before examining the outcomes of the project, it would be useful to consider the strengths and weaknesses of the methodology used.

*   The first thing to emphasise is that the project did, in fact, run largely according to plan. This was testimony to the perseverance of participating staff, as well as their conviction of the importance of the issue. They were sufficiently concerned with the problem of seminar teaching to stay involved despite many other pressures.
*   Fluctuations in student participation proved something of a problem. What had begun as large seminars often became much smaller as attendance levels rose and fell. Of course, 'deep learning' might have been easier to achieve in smaller groups, but that was not what the project was about. Techniques geared to large numbers often became unworkable with smaller groups, while questionnaires designed to elicit responses to large-group teaching became largely meaningless when filled in by students who had attended a small-group seminar.

- The design of questionnaires also raised a number of issues. Multiple-choice questions were felt by some tutors to be less productive than text-based ones – hence the change in format half-way through the year. On the other hand, the text-based questionnaires often gave rise to varied and disparate comments, or continued to duplicate in a textual way the high number of apparently unreflective responses previously collected. In some respects, therefore, their message may have been less conclusive than the multiple-choice questionnaires, which did give decisive statistical feedback in certain cases.
- There was an element of artificiality about the way the project took place which perhaps limited its findings. In particular, those techniques tried at Kingston University which involved students in completely new activities (role play, debates, multiple-group work) and exercised new skills (text analysis, tasking, group presentation), given time and repeated application, might have proved useful. However, they were often sprung on the students with little warning, and perhaps needed more preparatory work in order to succeed. At Newcastle, large classes were in themselves something of an innovation for tutors and students: to some extent the novelty may have diverted attention from what was actually going on in the seminars.

The outcomes of our project are based on the recorded discussions of staff and students at meetings, the national questionnaire sent to all history departments, and the staff and student questionnaires. One of the most valuable outcomes was the involvement of staff at Kingston and Newcastle in the exercise itself, and the discussion it generated about the way group teaching is conducted. Despite worries expressed by some theorists that the methods of action research may be too eclectic,[7] lecturers and tutors often voiced their appreciation that a forum had been created in which they could discuss teaching and unburden themselves of worries that had preoccupied many of them for some time. They greatly appreciated the opportunity to discuss their experiences: staff had tried techniques which others thought might be useful to them, or had encountered problems with which others could offer help. The input of educationalists was also appreciated, and the project also provided staff with a reason and a support for innovation.

The project has also gone some way to answering the questions it initially raised: How have history departments responded to the challenges posed to seminar teaching by the growth of class sizes? What ought seminars to be about, and can their goals be achieved in the context of larger student numbers? It has also produced many other, more general findings. In some cases these provide a good context for understanding particular outcomes; in others they represent significant points in themselves:

- Over recent years, the increase in student numbers has led most history departments to increase the size of seminar classes. In those which responded to the national questionnaire, some 89 per cent of staff recorded that the number of students in seminars had increased. Their responses indicate that, since 1992, history departments have increased seminar class sizes by the addition of between five and ten students. Most appear to be now operating with groups of fifteen or more. Those exceptional cases where small tutorials are still held regularly appear to maintain this system on the basis of preferential funding. The fact that many institutions are now operating with large seminar groups is something which perhaps needs to be addressed more fully in educational literature.

• Both the national questionnaire and staff discussions at Kingston and Newcastle revealed a high degree of staff antipathy towards large seminar groups. According to comments written on the questionnaires, as well as minuted discussions, tutors felt that large seminar groups often produced irregular attendance patterns. They required a much greater staff input in terms of preparation time and planning. Moreover, tutors felt that large groups made it more difficult to achieve those qualities which were most valued in seminars, namely high levels of student participation, staff interaction with the individual student and identity formation among the group. In the national questionnaire, 69 per cent of respondents said that seminars had become more difficult to teach as a result of increased class sizes, and 75 per cent said that seminars were now too big. Some, indeed, felt that seminars ought to be given up altogether and a completely new type of teaching introduced. Though students' responses to the same kind of question must be qualified by their more limited experience, the national questionnaires revealed that they too, where they had commented on increased seminar size, had done so negatively (41 per cent) rather than positively (11 per cent). These results raise important questions regarding the level of resources being made available for increased seminar sizes and the quality of the teaching being delivered, as well as in relation to staff and student morale.

• The national questionnaires and staff discussions at Newcastle and Kingston show that in response to the increase in numbers, staff have changed the way they teach groups. The national questionnaire revealed that some 72 per cent of staff had found new methods to deal with large seminars. Against this figure, however, only 47 per cent of staff recorded having received advice from their department on changing teaching practices, and over 60 per cent said they required more information on seminar teaching. In most instances, the tutorial-style approach, with one student offering a presentation, had been dropped for practical reasons, and seminar-style discussion adopted.

• At the national level, a variety of techniques were suggested by history tutors as ways of dealing with large seminars. These included: pairing students; small-group discussion with the tutor circulating between groups followed by a plenary session; buzz groups; preparation of written reports (c. 400 words) which are then submitted for peer assessment; and student role-play (e.g. chair, presenter, reporter). Most of the techniques revolved around the creation of smaller groups within larger groups.

• With regard to the purpose of seminars, staff at Kingston and Newcastle felt that seminars should: enable students to gain confidence in a subject; develop analytical skills; challenge and disturb students; inspire students to go further in their studies; be enjoyable; and allow students to follow a model for research and historical understanding as presented in the person of the lecturer. They also felt that such things could best be encouraged by techniques which allowed student participation, activity, interaction with the tutor and the subject, and argument. To this extent the ideas of the participants were similar to the textbook definitions of 'deep learning', but there were also important differences. Many staff felt that seminars should have an element of informational input and should be geared towards assessment, both through preparing students for exams and assessing their performance within the seminar – if only as an incentive for students to attend. These views were held far more strongly by students, many of whom believed that seminars should not merely offer an opportunity to clarify information, but should contribute towards their overall assessment results. Indeed, many students revealed a depressingly utilitarian approach to learning – but one probably encouraged by other changes in higher education, such as semesters and modularised teaching. The attitude appears increasingly to be 'Why should I do any work for which I do not gain a credit?'

More positively, seminars were viewed by staff and students as important in creating cohesion in history classes and social interaction between students – something which the students in particular felt was important to motivation. Many tutors thought that seminars should enable students to develop important transferable skills and personal qualities, such as decision making and management of self and group. Rather than being something completely different from 'deep learning', however, it might be argued that most of these transferable skills are themselves exercised in seminars in which students are encouraged to adopt a 'deep' approach to their learning.

- A number of techniques appeared to diminish the number of student objections to large seminar groups, and produced responses in the questionnaires which were associated with 'deep learning'. The following techniques in particular groups evoked positive responses from students and staff, either at Kingston or at Newcastle: the use of video materials as primers for discussion; buzz groups; presentation by groups; student-led sessions; brainstorming; role-play; debates; and textual analysis. Though the results of 'deep learning' on assessment levels were not provided by this project, the comments on questionnaires and in oral responses suggested that the prerequisites for 'deep learning' were, indeed, in place.

- The use of such techniques appeared to produce secondary problems for staff. By far the largest was that of time. Some techniques proved extremely time consuming, in terms both of preparation and of organising students within the seminar hour itself. Students themselves appeared to feel the time pressure more acutely in larger groups: the number of students saying seminars were too short began to grow. Environmental problems also loomed larger: size of room, flexibility of seating and acoustic suitability were mentioned more frequently. Moreover, attendance levels appeared not only to fluctuate more widely in larger groups, but also to become more harmful to the way seminars progressed when such techniques were being used. This was cited repeatedly by staff and students in the questionnaires, as well as in discussion, as a factor in the success of the techniques used for large groups: the more complex structures of larger seminars placed a greater onus on regular attendance, yet the students felt less pressure to attend when the class was large.

- In interviews at Kingston, students expressed the strong conviction that some form of assessment should be introduced into seminars, both to ensure regular attendance and to reflect the work being done on presentations. However, tutors highlighted the practical difficulties of the suggestion: issues such as the non-involvement of external examiners in this form of assessment, wide deviations in tutor marking and poor student performance in front of groups. At Newcastle, there were strong feelings among the tutors that the voluntary principle of seminar attendance ought to be maintained. As at Kingston, however, many students wanted seminar contributions to form part of their individual assessments. On the other hand, they expressed strong objections to group assessment, which they saw as inexact and likely to burden them with the marks of weaker students.

- Although the historians at Kingston had drawn up a long list of possible techniques for dealing with larger groups, the techniques chosen for development were somewhat conservative. They did not choose, for example, to use fishbowl, tasking or tutorless groups. Neither did their initial list include the use of the Internet, as had been the case at Newcastle. In the reports explaining their selection it was noted that many of the techniques initially suggested – which had often been drawn from educational literature – were unsuitable: in addition to the problems already mentioned, staff felt that many of the techniques were too involved for the time available (50 minutes), often patronising in tone – given, in particular, the high proportion of mature students at Kingston, but even with eighteen-year-olds – and unrealistic given the resources at hand.

At Newcastle, where staff were given much freer rein, there was more innovation. Some tutors had been experimenting for years, so that the use of techniques such as buzz-groups or debates did not strike them as particularly novel. In other cases, quite elaborate techniques were introduced. In an American history course, for example, seminar time was doubled to two hours. (This would not have been possible at Kingston due to timetable constraints.) Within that time a highly structured combination of small-group presentations (sometimes multimedia) and plenary discussion was employed. Students were also encouraged to assess one another's presentations – though this did not contribute to their formal assessment. Another example of innovation was the use of Web sites to deliver material to students (e.g. in Scandinavian history) and, in one case (early-modern British history), to send their comments on the material by e-mail to the lecturer in advance of the seminar. Here too, however, such techniques were found to produce enormous secondary burdens – above all, in terms of time – both for staff and students. The message seems clear: teaching large groups using innovative techniques requires more resources.

Conclusion

In addition to our specific findings, there were two important general ones which merit particular attention.

• At both Kingston and Newcastle, staff seemed generally enthusiastic about the project, and curious about its purpose and results. In particular, the TLSS and AQEU were keen to get involved and give advice – and their support was much appreciated. However, at Kingston there were also some expressions of opposition towards the project from staff who felt that it might, as it were, be appeasement in the face of larger student numbers. The effects of the enormous changes that British higher education has undergone also appeared to have caused an element of cynicism and an attitude that staff had 'seen it all before'. Rises in student numbers, modularisation, semesterisation – to name the most obvious changes – have perhaps left staff feeling powerless. Such voices were not in the majority however, and most staff felt the issue important enough to support the project strongly. In both universities the project also faced stiff opposition to its execution due to other demands placed on staff time. The project recorded at both Kingston and Newcastle, as well as nationally, that the demands of research and administrative tasks meant there was little time to devote to teaching methods and practices. Educative centres such as the TLSS and AQEU are all well and good, but the questionnaires and discussions revealed that history staff do not use staff and educational development units on a regular basis.
• One of the main messages that emerged from discussions and the questionnaires is that staff and students appear to agree that seminars now constitute the linchpin of their university teaching. It is here that staff get to know students and students get to know one another. Indeed, according to interviews at Kingston, mature students, who are often part-time and geographically isolated, value the interactive and social aspects of seminars even more highly than younger students. Here, too, students get to act out the role of being historians: in other words they practise the cognitive and analytical skills which make up the historical discipline and which are often prized by employers, even though the great majority of students do not go on to become professional historians.[8] This project has found, however, that it is these parts of the seminar experience – the social interaction, the personal guidance by tutors, the active involvement of students, the exercise of historical skills – which are most diminished by the growth of student numbers. If the history seminar is

to lose such attributes, what is to distinguish the student's university experience from that of a correspondence or Internet course? This poses important questions for higher education in general, where, it has been remarked, increased student numbers have tended to lead to a reduction in such interactive group sessions in favour of lectures.[9] How much is the student drop-out rate linked – as attendance appears to be – to larger numbers and the lack of identity of students with their departments? Should more radical reforms be undertaken in the way that teaching is delivered in order to realign it with the growth in student numbers, or should we insist on increased teaching resources to recapture something of the old qualities of seminars?

Notes

1 The questionnaire we issued to all history departments indicated that less than 10 per cent of history seminars were composed of ten or fewer students. Approximately 66 per cent had fifteen or more students per seminar group.

2 Literature on this includes: A. Booth, 'Learning history in university: student views on teaching and assessment', *Studies in Higher Education*, 18 (1993), 227–35; A. Booth and P. Hyland (eds), *History in Higher Education* (Oxford, Blackwell, 1996); P. J. Frederick, 'Motivating students by active learning in the history classroom', *Perspectives* (October 1993); and I. Steele, *Developments in History Teaching* (London, Open Books, 1976). See also various issues covered in *Teaching History: A Journal of Methods*.

3 See, for example: G. Brown and A. Atkins, *Effective Teaching in Higher Education* (London, Routledge, 1988); G. Gibbs, S. Habeshaw and G. Habeshaw, *53 Interesting Things to Do in Your Seminars and Tutorials* (Bristol, Technical and Educational Services Ltd, 1987); G. Gibbs and T. Habeshaw, *Preparing to Teach: Introduction to Effective Teaching in Higher Education* (Bristol, Technical and Educational Services Ltd, 1992); P. Race and S. Brown, *500 Tips for Tutors* (London, Kogan Page, 1992); University of London Teaching Methods Unit, *Improving Teaching in Higher Education* (London, Institute of Education, 1976). Some exceptions include: G. Gibbs, *Discussion with More Students* (Oxford, PCFC, 1992); G. Gibbs, *Teaching Large Classes in Higher Education* (London, Kogan Page, 1992).

4 See S. Fearnley, 'Class size: the erosive effect of recruitment numbers on performance', *Quality in Higher Education*, 1:1 (1995), 59 65; G. Gibbs, G. Lucas and V. Simonite, 'Class size and student performance: 1984–1994', *Studies in Higher Education*, 21 (1996), 261–73; S. Mahler, L. Neumann and P. Tamir, 'The class-size effect upon activity and cognitive dimensions of lessons in higher education', *Assessment and Evaluation in Higher Education*, 11 (1986), 43–59.

5 General literature relating to this includes: L. Cohen and L. Manion, *Research Methods in Education* (London, Routledge, 1994); J. Elliott, *Action Research for Educational Change* (Buckingham, Open University Press, 1991); P. Hague, *Questionnaire Design* (London, Kogan Page, 1994); P. Hyland, 'Examining action research to improve seminars through assessment', in G. Gibbs (ed.), *Improving Student Learning: Using Research to Improve Student Learning* (Oxford, Centre for Staff Development, 1992); O. Zuber-Skerritt, *Action Research in Higher Education:*

Examples and Reflections (London, Kogan Page, 1992).

6 On 'deep learning' see: E. Berenson, 'Active learning in the university classroom, or what I learned from elementary school teachers', *Perspectives*, 17–18 (1996); J. Bradbeer, 'Society, nature and place: a final year core course in contemporary philosophical debates in geography', *Journal of Geography in Higher Education*, 21, (1997), 373–9; N. Entwistle (ed.), *Encyclopaedia of Educational Research* (London, Routledge, 1987); Gibbs, *Improving Student Learning*; P. James, 'Progressive development of deep learning skills through undergraduate and postgraduate dissertations', *Educational Studies*, 24:1 (1998), 95–105; P. B. Lowe and C. M. Kerr, 'Learning by reflection: the effect on educational outcomes', *Journal of Advanced Nursing*, 27:5 (1998), 1030–3; J. Sandberg and Y. Barnard, 'Deep learning is difficult', *Instructional Science*, 25:1 (1997), 15–36; L. Norton and E. Scantlebury, *Encouraging a Deep Approach to Learning: A Pack for Teachers* (Liverpool, Liverpool Institute of Higher Education, 1997).

7 Hyland, 'Examining action research', pp. 7–9.

8 On transferable skills see, the *Times Higher Education Supplement*, 1 January 1988, and the *Sunday Times*, 11 December 1988.

9 D. Laurillard, 'I.T. and Dearing: the implications for higher education', in H. Beetham (ed.), *Proceedings of the C.T.I. Colloquium . . . on Thursday 31, July 1997* (London, CTISS Publications, 1997).

I I   John Peters, Christine Peterkin and Chris Williams[1]

Progression within modular history degrees: profiling for a student-centred approach

Student progression in learning is central to the purpose of higher education. Students attend universities and colleges in order to acquire or develop knowledge, skills and other attributes which will be rewarded at the completion of their studies by the award of a degree. Yet in Britain, providing evidence of progression in terms of curriculum design has become increasingly difficult with the widespread introduction of modular and semesterised degree programmes. For modularisation and semesterisation have often fragmented institutional or discipline-designed systems of progression without providing any obvious replacement. At the same time, fee-paying students, employers and government agencies are demanding more exacting evidence of student progression and skills acquisition.[2] The implementation of a formative student profile document is tested here as a possible solution to this problem.

This chapter outlines the issues relating to progression within modular history degrees and the possibilities offered by profiling, and examines the general debate surrounding profiling as a means of recording progression. The concerns which have to be faced in designing and delivering a specific formative history student-centred profile will be addressed, and the evaluation of that profile will provide the basis for discussion of the issues raised by such profiling.

Progression and modular degrees

If challenged to demonstrate the progression required of undergraduates a decade ago, most history departments in Britain would probably have responded by presenting the structure of their degree programme: first-year courses provide a broad chronological overview; second-year courses focus on more specific areas or periods; and third-year courses require either detailed work through 'Special Subject' courses and dissertations or demanding comparative work on thematic courses. So, it could be argued, the degree programme grew progressively more challenging over the three-year period, requiring students to develop and demonstrate their historical ability at higher levels and in greater depth.

Whether it was the degree programme itself which imposed the progression or whether this came more from the demands made upon students in each year-group by tutors is open to debate. Certainly, this system presented progression as being embodied in the programme and the teaching of year-groups, rather than in individual student advancement.

The widespread introduction of modular degree programmes, where students from different year-groups attend the same modules and choose their own routes through a range of usually shorter course units or modules, has seen highly structured programmes largely overtaken by student choice. While greater student choice of modules and modes of study is to be welcomed, this has repercussions for structured progression within programmes. At the worst, most superficial level, it could be said that the only remaining progression is the accumulation of module credits towards the number required for a degree. The challenge is to establish a system which accommodates the benefits of a flexible modular system while guaranteeing the progression considered to be inherent in the traditional structures.

The introduction of formative student-centred profiling may offer a solution to the problem of demonstrating progression within modular degrees. The term 'profiling' is used here because, if the system is formative and student centred, the process undertaken by students should be the focus rather than the profile document itself. The document should merely function as a means to the end of student planning, reflection and recording. Such profiling would encourage students to take responsibility for the construction of their own progression through undergraduate study by targeting the acquisition and development of skills and attributes practised in study for a history degree. Profiling can counteract the fragmentation which can occur in modular schemes by 'pulling together otherwise disparate learning experiences'.[3] The profiling process also allows students to use the flexibility of modular degrees to create an individual progression which is more meaningful and relevant to them personally than the traditional structures.

Yet profiling is by no means unproblematic. The term has many meanings and covers a wide range of materials and practices, such as records of achievement, portfolios, personal development files, learning contracts and many other ways of recording student performance. The distinctions are usually made in superficial terms, on the basis of the document format for such records. However, more fundamental distinctions can be made which often cut across the formats of such systems. These distinctions can be based on the nature of the inputs, processes and outputs required.[4] The main input may be from the tutor, student or a combination of the two, and might apply to academic performance, skills and personal attributes, and/or extra-curricular activity. The process might be specific or cumulative, summative or formative. Finally, the output might be formal and institutionally validated, such as a Statement of Achievement; it might remain personal to the student; or it could even be withheld from the student as an institutional record. Further differentiation between systems could be provided by isolating the objectives underlying different examples.[5]

In the circumstances, it is no surprise that Bill Law's suggestion that the term 'profile' be used generically to cover the 'whole range of methods of student portrayal which have been developed to replace – or at least supplement – conventional assessment formats'[6] has been taken up by writers on British higher education as a means of avoiding confusion.[7] Nevertheless, it is necessary to be aware that this generic use of the term merely masks important divisions about the nature and purpose of profiling. These divisions lie very close to the surface and can be analysed in recent British government advice. The Dearing Report (1997) contains an important recommendation on profiling: 'We recommend that institutions of higher education, over the medium term, develop a Progress File. The File should consist of two elements: a transcript recording student achievement . . . [and] a means by which students can monitor, build and reflect upon their personal development.'[8] This emphasises the importance of profiling as an area for development in British higher education. Government pressure to use profiling has emerged from concern that the education system meet the requirements of the labour market. Transcripts would supply employers with much greater information about the individual graduate in a commonly understood language of transferable and key skills than is provided by degree classifications. More pertinent is the requirement that in a changing labour market, with fewer permanent jobs, a flexible workforce needs to be willing to acquire new skills when necessary. The 'graduate as finished article' would be swiftly outdated; better to produce life-long learners who are capable of reflecting upon, planning and expanding their own learning as required. As one influential piece of advice to undergraduates puts it: 'The self reliant graduate is aware of the changing world of work, takes responsibility for his or her own career and personal development and is able to manage the relationship with work and with learning throughout all stages of life.'[9]

Profile documents have been used for some time in higher education,[10] and a number of projects across higher education in Britain are currently seeking to develop profiles and the recording of skills.[11] These projects focus primarily on generic profiles rather than working from a specific subject base. They differ from the more traditional use of profiles in British higher education to provide evidence of professional competence on vocational courses. Many of these vocational profiles are what Assiter and Fenwick refer to as a 'prescribed learning outcomes profile', in which all the outcomes have to be assessed and met in order to qualify for admission to a profession.[12] This form of profile is summative and rather inflexible, and is not as effective in the development of the student's own reflective practice as a 'personal development profile'. A more flexible, student-owned, formative approach provides a means whereby students can reflect on skills and experiences they already have, identify those they need to develop, plan their degree programme in order to practise them, and record their achievements as they progress. Clearly, there are tensions between the use of a profile as an institutional document proving a student's graduate skills and abilities to employers, and its use as a formative tool for enhancing reflective practice and progression in learning.[13] A formative profile must surely place the emphasis on student ownership, and therefore avoid the intrusion of institutional assessment. So the document must be for the student and must belong to the student.

Student-centred profiling can also be 'catalytic' in the development of higher education practice.[14] Recent moves to make the process of education more explicit have resulted in greater engagement with educational theory. As a result, the rhetoric of higher education is changing to acknowledge the value of something that practitioners have always known: a great deal of student learning goes on outside the lecture theatre and seminar room. In order to demonstrate the full value and purpose of studying in higher education it is therefore necessary to go beyond what tutors teach and to focus on what students learn. Thus there is a transformation from viewing higher education as a lecturer-centred teaching paradigm, to seeing it as a student-centred, learning paradigm.[15]

Formative profiling encourages students to focus on their own learning, and to become partners in the education process rather than viewing themselves as mere recipients of knowledge or information. They are thus more engaged in active learning. By focusing on skills and processes, rather than on tutors' transmission of information, a formative profile can foster a more effective, 'deep' approach to learning.[16]

In relation to the study of history, a 'surface' approach would focus on the acquisition of information about the past whereas a deep approach would emphasise the process of 'doing' history. History moves from being a collection of facts to become the application of a wide variety of skills to the evaluation of source material and the construction of an interpretation. It is obvious that this latter approach is more satisfactory, and should result in students gaining higher grades. At many institutions this should be axiomatic because degree classification criteria distinguish positively between work which is evaluative and that which is largely descriptive.

Designing and implementing a history student profile

The construction and trial of a history student profile (hereafter, the Profile) meant engaging with general debates about the purpose and function of profiling. It also required a number of specific issues to be resolved, such as the use which was to be made of skills descriptors and levels of attainment, and the relationship of generic descriptors to the study of history. The design of the Profile and its integration into a modular scheme had to be established. All this was done by a small group of history tutors from University College Worcester and Cardiff University. Finally, the Profile was used by all history students at Worcester and a pilot group of history students at Cardiff in the academic year 1997–98.

In order to function as an effective student-centred document, the Profile had to establish a language of skills which was obviously relevant and accessible to its users. This proved problematic because of the ongoing debate over the best way to categorise skills. 'Key skills' descriptors offer a nationally recognised framework, while more specific and lengthy lists of 'graduate attributes' have greater currency within academic departments. However, both categories have their weaknesses, and it was decided that a list tailored specifically to the experiences of history students, and described from the perspective of historical study, would best serve our purpose.

There is increasing pressure for British universities and colleges to adopt the language of key skills. The general headings for these are communication, information technology, application of number, improving own learning, working with others and problem solving. They are nationally recognised because they are used to underpin the National Record of Achievement in secondary schools and in many vocational courses, such as General National Vocational Qualifications (GNVQs). Thus they have currency with employers, and provide a simple, basic list of skills together with a detailed breakdown of more specific skills and levels of competence. The difficulty with key skills is that they are often considered an unwelcome and unhelpful imposition.[17] The paperwork associated with GNVQs has earned them a reputation for being over-bureaucratic in operation, and of applying descriptors and levels which are not easily related to specific degrees or to degree classifications.[18] Fundamentally, as highly generalised descriptors, they fail to emphasise many of the qualities which academics consider central to undergraduate education, such as having an enquiring mind and critical awareness. Finally, because of their origins outside universities, key-skills descriptors are presented in a language which is not easily accessible or clearly relevant to history tutors and undergraduates.

Lists of graduate attributes have the advantage of being products of higher education.[19] They usually build out from the subject area and provide an eclectic mix of transferable skills, personal attitudes and competencies. Various lists are used with some success in many British universities and colleges in order to categorise what students learn. However, such lists can become lengthy and the mix of different types of attribute makes the application of level-of-attainment descriptors difficult. Nevertheless, the descriptors remain readily identifiable, and useful in presenting graduate qualities to employers. Furthermore, the flexibility and inclusiveness of this approach make it easier to present the full range of what history graduates might be expected to learn, and to present it in a way which makes it evident that skills are an integral part of studying history rather than extraneous employment skills.

The Profile used seventeen headings in seven groups. It began with subject-specific material, which was divided into the two headings of 'subject's content' and 'subject's nature'. The other groups were cognitive skills, personal attributes, communication skills, social skills, research skills and practical skills (which included languages, information technology and numeracy). Some of these might not be considered central to, or even necessarily available through, historical study. However, the flexibility of modular schemes, which often allow even single-honours history students to pick up other subjects, put opportunities to practise these skills within the reach of history students. If the Profile was to be student centred, it had to allow for the full student experience rather than just focusing on areas provided by history tutors. Further, the itemising of skills which were less familiar to students provided the scope to raise awareness of the opportunities open to them and to highlight the wider value of some of these skills.

The mere itemisation of a list of skills or attributes in the Profile would not allow for the recording of progression. In order to document progression there must be readily understood level-of-attainment descriptors for each skill or attribute, otherwise the profile document might produce an unwanted surface approach to learning by encouraging a 'tick box' attitude to skills acquisition. With level-of-attainment descriptors for each skill, students are required to establish their current level of ability, set themselves targets and document the improvement in their application of skills as they rise through the levels during their degree programme. Unfortunately, level-of-attainment descriptors are as fraught with difficulty as lists of skills.

Level-of-attainment descriptors are available for key skills. However, these are highly bureaucratic and do not easily match the degree classifications by which students are ultimately judged and by which they measure themselves. Level descriptors are also used widely in credit accumulation and transfer. However, though these levels were developed for higher education, they do not relate to degree classifications. Levels provided by organisations such as the South East England Consortium for Credit Accumulation and Transfer, based at the University of East London are linked to the standards expected to be achieved by year-groups. Yet it is evident that individual students achieve different levels of performance in different skills at different stages of their degree programme. To suggest otherwise in the Profile might de-motivate students by establishing targets which are too low for some, yet too high for others.

In order to make the Profile as relevant and responsive as possible to individual student experience, it seemed appropriate to apply degree-level descriptors to skills and attributes. It proved possible, in part, to apply a set of generic degree assessment criteria which was already used by students at Worcester. Set out in largely Bloomian terminology, this provided an obvious foundation for the skills-level descriptors.[20] Bloomian descriptors have some weaknesses, because they are much clearer about the assessed outcome of students' work than the approaches required to achieve that outcome. Thus they are not particularly helpful for informing students of the best approaches to achieving improvement. This weakness was addressed by including a specific-skill descriptor, namely cognitive skills, which was explicit about the way certain approaches to learning shaped the outcome achieved. A great advantage of Bloomian descriptors is that they allow high-order information management skills – such as analysis, synthesis and evaluation – to be embedded across all the skills descriptors. Thus, generically, the lowest level of attainment in the Profile, level one, consisted of basic competence and ability to describe and provide a historical account; level two involved analysis and synthesis; level three introduced evaluation; and level four emphasised the ability to challenge preconceptions.

The application of degree assessment criteria to the skills and attributes was not an exact science, particularly in terms of competencies such as information technology or attributes such as personal responsibility. However, what emerged was a list of skills and attributes, with four levels of attainment for each skill, of which it could be said that the levels approximated to 3rd, 2ii, 2i and 1st class degree classifications, respectively. Students could thus make judgements about their progress across the full range of skills and attributes, in terms of levels of attainment with which they were familiar. For example, the levels of attainment for 'subject's nature' and 'cognitive skills' were described as follows:

Subject's nature
Level 1   The ability to provide definitions of key terms, such as historiography, the Whig interpretation, methodology and 'history'.
Level 2   The ability to identify and explain the key historiographic schools. Awareness of alternative definitions of the nature and uses of history and different historical methodologies.
Level 3   The capability to debate the nature of the subject, its methodologies and historiography. The ability to defend your own conceptualisation of history and your own methodology.
Level 4   The ability to work with and critically evaluate historical paradigms and methodologies. The ability to adopt different methodologies and paradigms, as they are appropriate, and to explain and defend your choice.

Cognitive Skills
This heading is not about IQ or intelligence as such, but is about *the way you think*. It is of central importance because the way you think drives your approach to the subject and to all other skills. So, though this could be included as a personal skill it is considered important enough to have its own section.
Level 1   The ability to comprehend written, numerical and spoken material. The ability to remember information. Knowledge is conceptualised as collected information or facts, received from other people or sources of information.
Level 2   Knowledge is conceptualised as the collection of experts' ideas and interpretations. The ability to categorise information or ideas and offer a simple analysis.
Level 3   The ability to engage in debate and present a clear, well-supported, individual point of view. Knowledge is no longer to be collected as an end in itself but to be used to construct a personal interpretation. The ability to evaluate evidence and arguments.
Level 4   The ability to use and evaluate complex ideas and paradigms. The ability to make intellectual leaps and apply principles deduced from one situation to deal with others. Knowledge is actively used and applied in problem solving.[21]

In each case there is a clear progression through the levels from description, to analysis, to evaluation, and on to the ability to make conceptual leaps beyond established boundaries.

With the production of the skills and attributes descriptors, each broken down into four levels, the core of the document was completed. The rest of the design was undertaken in such a way as to create a document which was coherent and capable of stand-alone use by students. This required the provision of: an introduction (setting out the nature of the trial and the ideas behind profiling, skills and personal progression); a list of transferable skills and graduate attributes; a matrix of skills and levels; guidance on how to use the profile document; module record sheets; other record sheets (for semesters, work experience, student union activity and other learning experiences); and three exercises (one for each year of full-time undergraduate study).

A group of 36 students in their second year at Cardiff University and all 199 students completing history modules at University College Worcester in 1997–98 were provided with a copy of the Profile. It was made clear to students that the document now belonged to them for their private use. The Profile was capable of stand-alone use, but care was taken to provide a formal presentation to students in order to introduce the document and its expected benefits. The introduction to first-years at Worcester seemed the most satisfactory, because it involved the whole year-group and allowed the completion of the first exercise during timetabled seminar sessions. Presentations to second- and third-year students at Worcester were more fragmented and brief because the modular system did not present the opportunity to work with them in year-groups.

History tutors were asked to make time for the completion of module record sheets at the beginnings and ends of their modules. They were also asked to highlight to students the skills or attributes which could most appropriately be practised in the course of completing each particular module. For example, modules which were partly assessed by oral presentation lent themselves to a focus on oral communication; a demographic history module provided the opportunity for a focus on numeracy or information technology, and so on. Students were also advised that the Profile might provide the basis for some discussion with their personal tutor about their academic progress.

The various record sheets in the Profile formed the heart of the document and amounted to half its total of sixty-three pages. Only by completing them did the student transform the document into a profile and record of their achievements. Each module record sheet allowed students to identify skills they might wish to target for development in a particular module. The sheet asked them to indicate the target level and to establish both the opportunity that module offered to practise those skills and the criteria by which they would judge their own success. As the module progressed, or at its end, students were asked to explain how they practised the skills and to provide evidence of their progress. Finally, they were encouraged to identify skills to work on in subsequent modules.

Integrating a profile into the student experience is vital to its success. This was difficult given the experimental nature of the project, but three exercises were included in order to embed it in the student experience. These acted as periodic reminders of the value of the Profile and aimed to ensure that it was not seen by students as divorced from their degree programme. No major alterations were made in the timetable or in the weight of assessed work facing undergraduates in order to release time to complete the Profile, so the exercises were designed to be completed within the timetabling of core history modules.

The first exercise was completed by first-years at the beginning of semester one. It introduced the Profile and the nature of skills and attributes. Students were asked to reflect on the skills they had already developed before coming to higher education, to discuss their expectations of a history degree, and to establish the areas that they wanted to develop. Exercise two was a skills audit completed by second-years in semester two, with the aim of establishing progress and planning the final year of study. Exercise three was completed by third-years in semester two. This involved studying some job advertisements and writing a letter of application using the evidence previously gathered in the Profile. Thus while the first two exercises stressed planning and progression, the final exercise highlighted the value of the completed Profile as a tool for self marketing beyond college.

Evaluation process and findings

The student-centred nature of the Profile placed some limits on the evaluation process but also suggested exciting possibilities. If the Profile was to be for students' use, then it was quickly realised that copies could not be collected by tutors as part of the evaluation process. This might unduly influence its use during the trial and detract from its student-centred nature. The Profile was intended to be used by students as a valuable part of their individual learning process and, in part at least, to encourage them to take responsibility for their own learning. Thus it seemed logical to involve them actively in all stages of the evaluation. Hence five students from Worcester and two from Cardiff were employed to undertake a major role in collectively designing and implementing an evaluation process. The method of evaluation which was employed emerged from the discussions of the student evaluators.

The first stage of the evaluation consisted of a series of interviews designed to locate issues of concern to Profile users. Having explored the advantages of individual and group interviews, the evaluators decided to use a combination of both in order to elicit a wide range of views. The same framework of questions was used for both the individual interviews and the focus-group discussions, though the more generalised questions were used to encourage debate in the focus groups.

The second stage of the evaluation involved designing a questionnaire using data from the interviews to identify key issues. Respondents were asked to provide brief but anonymous personal details and then to signal their level of agreement with forty-five statements. These covered the main areas of whether the Profile should be compulsory, its format and implementation, its relationship to modules, the skills and attributes, the role of tutors, and possible means of improving the Profile. All participating students at Worcester and Cardiff were invited to complete the questionnaire. At Worcester 108 out of a possible 199, and at Cardiff 10 out of a possible 36 students, completed the questionnaire. At Worcester a range of age groups were represented in completed questionnaires; at Cardiff respondents were all from the 18–21 year group. Clearly, the low rate of questionnaire completion at Cardiff renders the student evaluation there less meaningful than might otherwise have been the case. Nevertheless, in general the balance of response by Cardiff students was largely consistent with that of the main trial at Worcester.

In stage three of the evaluation, tutors whose students were using the Profile were interviewed individually. Pilots of all three stages of the evaluation were carried out, in order for student evaluators to practise the interviewing process and to ensure that the printed questionnaire did not contain ambiguities which would impede the effective gathering of data.

The main findings of the evaluation fell into three key areas:

Student perceptions of profiling

General attitudes towards profiling on the part of a majority of respondents were either positive or undecided, although attitudes were more negative at Cardiff than at Worcester. At Worcester the idea was most popular among first-years and among those in the 18–21 age-group. During interviews, even those students who said they had not used the Profile extensively were often sufficiently interested in the idea of profiling to offer suggestions for improvements. However, there was some evidence that negative attitudes towards profiling were being reinforced or even increased by the experience of using the Profile. For example, just over three-quarters of the students said they had not used the Profile extensively, over a third considered that it should not be employed in its present form, and only a small minority considered that it should. These responses were also reflected in the reports of the interviews, where some students indicated that they had used the Profile only when forced to and a number claimed not to have used it at all.

Responses relating to questions about students' perceptions of the purpose of the Profile indicated that a majority considered it to be useful as a personal record of, and a means of support for, individual development, and should be primarily for the student's own use. This finding is not necessarily undermined by the view of half of the students, who thought that the completed Profile should be available to their personal tutor in preparing their college reference. Questions on whether the Profile should be compulsory elicited strong negative responses. Questionnaire responses indicated that only a small minority considered that the Profile should be compulsory and even fewer thought it should be formally assessed. A small majority also rejected the idea that discussion of the Profile with a tutor should be compulsory. In interviews, students were divided on the issue of whether or not to introduce a compulsory element into the use of the Profile. The view was expressed that it should remain a personal record of progress, and that compulsion would tend to make students less honest in assessing their own performance. Despite the tendency of many students to reject compulsion, several students suggested that, given the other demands made on them during their degree, many would not bother with the Profile unless it were assessed, or at least until its completion was made compulsory.

These findings raise the issue of student motivation as being vital to the success of any Profile. The complexity and variety of student responses should be no surprise to those who stress the need for formative profiling because it allows for the variety of student attitudes, experiences and approaches to learning. It was frustrating to find that students saw the value of formative profiling, and so rejected formal assessment or compulsion, yet were candid enough to admit that without compulsion they were unlikely to undertake it. Despite the hopes of some authors on profiling, persuading students of the long-term value of profiling was not always enough, given what were perceived to be the more urgent demands made on them by assessed assignments.[22]

Implementation and format of the Profile

Questions to students concerning the issue of how the Profile was introduced focused on the point of introduction within the degree programme and the most appropriate methods of introduction. There was substantial support for introduction of the Profile at the beginning of year one. The most popular method of introduction was that which took place over several sessions to small groups of students, as this afforded opportunities for them to ask questions and explore a range of issues relating to the Profile. This was also the authors' preferred method of introduction because of the freedom it provided for discussion, and because assigning a significant amount of teaching time to the Profile early in the undergraduate programme gave an indication of the importance which tutors attached to it. This form of introduction served to embed the Profile in the student experience and to establish student expectations at the earliest possible opportunity.

Students responded well to some aspects of the document; for example, over three-quarters recognised the skills set out in the Profile as appropriate to history students, while almost three-quarters felt they understood the differences between the various levels of skill. The Profile therefore seems to have met some of its central purposes. It had made 'explicit the characteristics we seek to develop in our students'[23] by increasing their recognition of the range of skills practised in historical study. It had also established a set of explicit, clearly understood criteria which allowed the measurement of progression. Unfortunately, only about half of the students found the levels useful in reflecting upon their development, though a significant number were undecided, and less than half considered that the Profile helped them to plan their development. Although findings varied between Cardiff and Worcester, less than a third of all students found the module record sheets helpful in targeting their learning. Less than a quarter considered that the semester record sheets helped them to plan their future learning. Similar negative responses occurred when students were asked whether they found the exercises helpful.

Some very direct explanations for student resistance to this Profile were offered. In interviews, students at Worcester suggested that the Profile was 'too cumbersome and complicated', and students at Cardiff considered it to be too long and 'very patronising and repetitive'. Given the general support for the Profile's skill and level descriptors, it seems apparent that much of this criticism was aimed at the record sheets. Thus it appears as though the problematic element of profile design – achieving a set of readily understood skills and levels of attainment – had been overcome, only to find that this did not necessarily translate into student practice of record keeping. It might be possible to ameliorate the student concerns by redesigning the record sheets, or by presenting them for completion individually rather than *en masse* as part of a bound document. However, the fundamental issue again appears to be motivation; the skills and levels are understood but the task of record keeping is resisted.

The role of tutors in the profiling process

Student responses to questions on the role of tutors indicated a wish to receive more support – possibly from both module and personal tutors – in using the Profile. Discussions with students indicated that the amount of direct support given by module tutors at Worcester had varied considerably. This led to stage three of the evaluation, the interviewing of tutors by a student evaluator in order to identify tutor attitudes towards the Profile. The evaluation raised important issues about the necessary extent of tutor support for the profiling process.

Although over 60 per cent of Worcester students responding to the questionnaire agreed that they were capable of deciding which skills to focus on in each module, only 30 per cent of Cardiff students gave this response. Three-quarters of those responding across both institutions considered that skills sessions, which would help to identify and assess their needs as learners, would be helpful. However, very few students rejected the proposition that history staff should provide these skills sessions, so perhaps there was a wish to see skills discussed explicitly but within the discipline.

Only a small minority of students rejected the proposition that discussion of the Profile with other users and with a tutor would be helpful, although about a quarter were undecided on this issue. When the personal tutor was specifically mentioned as the individual with whom the Profile might be discussed, a majority of students responded favourably. In the interviews, the possibility of greater personal tutor involvement was frequently supported. One interviewer recorded, 'the role of personal tutors was an important issue for all those interviewed'. Another found that 'students felt this [greater student/tutor interaction] would have made the use of the Profile more appealing and more simple'.

Personal tutors at both institutions are usually provided from within the main field of study, so the emphasis on the personal tutor system indicated a wish for more formal support from within the history discipline but outside specific modules. Research indicating the importance of tutorial support for the profiling process had not been ignored during the trials.[24] Given the demand for more personal tutor support expressed throughout the questionnaire, it was somewhat surprising that few tutors reported being approached by students to discuss the Profile. This was despite students being advised to discuss the Profile with tutors both in introductory sessions and in the documentation itself. Again, the provision of support was no guarantee that it would be used. The respondents seemed to be suggesting the need for a more formal system of tutorials which, initially at least, would both compel and assist them to use the Profile.

Law has suggested that profiling acts as a catalyst to curriculum development, by encouraging staff to reflect on the skills content of their modules and by providing more information on the student experience.[25] This – together with indications that the way in which students perceived and responded to profiling had been influenced by the attitudes of staff teaching the modules – led to an evaluation of the interaction between the Profile and tutors involved in the trial. Most tutors did not appear to reject the concept of profiling; rather they expressed negative as well as positive views on the Profile. Some considered that a major disadvantage of the scheme related to the demands it made on students' time. One stated: 'It takes up time which could be better spent on assessed work, given the pressure of deadlines.' Tutors were also concerned that the current Profile format was too close to school Records of Achievement to be popular with students. Only a little over 35 per cent of Worcester students and 20 per cent of Cardiff students responding to the questionnaire endorsed this view.

Positive tutor comment suggested that the Profile would 'focus students to think about their learning', and the implication was that this would enhance the learning process. Some tutors could also see value in the Profile as a record providing 'tangible evidence of the practical skills students have acquired during their degree'. When asked to reflect upon the question of whether or not the Profile had affected their teaching, some tutors indicated that although they were already aware of the skills associated with the study of history, the profiling process had enhanced their awareness of the need to relate skills to planning. One tutor stated: 'When I plan sessions I think about what the module aims to achieve . . . and consider at what point we test those skills.' Another noted, 'It has made me think about the learning process, and what the students get from the modules.'

Conclusions

The trials have produced a number of very positive results. Students do see the value of formative, student-centred profiling. The majority considered that year one was the best time to introduce the Profile, and that it should stand largely as a personal record of progress and achievement, the completion of which should not be compulsory or assessed. Most students were happy with the descriptions of subject-specific skills, key skills and graduate attributes offered in the document. The Profile successfully covered the whole range of student skills acquisition, rather than just focusing on professional competencies, allowing the inclusion of what Hitchcock has identified as the four necessary areas: 'personal qualities', 'personal achievements', 'cross-curricular skills' and 'academic attainment'.[26] The responses confirmed the value of beginning with the subject, and explaining skills in terms which are clearly understood and considered appropriate by the target audience. Developing the Profile descriptors from a subject perspective rather than seeking to introduce them as generic, bolt-on employment skills led students to embrace them. Equally, providing level-of-attainment descriptors for the skills which were constructed on the basis of degree classifications made them acceptable.

Yet, despite these successes, there were problems with the trials. Student acknowledgement of the value of profiling in theory did not necessarily produce engagement with the exercises and record keeping in practice. Certainly there was some criticism of this particular Profile on the grounds of format and, in particular, the record sheets. By presenting them as a large number of similar pages in a bound document, the repetitive nature of the format was emphasised. More creative design and packaging might help. Presenting the record sheets as and when required might well have been less daunting and less cumbersome. With greater integration and a larger trial the module record sheets could have been available in modules, the semester record sheets at personal tutorials, the work experience sheets through the careers office, and the student activity sheets from the students' union. The students could then have actively constructed their own set of records from a variety of sources. However, these changes in the operationalisation of the Profile would only scratch the surface of the student resistance to record keeping which was encountered at both institutions.

Student motivation emerged from the trials as the central issue in developing a successful profiling process. Contrary to the expectations of some proponents of profiling, many of our students did not demand greater responsibility for their own learning or the right to keep a profile and use it to plan and influence their development.[27] It is perhaps too strong to say that they declined any such responsibility, but many certainly did not make time to use the Profile or to manage its use so as to make the most of the personal tutor support which was available to them. There are a number of issues which may well impact on student commitment to profiling and their motivation to perform the tasks involved; these include the degree to which the profiling activity is integrated within the normal student experience and institutional culture, student workloads and tutor support.

To be successful, any profiling activity 'should be fully integrated into teaching and learning processes'.[28] The Profile was successfully integrated into the language of the history discipline in terms of the skill and level descriptors used. Yet in operational terms the trials were less successful. The trials were designed in such a way that the operation of the Profile was partially embedded in the history programme, by the allocation of time in normal teaching sessions for the exercises and the completion of module records. This worked particularly well with the introductory exercise for the first-year. However, this did not prove to be enough. Module tutor support varied, voluntary personal tutor support was rarely sought, and the resulting – not entirely ill-founded – impression was of a hastily constructed and partial attachment of profiling to an otherwise largely unaffected history programme. As the modular degree scheme allowed all the students involved in the trial to pick up modules outside the history field, some parts of even their academic experience were untouched by profiling. Full integration might not require any major overhaul of current degree structures, but more convincing means of embedding profiling are required. Provision of record sheets and, vitally, support for completion of those records from different but appropriate sources would help here. This would mean inputs from other subject areas, the careers service and the students' union. The nature of modular degrees is such that it is often very difficult for one subject area to develop a wide-ranging profiling process without broader institutional involvement.

It is sometimes suggested that the only way to get students to value something is to assess them on it. This is not just an uncharitable, but also a far too mechanistic view of student motivation. Besides, such an approach would be unacceptable in this case as there was strong student opposition to the formal assessment of the Profile, and any such assessment would undermine the sense of student ownership of the profiling process. Nevertheless, it was clear that many students considered the Profile to be a chore which lost out in the competition for time when contrasted with summative items of assessment. With the unrelenting demands made on student time by the often heavy elements of continuous assessment on modular programmes, the student response was not unreasonable. A formative Profile is not going to succeed without, at the very least, some formal institutional recognition and indication of time which should be set aside within student workloads. Profiling need not be summatively assessed or made compulsory, but time must be allocated for it and an institutional culture created which attaches value to such work.

The student–tutor relationship is central to education and fundamental to the profiling process. Our trial did not place enough emphasis on the formal provision of tutor support for completion of the Profile. This shortcoming was reflected in the numerous requests for a greater level of tutor support. Most of the problems of student motivation might well be met by provision of appropriate personal tutor meetings. Input from a personal tutor is required in order to encourage and guide student reflection.[29] Many students were not entirely comfortable assessing themselves and, initially at least, required some assistance and encouragement. While summative assessment might be damaging to student-centred profiling, formative assessment is important to it.[30] Module tutors often provided this indirectly through comments about skills on module-specific work, but only the personal tutor could have provided such input on the Profile itself. A simple requirement that semester record sheets be completed at formal personal tutor meetings would have corrected this shortcoming. Student-centred profiling should not mean purely tutor-less activity.

In responding to the issue of student motivation a number of complementary solutions have been identified. They, in turn, raise concerns about institutional commitments to profiling. It is ironic that documentation specifically written to meet the needs of history students should raise so many institutional questions. There is only a small chance that developments championed within a history department might drive institutional change. Nevertheless, integrating the Profile in the broad student experience, taking profiling into account in student workloads and the provision of personal tutorial support all require a commitment to profiling at an institutional level. The provision of tutorial support in particular requires the commitment of resources to some staff development and the staffing of personal tutorials. Yet if these resources provide an institution with a system for embedding student-centred progression within its modular scheme, the benefits surely outweigh the costs.

Notes

1 We would like to thank students – particularly Karen Ablett, Jo Baldwin, Sue Chilcott, Lorraine Eustace, Elizabeth Ray, Bryony Skelton and Helen Squire, who acted as student evaluators – and colleagues at University College Worcester and Cardiff University.

2 See, for example, attempts to define 'graduateness' in Higher Education Quality Council (HEQC), *Graduate Standards Programme Final Report* (London, HEQC, 1997).

3 G. Gibbs, 'Assessing skills and competencies', in G. Gibbs (ed.), *Assessing Student Centred Courses* (Oxford, Oxford Centre for Staff Development, 1995), p. 65.

4 B. Law, *Uses and Abuses of Profiling* (London, Harper and Row, 1984), p. 153.

5 G. Hitchcock, *Profiles and Profiling* (London, Longman, 1990), ch. 2.

6 Law, *Uses and Abuses*, p. xiii.

7 A. Assiter and E. Shaw, 'Records of achievement background, definitions and uses', in A. Assiter and E. Shaw (eds), *Using Records of Achievement in Higher Education* (London, Kogan Page, 1993), p. 20.

8 The National Committee of Enquiry into Higher Education, *Higher Education in the Learning Society: Report of the National Committee* (London, HMSO, 1997), [Dearing Report], p. 141.

9 Association of Graduate Recruiters, *Skills for the Graduate in the 21st Century* (Cambridge, Association of Graduate Recruiters, 1995), p. 19.

10 Council for National Academic Awards, *Profiling in Higher Education* (London, CNAA, 1992).

11 Promising examples of profiles delivered through information technology include the LUSID project being developed by Liverpool's universities and the ProFile at Bangor

University. Two projects which have been helpful to this trial are 'PADSHE: Personal and Academic Development for Students in Higher Education' at Nottingham University, and 'Skills Development: The Management of Change' at Newcastle University.

12 Assiter and Fenwick, 'Profiling in higher education', in Assiter and Shaw (eds), *Using Records of Achievement*, p. 26.

13 A. Paczuska and I. Turner, 'Recording achievement: the tensions between personal development and academic standards', *Innovations in Education and Training International*, 34:2 (1997), 76; G. Gibbs, 'Using profiles', in Gibbs (ed.), *Assessing Student Centred Courses*, p. 124.

14 Law, *Uses and Abuses*, pp. 4–5.

15 R. Barr and J. Tagg, 'From teaching to learning – a new paradigm for undergraduate education', *Change* (Nov./Dec. 1995), 13–25.

16 See, for example, G. Gibbs, *Improving the Quality of Student Learning* (Bristol, Technical and Education Services, 1992), pp. 2–11 or D. Laurillard, *Rethinking University Teaching* (London, Routledge, 1993), p. 51.

17 History at the Universities Defence Group (HUDG), 'Standards in history: final report of a working party of the History at the Universities Defence Group to the quality assurance agency' (April 1998). Available from HUDG, Institute of Historical Research, University of London, Malet Street, London WC1E 7HU.

18 Gibbs,'Using profiles', pp. 125–6.

19 HEQC, *Graduate Standards*, vol. 2, annexe c, HEQC pilot graduate attributes profile.

20 B. Bloom, *et al.*, *The Taxonomy of Educational Objectives* (London, Longman, 1956).

21 J. Peters, 'Worcester history student profile', pp. 11–12. Available from Dr John Peters, University College Worcester, Henwick Grove, Worcester WR2 6AJ.

22 M. Wedgewood and J. Godfrey, 'The record of achievement as a learning resource for all students', in Assiter and Shaw (eds), *Using Records of Achievement*, p. 78.

23 L. Cooke and M. Taylor, 'Maintaining the ethos of records of achievement in the higher education sector', in Assiter and Shaw (eds), *Using Records of Achievement*, p. 65.

24 B. Starr, 'Profiling and assessment of professional and personal transferable skills acquired by students on a BSc honours course in psychology', in Assiter and Shaw (eds), *Using Records of Achievement*, p. 85.

25 Law, *Uses and Abuses*, pp. 4–5.

26 Hitchcock, *Profiles and Profiling*, pp. 143–4.

27 Assiter and Shaw, 'Records of achievement', p. 21.

28 Assiter and Fenwick, 'Profiling in higher education', p. 27.

29 Dearing Report, p. 140.

30 Gibbs, 'Assessing skills', p. 63.

Teaching oral history to undergraduate researchers

Oral history projects – involving 'the interviewing of eye-witness participants in the events of the past for the purposes of historical reconstruction' – are just one of many different types of undergraduate historical research.[1] In Britain, most undergraduates majoring in history are required to undertake a historical research project at some point in their degree. There is evidence that history teachers favour research projects as a mode of assessment and that students experience the project as a highlight of their experience in higher education.[2] Yet very little is written about student research projects in history, or indeed more generally about undergraduate research projects.[3] By contrast, there is a wealth of literature about undergraduate oral history courses in which students conduct research projects based upon interviews. This chapter synthesises three pieces of research: a survey of the international literature about teaching oral history in higher education; a questionnaire analysis of British courses in which under-graduates conduct life-history research projects (two-thirds of the courses involved oral history though they also included research using published and unpublished life-story writing); and an analysis of learning diaries by students taking the Certificate in Life History at the University of Sussex.[4]

Pedagogical principles and structures

Oral history is a trans-disciplinary research method which is used in a wide range of academic and professional fields.[5] Although many oral history courses are taught within history degrees, they are also taught in degree programmes such as anthropology, sociology, women's studies, geography, education and health studies. Conversely, undergraduate historians taking oral history are required to grapple with the trans-disciplinarity of oral history.

The pedagogical principles outlined by Australian oral historian Janis Wilton provide an excellent starting point for teaching oral history. In summary, 'the principles entail an interactive and reflective teaching method, the incorporation of theory, and the insistence that students learn by practising and applying oral history methods and understandings'. The focus on interactive teaching methods and materials 'entails a strong use of exercises which invite reflection and learning', and '"reflection" means constantly examining what is being learnt . . . by both student and teacher'. Theoretical and conceptual understandings, for example about memory and the interview relationship, should inform oral history practice, but not dominate: 'at the core . . . is the requirement that students should practise and apply oral history method and theory'. 'They must get out there and interview. They must prepare for and process the interviews they conduct. They must do something with the interviews . . . they must explain and analyse both the oral history process and the product which they have created from that process.'[6] In many ways these principles for teaching oral history mirror current ideas about effective teaching and learning in higher education: learning should be active, participatory and interactive; theory should be integrated with practice; students should think critically about the nature and use of knowledge; and both students and teachers should reflect upon the process and outcomes of learning.

These principles require a substantial investment of tutor and student time. The most common complaint of participants in oral history courses is that they do not have enough time to deal with the practical, personal and conceptual demands of this research. Oral history involves the creation of research sources and an active relationship with those sources. People are not paper, and ill-prepared researchers can cause damage to themselves and their interviewees. Undergraduates (or any other students) should not be expected or encouraged to undertake oral history research – for example in their dissertation – without initial training. A term or semester of weekly seminars, or an equivalent series of training days, is probably the minimum requirement.

Because of the labour-intensive processes of teaching interview skills and supporting interview-based projects, oral history courses work best with relatively small groups of students. Seminar-sized groups of between ten and twenty students allow for interactive workshop activities. The obvious and very successful exceptions are distance learning courses such as those offered by the Open University in Britain and the University of New England in Australia, which are designed to be taught to large numbers of students through carefully designed distance education methods and resources which guide independent study.

Students may come with their own research topics, in which case the challenge for tutors and students is to ensure that the proposed research is manageable within the constraints of the course, and the common element for analysis will be the process and products of oral history itself. On the other hand, if the class undertakes a project on an agreed subject, then students can collaborate in background research and project planning and discuss how their collective work may contribute to historical understanding. The degree to which the research is then undertaken as a group project (as opposed to individual research on the same subject), and the extent of collaboration between students and of student control over the research process and agenda, may vary. In a historical studies degree at the University of Portsmouth, Sue Bruley devised an oral history course which involved students in decision making at every stage. She reports that after an initial exploration of twentieth-century British women's history, and of methodological issues raised by feminist oral historians, 'we met to thrash out the aims of our study . . . [and] eventually decided to interview women who had been full-time housewives in the 1930s, and a similar group from the 1950s'. Students researched what proved to be a scanty literature on domesticity in this period, developed criteria for selecting respondents, and decided on the framework for the interviews. After the interviews the students discussed a photocopied summary of each interview in terms of oral history practice and its contribution to historical understanding. As the students gained confidence and expertise, the tutor became less a teacher and more an external adviser and technical facilitator.[7]

Group projects have their drawbacks. The Portsmouth group was undermined by unavoidable student absences which delayed the formation of group identity, and 'the disparity in enthusiasm and/or abilities between different members of the group' can also be a problem.[8] On the other hand, though group projects need to be carefully structured and coordinated, they can be an empowering exercise for students, who must develop the skills and relationships to work effectively as a group and to coordinate each stage of the research.

Teaching oral history interviewing

For most students, interviewing is a novel experience in which they are required to learn about 'unfamiliar things' which might not otherwise be part of their degree: 'things like dealing with live people, and with ethical and legal issues, using technical equipment, and developing techniques of interviewing and editing'.[9] To a certain extent, students learn oral history interviewing by doing it, yet there are a number of strategies to prepare students for their first interview in the field.

Training should interweave theory and practice.[10] The following extract from a learning diary by a student taking an oral history course at the University of Sussex shows how theoretical reading can inform oral history practice while, in turn, project work brings the issues of oral history to life:

> I've just been reading Raphael Samuel's 'Perils of the Transcript' and wondered about his critique of Ronald Blyth's transcripts of 'Akenfield'. Samuel suggests Blyth has 'tidied up' the interviews by omitting link phrases, adding punctuation, not showing hesitations, ie. not conveying the feel of spoken word . . . I am transcribing my own interview almost exactly as I heard it, just missing out the occasional 'err' . . . Yet it fits Samuel's description [of Blythe's transcription] because that's how Mr H. *talked*. He had his memories prepared, and talked as though reading from a book. . . . Samuel is assuming they spoke in a different way to how Blythe transcribed them. Is he right to make this assumption?

Theoretical writings about memory often make most sense for students when related to their own remembering. At the University of New England in Australia, Janis Wilton facilitates group workshops in which her students explore issues about memory by tapping and analysing their own memories of a topic such as a childhood home:

> Using these offered memories as a starting point discussion centres on, for example, the different types of things people remember, how they reconstruct memories, the sorts of things we do not tend to remember, the different factors (past and present) which influence what and how we remember, how memories are created in the first place and the types of information which can be tapped through asking people to recall past experiences.[11]

Through exercises like this, students come to understand the use of memory in their own oral history, and the implications of Alessandro Portelli's claim that 'what is really important is that memory is not a passive depository of facts, but an active process of creation of meanings'.[12]

Oral history teachers can use a number of innovative approaches to prepare students for the practical complications and dilemmas of interviewing. North American oral historian Charles Morrissey embodies the 'hazards' of oral history in the story form of real-life 'scenarios' based on 'my own experience since 1962 . . . While all of these oral vignettes pertain to oral history concepts, methodologies, strategies, and ethics, none of them – as classroom discussion routinely demonstrates – have answers that are necessarily "right" or "wrong".'[13]

An essential preparatory exercise is the practice interview between members of the class. These may be conducted in pairs and take anything between fifteen minutes and an hour, with each side taking a turn as interviewer and interviewee. Alternatively, a third person may act as a time-keeper and observer, with the roles rotating. The practice interview enables students to gain confidence in the use of tape-recording equipment, to learn about asking questions (they soon come to see the effects of closed or leading questions, and to hear with dismay their own repetitive verbal affirmations), and to recognise the usefulness of an interview guide – but also the importance of flexibility and the need to listen to what is being said and to respond where appropriate. The student being interviewed begins to understand what it is like to be on the other side of the microphone. The interview pairs or groups should have time to evaluate their own practice and, where possible, sections of interviews can be played to the larger group for discussion and analysis. Of course, a practice interview conducted in the artificial setting of a classroom is still a real human interaction, in which even the 'safest' of subjects ('first day at school', 'your childhood home') can provoke powerful and even painful remembering for interviewee and interviewer. So the teacher needs to prepare students for such eventualities and be ready to provide support if necessary. In effect, students are learning how to deal with the human issues of interviewing, but in a comparatively safe space and context.

Many students are particularly worried about the technical aspects of recording an interview. Students need to be comfortable and competent with tape-
recording equipment so that they can produce tapes with reasonable sound
quality and, most importantly, so that they can concentrate on what is being
said, on their own interventions and on the progress of the interview relationship. One problem is that many history departments do not have sufficient tape
recorders of adequate quality for use in practice interviews and oral history fieldwork. Students often provide their own tape recorders, which will produce interviews which can be transcribed and analysed, but which may not produce the
sound quality required for audio presentation or archiving. Teachers need to put
pressure on their own departments or institutions to provide sufficient and adequate recording equipment, using the argument that it is an essential and invaluable learning resource which will enable the production of archive-quality
interviews. At the very least, a small number of good quality tape recorders (such
as the Marantz or Sony Professional) and microphones enables the teacher to
show students what can be achieved on better equipment, the advantages of an
external microphone, the differences between tie-clip or hand-held microphones, the value of Dolby, and so on. If video equipment is available students
will have a chance to develop their skills in both audio and video recording.

Preparation for the interview

Students will prepare for their first 'real' interview with background reading on
the research topic and by producing an interview guide based upon the historical factors and issues highlighted in the reading, and any information they might
have about their prospective interviewee. In teaching situations there is rarely
sufficient time for a preliminary meeting with the interviewee, unless he or she is
already known to the student. However, an introductory letter on headed note-
paper followed by a phone call allows the student to explain the aims and process
of the interview and to glean background information which might be relevant
to the interview.

In a group project, students and tutor can collaborate in the creation of an
interview guide, and for individual projects the tutor can offer advice and students can learn from assessing each others' drafts. The students will have discovered during their practice interviews that they need to have an outline for their
questioning (as a reminder of their aims and focus, and so they can keep an interview on track), but also that it should not be too detailed (so they get lost or con-
fused) or too inflexible (so they are unable to follow unexpected responses and
the particular patterns and meanings of the interviewee's story). As students
develop confidence in the subject area and their own interview skills they gradually use the agenda more as a guide and back-up than as a set of questions.

The strategies for selecting interviewees vary between group and individual
projects, though the principles are much the same. The constraints of a degree

timetable suggest that a sharply defined geographic and thematic focus is both necessary and useful.[14] Students then need to consider whether potential interviewees match the aims of their research and are practically accessible. For a group project it might be possible to discuss sample criteria (and issues about samples and 'representativeness') and to arrange interviews with people with different experiences of the topic, which will allow for comparison. Students working on unrelated individual projects usually do not have the time to generate a sample of interviews, and are more likely to use one or two interviews for a case study about issues on a particular subject, or to explore the value and limitations of a life-history interview.

Opinion varies about whether or not it is a good idea for students to interview family members or close friends. These people will be easy to access and often happy to help the student in their research. But the interview will not necessarily be straightforward. An interviewee may wish to protect a younger relative from troubling aspects of the family history, and the interviewer might not wish to engender painful remembering, not least because the interview will impact upon an ongoing relationship. On the other hand, Kathryn Castle, who teaches oral history on a Women in History course at the University of North London, reports that students 'who interview members of their own families or close acquaintances often report a new perspective on the lives of those they thought they knew well'.[15] My own advice to students wanting to interview family members or friends is that they should recognise that the interview might have a significant effect on an important, ongoing relationship, and they should take care. Whether students ask to interview a family member, a friend or someone they have not previously met, the response is usually positive: 'in practice, most respondents engage in the process in a spirit of public service, for reasons of personal catharsis or simply so that their story is told and recorded.'[16]

One final preparatory suggestion is the research diary. Janis Wilton explains the use and value of the diaries kept by her students:

> The idea is that from day one of an oral history project students should keep a dated, detailed and personal record of their project as it unfolds. They should record what they do, any ideas they have about the project, where and what they learn about the oral history process, how effectively they manage to acquire and use oral history skills and techniques, how they feel about the experience, the extent to which they are influencing the outcome of the project, their responses to the interviewees and the ways in which interviewees are involved in the project. Essentially, the diary becomes a very personal account of the oral history process and its outcomes. In the long run the material noted in the diary can also provide some of the substance for explanatory reports, commentaries and/or introductions to the final oral history project.[17]

To familiarise the students with the use of a diary, and to demonstrate its potential in research, Wilton introduces the students to publications in which researchers are explicit about the personal processes of the research. This, in turn, raises issues for discussion about the autobiographical nature of research.

The interview

For most well-prepared students the first 'real' oral history interview is a nerve-wracking but ultimately positive experience which generates tremendous excitement about the process and relationships of living history. It has been suggested that some younger or less mature students may struggle with the interpersonal and ethical issues of the interview, and that they may find it difficult to empathise with older interviewees.[18] My own experience is that an interest and enthusiasm in other people's lives and stories tends to be more important than the age of the student interviewer. Some students of all ages develop an impressive and effective affinity with their interviewees; others do not. It may be that oral history is best suited to certain kinds of student with particular learning styles. Most obviously, it suits students who are comfortable with practical activity and social interaction.

Students should write an account of the interview as soon as possible and while it is still fresh in the memory. This account might describe the interview setting and relationship, and other factors which will not be apparent on the tape but which will have affected what was said. Students should also produce either an index of the interview tape or a transcript of the interview. Though transcription is very time consuming, it does require the student to listen carefully to his or her tape and to consider the effects of the translation from an oral to a written version of the interview. A copy of the transcript can also be sent or delivered to the interviewee, together with a thank-you letter and a copy of the tape. This gesture is usually much appreciated.

Of course, students encounter all sorts of problems during their first interviews. For example, Sussex students conducting their first interview for an oral history of the Ouse Valley had problems with interviewees who would not shift from a very fixed and formal account of public life or who uncovered painful memories. One student from overseas struggled to communicate with an old farm worker who had a strong Sussex accent, and another felt constrained by the controlling influence of an intermediary who had set up the interview. Though a difficult interview may be frustrating or disappointing for the student, and perhaps also for the interviewee, within the course it is crucial that lessons are learnt from the review of extracts from student interviews. The review process covers recording techniques and tape quality, the effectiveness of the interviewer's questions, contextual factors affecting the interview, and the nature of remembering and recall.

Above all, students are confronted and challenged by the human issues of the oral history relationship. They may recognise the need for discretion and confidentiality in certain circumstances, in particular where they are investigating a small and sensitive community.[19] Students at the University of the South Pacific in Fiji taking Doug Munro's oral history course found that the guidelines for oral history interviewing needed to be adjusted according to particular cultural expectations:

In most Pacific Islands societies great deference is shown towards age and kinship, particularly if that person is of high rank. In Fijian culture, moreover, the formal relationship between uncles and their siblings' children impacts drastically on an oral history interview because the niece or nephew cannot, for cultural reasons, ask follow-up questions. The uncle says his piece into the tape, and that is that.[20]

Most frequently, students worry about dealing with the painful or emotive memories which may be invoked during their interview. Sue Bruley's advice makes good sense:

If we want students to practise oral history . . . then they must interact with real people about their life experiences. Of course extreme care has to be taken that the students concerned are trustworthy, sensitive and adequately briefed. Also, it is essential that the elderly person knows what the interview is for and has freely agreed to it.[21]

A related issue is the ownership of interview material and the degree of reciprocity in the researcher–researched relationship. While it is relatively easy to give the interviewee a copy of the tape and either a transcript (if one is made) or perhaps a narrative account of the recorded life-story, the exchange is more complicated in relation to student essays, which may not be produced in a language and form that is readily accessible to the narrator, and which may make challenging comments about the interview relationship and remembering. In such cases students may need to produce rather different products for the course and for the interviewee. Maggie Wilson offers this excellent code of conduct which is followed by her students:

A code of ethics in this context includes the acceptance of hospitality and of the social nature of the occasion for many; allowing the respondent to vet the testimony before submission; offering the use of pseudonyms; presenting a well-bound copy of the testimony to the respondent and fashioning a verbal or written contract to regulate any use made of material. In this the tutor also bears a responsibility to safeguard material of a sensitive nature.[22]

Assessment and learning outcomes

Assessment tasks should contribute both to the learning about oral history and to the assessment of that learning. Oral history courses are typically assessed through the production of one or more of the following: the presentation of an interview tape, together with some form of documentation (either a transcript, an index or a summary); an account of the interview which considers issues about oral history theory and method; a narrative of the life-story situated within its historical context; and a critical assessment of the contribution of the interview to the understanding of a particular historical topic. The aim is for students to produce evidence of their practical work, together with some form of critical and reflective writing. Group work can be assessed by allocating a proportion of marks to the achievements of a group, as identified in joint writing or a portfolio of group project materials.[23]

One particular issue in assessing oral history concerns the quality of the student interview. An interview might be affected – for better or worse – by the fortuitous choice of a 'good' or 'bad' interviewee, or by other unavoidable circumstances. Most tutors agree that they are not assessing the quality of the student's interview, and are primarily concerned with the quality and insightfulness of the student's reflections on the interview process as evidence of what the student has learnt. Steve Pile reports that 'perhaps ironically, the best reports were provided by those who had had the "worst" interviews':

> Those with 'bad' interviews (one interviewee gave one-word interviews throughout, another would only talk about Hollywood films and mystery novels) at first thought that their interviews were 'rubbish', but found that they did indeed have interesting material when they sat down and started to ask themselves why it was that these people replied in the way they did.[24]

Moreover, listening to student interviews for the purposes of assessment can be very time consuming. While tutors may need to limit themselves to selected extracts, they also need institutional recognition that supporting and assessing oral history projects is labour-intensive work and should be adequately recompensed. This is not an easy argument to win in an under-resourced higher education system, though the evidence suggests that this investment of time and money is more than repaid in terms of student learning outcomes and other benefits.

Martyn Lyons at the University of New South Wales lists the main problems with his oral history course – achieving the right blend of theory and practice; the time taken in assessing student work; and the lack of time for the production of tangible outcomes – but concludes on a very positive note about the outcomes of the course:

> On the plus side, the friendly co-operation of interviewees has been very encouraging, and so has the extraordinary commitment of students. Many expressed the feeling that they had learned something very useful, and I believe they have found the experience liberating. They have tested themselves in a new field, and discovered something in the process about their own personal capabilities. A few have re-learned the lost art of listening, and they have all been forced to re-assess the discipline of history.[25]

This summary is typical of the positive outcomes reported by tutors and students on most oral history courses. First, oral history project-work can engage students in a particular historical topic and generate significant historical insights. Helen Andreoni, for example, reports that 'the major issues of multicultural studies just fall out of the recorded conversations and the experiences in collecting them'.[26] More generally, the experience of actually 'doing' history forces students to reassess the discipline of history. David Blake notes that trainee teachers felt that 'even a limited introduction to the process of oral history had challenged their preconceptions as student teachers about the nature of history' and about how it might be taught in schools.[27] Through oral history, students also learn a range of research skills, including project preparation, interview and recording techniques, source documentation, and the analysis and use of different types of evidence. Equally important, they develop an understanding of some of the issues about doing qualitative research of this kind: about memory as a source; about sampling and representativeness; about research relationships and responsibilities; and about the creation and use of social or historical knowledge. In short, research projects 'produce students better equipped to make critical use of knowledge'.[28]

Oral history courses lend themselves to the development of a range of personal and transferable skills, such as organisation and strategic thinking, listening and communication skills, verbal and other forms of social interaction, and the ability to work effectively in a group.[29] Personal confidence often blossoms as students develop faith and pride in their abilities, and students who have been less successful in more conventional academic situations sometimes come into their own through project work: 'the less articulate, for instance, may excel their more scholarly contemporaries when it comes to interviewing technique or organisation and improvisation'.[30] Oral history interviews can also generate understanding of, and respect for, people of different ages and backgrounds. For Steve Pile, one of the benefits of conducting interviews in a day centre was that the students learned about the lives and world-views of an older generation.[31] Students on Helen Andreoni's Multicultural Studies course at the University of New England in Australia gained direct insights into the migrant experience by visiting members of particular ethnic communities in their homes and listening to their stories.[32]

The oral history project – particularly when the topic has a personal significance for the student – can validate and affirm the identity of both interviewer and interviewee. Anthropologist John Forrest writes perceptively about this potential and its realisation in the work of his student and co-author Elisabeth Jackson:

> We know full well that one of the purposes of fieldwork is to give the unrepresented a voice, but we rarely concede that they give us a voice. Under the right conditions the process can be entirely symbiotic. Elisabeth's interview with Danny [a black man whose struggles in life resonated with her own] shows how both the interviewer and interviewee can help each other to find a voice. By presenting *him* she was able to represent *herself*.[33]

Finally, oral history courses can produce important historical sources and valuable histories. Students are surprised, and then pleased, as they realise that by contrast with some of their other university studies – in which they assess and regurgitate other people's work – through oral history projects they can make history anew and for themselves. The evidence from oral history research courses and projects confirms that the best way to learn history is by *doing* history.

Notes

1 R. J. Grele, 'Directions for oral history in the United States', in D. K. Dunaway and
   W. K. Baum (eds), *Oral History: An Interdisciplinary Anthology* (Walnut Creek,
   Altamira, 1996), p. 63.
2 History at the Universities Defence Group, *Submission to the National Committee of
   Inquiry into Higher Education* (Hull, University of Hull, 1997), pp. 3–4.
3 See M. Luck, 'Undergraduate research projects – what are they worth?', *New
   Academic* (Spring 1997), 23–4.
4 The research is written up in full in A. Thomson, *Undergraduate Life History
   Research Projects: Approaches, Issues and Outcomes* (Brighton, University of Sussex,
   1998).
5 B. A. Lanman, 'The use of oral history in the classroom: a comparative analysis of
   the 1974 and 1987 Oral History Association surveys', *Oral History Review*, 17:1
   (1989), 215–26.
6 J. Wilton, 'Share and compare: ideas for teaching oral history', *Oral History
   Association of Australia Journal*, 18 (1996), 17–18.
7 S. Bruley, 'Women's history, oral history and active learning: an experience from
   Southern England', *Women's History Review*, 5:1 (1996), 119.
8 B. Harrison, 'Tape recorders and the teaching of history', Oral History, 2 (1972), 5–6.
9 A. M. Hyatt, 'Teaching oral history to post-Secondary students', *Canadian Oral
   History Association Journal*, 14 (1994), 30.
10 Course reading lists should include published oral histories (usually books but sometimes other media such as film or CD ROM) which demonstrate different ways of
   recording, analysing and presenting oral testimony; any one of several excellent text-
   books, such as P. Thompson's *The Voice of the Past: Oral History* (Oxford, Oxford
   University Press, 1988) or V. Raleigh Yow's *Recording Oral History* (London, Sage,
   1994); seminal works about the theory and method of oral history, such as S. Berger
   Gluck and D. Patai's edited collection, *Women's Words: The Feminist Practice of Oral
   History* (London, Routledge, 1991), A. Portelli's *The Death of Luigi Trastulli and
   Other Stories* (Albany, State University of New York Press, 1991) and M. Frisch's *A
   Shared Authority: Essays on the Craft and Meaning of Oral and Public History*
   (Albany, State University of New York Press, 1990); and a set of the appropriate
   national oral history periodical, such as the British journal *Oral History*. R. Perks's
   Oral History: An Annotated Bibliography (London, British Library, 1990) is an inval-
   uable resource for students looking for oral history writings on particular topics.
   Library resources vary within institutions and it is not always possible to ensure ready
   access to key texts, especially with large groups of students. *The Oral History Reader*
   (London, Routledge, 1998), edited by myself and Rob Perks and containing key articles written over the last thirty years by oral historians from around the world, is
   intended as a resource for students and teachers of oral history, and is arranged in five
   sections which loosely match the structure of an oral history course.
11 Wilton, 'Share and compare', p. 19.
12 A. Portelli, 'What makes oral history different', in Perks and Thomson (eds), *The Oral
   History Reader*, p. 69.
13 C. T. Morrissey, 'Oral history as a vocation: classroom questions of a perplexing
   kind', *Canadian Oral History Association Journal*, 14 (1994), 36. See also R. A.
   Sargent, 'International oral history research as vocation: inquiry and confusion –

teaching and learning oral history methods', *Oral History Forum*, 16–17 (1996–97), 89–94.

14 Bruley, 'Women's history', pp. 113–14.

15 K. Castle, 'Oral history for undergraduates: a skills perspective', in E. Assiter (ed.), *Transferable Skills in Higher Education* (London, Kogan Page, 1995), p. 145. See also Bruley, 'Women's history' and M. Wilson, 'Oral evidence work with undergraduates', *Oral History*, 20:1 (1992), 64.

16 *Ibid.*, p. 65.

17 Wilton, 'Share and compare', pp. 18–19.

18 See Bruley, 'Women's history', p. 116.

19 See Harrison, 'Tape recorders', p. 8.

20 D. Munro, 'Teaching an oral history course at the University of the South Pacific', unpublished paper, 1997, p. 8.

21 Bruley, 'Women's history', pp. 117–18.

22 Wilson, 'Oral evidence work', p. 65. For guidelines on student publication on the World Wide Web, see M. L. McLellan, 'Oral history in the classroom and on the World Wide Web', *Oral History Association Newsletter*, 31 (Fall 1997), 39.

23 Bruley, 'Women's history', p. 125.

24 S. Pile, 'Oral history and teaching qualitative methods', *Journal of Geography in Higher Education*, 16: 2 (1992), 141.

25 M. Lyons, 'Teaching oral history at the University of New South Wales', *Australian Historical Association Bulletin*, 62 (1990), 48.

26 H. Andreoni, 'Oral history: an inspired technique for exploring community relations', *Oral History Association of Australia Journal*, 6 (1984), 29.

27 D. Blake, 'Student teachers remember their schooling: an approach through oral history', *Oral History*, 23:2 (1995), 75.

28 Luck, 'Undergraduate research projects', p. 24.

29 Castle, 'Oral history', p. 146.

30 Harrison, 'Tape recorders', p. 9.

31 Pile, 'Oral history', p. 141.

32 Andreoni, 'Oral history', p. 29.

33 J. Forrest and E. Jackson, 'Get real: empowering the student through oral history', *Oral History Review*, 18:1 (1990), 35–7.

13 Ian Dawson and Joanne de Pennington

Fieldwork in history teaching and learning

In a recent discussion of fieldwork in history teaching at British universities, Christine Hallas concluded that 'generally the use of fieldwork in higher education history courses has been sporadic . . . occasions when some light relief is required from sitting in the lecture hall'.[1] This view was largely impressionistic, as little formal research has been undertaken to determine how widely fieldwork is used in history departments, what kinds of activity are undertaken and how highly students value fieldwork as a form of learning. Whereas geographers, archaeologists and others seeking to improve their students' learning through fieldwork can draw on a substantial body of case studies and analyses, historians have had to depend primarily on their own individual experiences.[2]

This chapter endeavours to begin to fill this gap by reporting the results of surveys of university departments and of recent history graduates, undertaken to establish the quantity, variety and purposes of fieldwork and its value in students' eyes, and by identifying a range of issues affecting the effective use of fieldwork. For the purposes of this research, fieldwork was defined as the study of physical, non-written evidence such as castles and other buildings or artefacts in galleries and museums.[3] Questionnaires were sent to all history departments in Britain. Forty-seven responses were received, of which the great majority came from the 'new' universities and university colleges. The questionnaire focused on five issues: who initiated fieldwork, the purposes of fieldwork, the types of place visited, the contribution of fieldwork to student assessment and future uses of fieldwork. The extent of students' experience of fieldwork and their perceptions of its value were investigated through a questionnaire sent to former history students studying for the Postgraduate Certificate in Education (a teaching qualification) at four universities and colleges. Eighty-three former history students who had undertaken their first degrees at forty-three different institutions completed the questionnaire. In addition to the questions asked in the departmental survey, the students were asked about the kinds of activity they had undertaken and about their perception of the value of the study of sites as historical evidence in relation to other kinds of source.

Policies and practices

In the survey of departments, nineteen of the forty-seven replies cited departmental policy as the major reason for their use of fieldwork. This was sometimes linked to the development of courses on such topics as heritage, landscape history, the built environment and research methodology. One respondent described his department's 'over-riding objective in fieldwork' as being 'to bring students into contact with *how history is used* in the "real world" and the *political, social and economic debates* which inherently have an historical component'. He continued, 'at Level One [first year], for example, we take students to Wigan Pier and to the Merseyside Maritime Museum in order to expose them to how historical issues are portrayed to a mass audience.' In the remaining twenty-six universities the use of fieldwork depended on lecturers' own initiatives. Replies indicated that in these cases the lack of a coherent and supportive policy increased existing difficulties in arranging and carrying out activities beyond the university. Much therefore depended on the confidence of staff in the effectiveness and value of the learning strategies being employed outside the normal classroom. The existence of staff with backgrounds as teacher-trainers, or the appointment of new staff with an interest in the historical importance of sites, were often key factors in building this confidence.

One result of this generally unsystematic approach to the initiation of fieldwork is that many students taking history degrees never visit a historical site as part of their course. Over half of the eighty-three students surveyed had not undertaken fieldwork during their degrees. These forty-five students were drawn from thirty universities. Many felt that there had been little opportunity because of, for example, the impracticality of fieldwork for courses on the history of other countries. However, there was the indignant lament, 'I did a course on medieval monasticism which *really* should have included St Mary's Abbey in York *and* what about Fountains etc?' More problematically, the student who commented, 'I didn't do any but still got a 2i', made this statement in support of his contention that fieldwork was of no importance in the study of history. This may be one flippant response, but the overall pattern of replies showed that students had significantly different understandings of the value of fieldwork and of sites as a source of historical evidence, depending on whether or not they had any experience of fieldwork.

The thirty-eight students who had experience of fieldwork recorded a total of eighty-seven visits during their three years of study: thirty-two in year one, twenty-four in year two, and thirty-one in year three. This pattern may reflect a desire on the part of tutors and departments to involve and enthuse new students through fieldwork in the first year of their course, and through using sites to add depth to the range of sources studied in the final year. Moreover, the range of places visited was extremely varied. It included the expected sites such as castles, stately homes, industrial sites, deserted villages, museums and art galleries, but also a sewage works, a funeral director and local cemetery, and more distant exotica such as Versailles, Amsterdam, Venice, a one-week visit to St Petersburg, and the sombre scenes of Western Front battlefields and Holocaust sites. Those students whose highlights involved exploring Victorian graveyards may not have sympathised with the complaint that it was too cold to take notes in St Petersburg.[4]

This range suggests no lack of imagination or enterprise on the part of tutors, although the ability to continue the more distant or longer visits was felt to be seriously at risk because of financial constraints. The use of properties owned by English Heritage and the National Trust was extensive, and it is possible that closer, structured links between these organisations and universities would be advantageous both in developing resources and in planning modules so that the use of a site is integral (and perhaps the starting point of enquiry) rather than being an entertaining flourish at the end of a lecture-based course. Overall, such a range of activities underlined the absence of a journal which could bring together case studies and thus promote ideas about the effective use of historical sites for fieldwork.

From a departmental perspective, the most highly rated purpose of fieldwork was its development of students' skills in critically analysing evidence, followed by the acquisition of contextual knowledge, with the improvement of staff–student relations in third place. Other objectives cited were extending knowledge of the local community and the development of transferable skills, although few replies referred to the enhancement of teamwork and independent learning, both particularly achievable through fieldwork. However, the student respondents had a different perspective on the objectives of the fieldwork they had undertaken. Only 25 per cent saw the development of evidence-handling skills as the key objective, while 38 per cent thought that the acquisition of contextual knowledge had been the most important objective. Nearly 20 per cent believed that 'general interest' had been the prime purpose of their fieldwork. Some students clearly felt that there was an appropriate emphasis on deepening knowledge and analysing a site as evidence. Other comments that fieldwork was a 'bringing together [of] work done on a Georgian town', and that 'it helped to clarify and make real what we had already learned', suggest the development of contextual knowledge and the value of field visits for pulling together the threads of a course. Fewer comments suggested the use of evidence-based activities, though one student identified the purpose of a visit to Hadrian's Wall as 'to prove or disprove theories', an intriguing and potentially exciting approach. Less positively, the number of times 'general interest' appeared as an objective was high, and it was reflected in comments such as, 'it didn't seem to provide much relevance to the course other than as general interest'. Although these differences about objectives may not be significant, it is possible, particularly in the light of the numbers citing 'general interest', that objectives relating to analysis of evidence are not apparent in the activities or assessments undertaken by many students. Comments suggest that field visits which are simply 'a pleasant diversion from seminars' are not popular with students. However laid back they try to be, students appear to prefer the rigour and value of field*work* to the relaxation and questionable relevance of field *trips*.

This perception that field visits were not sufficiently challenging was deepened by students' descriptions of the kinds of activity they undertook. Guided tours (either by the students' own lecturer or by someone connected with the site) predominated, providing the main component of thirty-four out of fifty-eight visits. Group or individual work made up the remainder. Students' own active involvement in learning during visits was dominated by discussion and written descriptions. Little use was made of investigative activities involving measurement and the collection of data. Fewer than 15 per cent of activities involved learning through independent or small-group completion of structured tasks. Just over half of respondents felt that the structure of the visit and the activities undertaken could have been improved. Since the lack of structure of visits was the most common complaint, it is reasonable to hypothesise that poorly structured visits fail to challenge students, thereby reducing motivation and making it more difficult for students to relate a field visit to the overall course.

It is instructive to compare these findings with the models of fieldwork developed by geographers. While 'Cook's tours' or guided 'sight seeing' visits were the major focus for fieldwork in the 1950s and 1960s, the 1970s saw the addition of 'problem-oriented, project-based fieldwork' involving 'inductive and deductive approaches, hypothesis generation and testing, data collection and statistical analysis, interpretation and report writing'. Passive student participation was being replaced by 'active student participation although often staff-led'. In the later 1980s these approaches were overlain by the introduction of objectives related to transferable skills.[5] The surveys undertaken in this research provide little evidence of history fieldwork having moved beyond the 'Cook's tour' stage. This is not to say that this approach is not valuable but, even allowing for the differences between the two subjects, there may well be room for the development of a wider range of approaches to fieldwork in history.

Replies from history departments indicated that few used fieldwork in formal assessment. Only sixteen departments had assessment strategies clearly related to activities undertaken on a fieldwork visit. Assessed tasks included specific examination questions based on a visit, oral presentations, reports, group-work tasks and the compilation of a fieldwork file in preparation for a dissertation. Among departments not using fieldwork in formal assessment, there was an acknowledgement of its value in informing personal studies such as dissertations. Moreover, tutorial and informal discussion of sites visited was common. Yet the absence of a relationship between fieldwork and formal assessment clearly downgraded the importance of fieldwork in students' eyes. Fewer than a quarter reported that fieldwork contributed to assessment, enhancing the view summarised by one student that fieldwork was 'more recreational than practical'.

Unsurprisingly, there was a marked contrast between students' views on the value of fieldwork depending upon whether they had direct experience of it.

Those who had undertaken fieldwork believed that their understanding of past societies and situations had been enhanced by the experience, as illustrated in Table 13.1.

Table 13.1 Student ratings of the value of fieldwork

	Students with fieldwork experience		Students without fieldwork experience	
	No.	%	No.	%
Vital importance	15	42	2	3.0
Important	9	25	17	42.5
Useful	12	33	18	45.0
Little importance	–	–	1	2.5
No importance	–	–	2	3.0

Why did these students see fieldwork as important? The majority of answers were at a basic level such as, 'it illustrated the points made during the course', another example of the 'let's go on a guided tour to round off the course' approach to fieldwork. More relevant to the purposes of fieldwork were the claims that, 'it brings home that evidence is not only about printed sources and artefacts. History is all around us'; 'History is a subject which works most effectively when it has penetrated a student's imagination. Visual aids (including visits) help this process enormously'; and 'Fieldwork gave me a real sense of being in touch with the history of an area, in a way that books alone could not have provided. My visit to Aldgate as part of a week long trip in London . . . was a real highlight.' What set these comments apart from nearly all others was their awareness of the contribution that the evidence of historical sites can make to a historical enquiry. However, few responses suggested that students had undertaken their fieldwork in a spirit of enquiry, seeking out answers to questions or testing hypotheses, and therefore it is not surprising that such responses were in the minority. The nature of the perceived objectives, the structures of visits and the nature of the activities undertaken all indicate a predominantly passive role for students. If students were required more frequently to think about the value of physical evidence, then their justifications for fieldwork might move more frequently beyond the banal 'it brings the past alive'.

Improving fieldwork

In their responses to a question about future patterns of fieldwork, even the most committed departments indicated that they faced increasing difficulties, particularly in financing visits and finding time for them. The constraints of departmental budgets (when available), increased travel costs linked to larger groups of students, and awareness of greater strains on students' finances and their ability to contribute to costs were frequently mentioned. Changes in the organisation of the academic year due to modularisation and a two-semester pattern further complicated fieldwork arrangements, especially if they were to be for more than a half-day and therefore intruded on others' teaching time. The development of information technology strategies for learning was also cited as another example of a new initiative that was pushing fieldwork down the list of departmental priorities.

Fieldwork was also seen as demanding in terms of preparation at a time when staff workloads appear to have increased, and because the 'academic return seemed small compared with archival and library study'. One department expressed the concern that fieldwork seemed irrelevant against the demands of the Research Assessment Exercise on staff time. Another occasional contributor to problems was a departmental ethos that did not see the study of historical sites as central to a history degree; one tutor commented dryly that some of his colleagues saw going to the library as fieldwork. It was apparent that staff confidence, both in their own expertise at using sites and in the value of fieldwork for learning, was increasingly important in maintaining the provision. In this respect, the attitude of most of those who made regular use of fieldwork was summed up by the comment that, 'constraints make it difficult for us to expand fieldwork but we remain committed to its use'.

Even in those institutions where fieldwork is pursued with conviction and confidence, it is felt to be threatened by, among other factors, financial constraints and competing priorities such as research. Therefore it is vital to be able to answer effectively the simple question: 'Why do we take students to historical sites?' Hallas's discussion of objectives for fieldwork deals effectively with transferable skills.[6] Outcomes more purely historical include the development of skills in asking questions and in observation and analysis by using the site to answer questions or test hypotheses; an understanding of the strengths and limitations of artefacts, buildings and other sites as historical evidence; deepening knowledge of events, people, attitudes and culture; and a sense of period, including the ability to identify similarities and differences between periods. Hallas's suggestion of 'empathy' as an objective in its own right is problematical in the light of the literature on empathy in teaching history in schools. Empathy is perhaps best seen as a means to enhanced understanding of motivation and causation rather than as a separate objective in itself.

Anyone who has led a field visit will recognise the truth in the assertion that 'effective learning cannot be expected just because we take students into the field'.[7] Objectives have to be clearly related to potential improvements in students' performance. Can the 'Cook's tour' deliver enhanced performance? The answer is that it may do, depending upon its purposes. If the prime objective is enhanced knowledge and the tour is simply a vehicle for conveying information to students then it is no more likely to be effective than a normal lecture, allowing for the distractions of a scenic backdrop or the boom of aircraft passing overhead. Using a historical site as the setting for a lecture imparting information would be a poor use of such a valuable resource. The nearest students may come in such circumstances to participative learning will be to nudge a neighbour and whisper, 'what did she say?' However, the guided tour may be much more useful if it is seen as a way of introducing students to a different objective – the analysis of the site as evidence. For this objective the tutor can pass on techniques in the tour, the first stage in preparing students for studying sites more independently. This approach would focus on passing on the tutor's skills and observational techniques rather than a quantity of information. Therefore what geographers term 'observational fieldwork' can be structured as a stepping-stone to 'participatory fieldwork'.[8] However, it is important that the literature on structured lectures be applied to this kind of introductory fieldwork; for example, the provision of brief tasks leading to feedback and the use of guidelines for note taking, including key quotations, skeleton notes and questions to be augmented by students' own answers or selection of detail as evidence.[9]

Perhaps the most valuable use of fieldwork lies in developing students' historical skills in asking questions of a site, suggesting hypotheses about its use or the society that created it, and using the detail of the site to test those hypotheses. If this approach is taken there are implications for the timing of fieldwork visits. Visits conducted at the end of a module may be useful for pulling threads together and consolidating understanding, but that too can take place effectively on campus. The best time to use a site may well be at or near the beginning of a sequence of work, so that the site can be approached with an open mind, questioned and combed for evidence, and then used as a case study against which to test further ideas and reading. This approach may also be the one best supported by developments in information technology, through the growing number of 'virtual reality' sites which can be explored by students and used to develop their skills of evidence analysis before going out to a site.[10]

Effective use of information technology is one aspect of a third area for objectives – employability. Developments in geography fieldwork have been significantly affected by Enterprise in Higher Education initiatives since the mid 1980s, developing transferable skills in leadership and group work, independent thinking and self organisation, communication and presentation. These skills do not develop through passive, lecture-oriented visits, but active, problem-solving fieldwork offers a particularly fruitful context for developing these skills, and may in turn have a constructive impact on students' ability to work together in the more familiar environment of the university.[11]

Another increasing problem for those wanting to use fieldwork comes from the rapid increase in the numbers of students in classes. There are few occasions when learning cannot be enhanced by fewer students having greater access to their tutors. However, if the need to provide fieldwork for large groups leads to a re-thinking of approaches to fieldwork, then some good may emerge. Historians can draw on the work of geographers and others on methods of dealing with large groups, particularly the use of worksheet-guided trails and group projects.[12] Such methods are valuable, not simply because they reduce the problems posed by large groups but because they make better use of the site as a historical source and require students to be active learners. They also encourage the development of skills as students may work in small teams, contributing and assessing ideas, and preparing and presenting conclusions.

Clearly, students will take fieldwork more seriously, will work harder and hopefully will learn more if it contributes to their formal assessment. The opportunities for using more varied forms of assessment are considerable, particularly in relation to the development of transferable skills. Oral presentation skills and organisational and group-work skills can be assessed alongside the traditional qualities of the historian. Oral presentations can prove to be a valuable stage in moving towards written assessment, as they provide an occasion for trying out ideas and structuring arguments and evidence.[13] Formative assessment of these skills may be more appropriate in year one, before moving to summative assessments in years two and three. However, traditional forms of assessment can be used successfully, both as assessment mechanisms and to help students focus effectively on fieldwork activities. An essay question such as 'To what extent can a visit to the site help to reconstruct the battle of Hastings?' will require students to discuss written sources and the site, and weigh up the value of the site as evidence in relation to the evidence from other sources.

Clearly related to assessment issues is the problem of ensuring students' progression in learning throughout their fieldwork activities. In terms of the progression of general skills, we have suggested that it may help to think in terms of a progression from guided observation to group and individual investigation. A more difficult aspect of progression is whether fieldwork undertaken in year three is more demanding in terms of the use of source analysis techniques than in earlier years. Given the limited quantity of fieldwork undertaken in history departments, there is no evidence of planned progression in the difficulty of tasks. This is clearly an area that would merit further investigation. In addition to helping students to see the value of their fieldwork, it would help tutors to identify standards and policies for this work. The existence of coherent, structured departmental policies should also assist in the process of gaining funding, both for field visits and for staff development. Departmental visits to sites need funding, but would also contribute considerably to the sharing of expertise and to the development of new ideas and teaching materials. With a departmental policy it is possible to move, albeit slowly over several years, towards creating progression in students' experience and learning through a coordinated approach to course construction and teaching.

Fieldwork in practice

A second strand of research was the analysis and evaluation of our own use of fieldwork. The following example is taken from a third-year Special Subject course, 'The Fall of the House of Lancaster, 1447–64'. The starting point for the planning of fieldwork was the assessment to be undertaken at the end of the year, which included one examination paper on the sources of the period. Students had to answer two out of four questions, three of which were based on the evaluation of documentary sources. The fourth question was designed to offer students the chance to consider the value of non-documentary evidence in relation to other forms of evidence as follows:

Either

How effectively can the battles of this period be reconstructed using written sources, artefacts and battle sites as evidence?

Or

To what extent do the buildings of the period and their contents support the view that mid-fifteenth century Englishmen were 'preoccupied with thoughts of civil war'?

Once the assessment needs were decided before teaching began, then field visits could be planned, designed to build students' knowledge of the range of non-documentary sources and their ability to evaluate and use them as evidence. Further objectives were the increasing of students' knowledge and understanding of events and of mid fifteenth-century society. The first of the three visits was undertaken early in the course, in the expectation that informal discussions would encourage students to contribute more freely in weekly classes. The first site visited was All Saints Church, Harewood (West Yorkshire) to see six pairs of effigies from the period 1400–1510. This entailed a twenty-minute journey each way and, at most, ninety minutes on site. Preparation for the visit was deliberately brief, consisting of an overview of the objectives, and the request for students to consider how sophisticated they thought fifteenth-century society was and the reasons for their views. This was intended to identify their preconceptions at the outset of the course, so that they could then more effectively observe any changes in their views. The visit was structured around an activity booklet which included three tasks. First, students were asked to complete a grid identifying the effigies and placing them in chronological order. This was not overly demanding as there were unavoidable information boards, so students were also asked to list the physical features that helped to decide the chronological sequence and in what ways they developed over the period. The second task focused on the livery collars, asking students to identify differences and to suggest why they differed and whether they could learn anything from them about the loyalties of the individuals. The third task ranged more widely, asking students to make deductions about a series of aspects of society from the effigies – the roles of religion, chivalry and warfare, the importance of ideals such as loyalty, and the prosperity of society. Each stage was undertaken by students working in pairs, with a specified time limit at the end of which they reported back to the tutor. Discussion then took place, with students comparing answers and key points being identified and developed by the tutor. Students had space in their activity booklets to add relevant notes. This helped to ensure that their notes had structure and were useable for further work and, ultimately, for revision. After each feedback session students moved on to the next task. Finally students were asked, on the basis of the evidence of the effigies and the discussions, whether fifteenth-century society was more or less cultured than they had previously thought and whether the effigies were more or less valuable as sources than they had expected, and to explain the reasons for their views.

The other two field visits were timetabled just a week apart, so that a visit to the Royal Armouries in Leeds to examine weaponry, armour and tactics paved the way for visiting the site of the battle of Towton, near Tadcaster in West Yorkshire. The preparation for the Armouries visit took five hours, working in conjunction with the Armouries education officer. The visit itself lasted five hours, and therefore had to be constructed to allow for the natural ebbs and flows in students' concentration over that time and, if possible, to enhance their concentration. The first hour was spent working in small groups on specified items of armour, investigating how the authenticity of the armour might be established and the suitability of armour and weapons for fighting. Tasks were again provided in an activity booklet, which also gave precise instructions as to where each item could be found because time wasted looking for items in a large museum rapidly de-motivates students. During the hour, the tutor worked with groups answering questions or prompting other lines of thought. At the end of that hour students spent half an hour with a museum curator, who talked to them about how the authenticity of armour can be established and the other issues they had been investigating. A half-hour break followed to allow students to relax before they spent another hour on a structured group activity, completing a table to identify a full range of weapons, which kinds of soldier would have used them, and their strengths and weaknesses as weapons. They were also asked to consider what evidence the armour and weapons provided about the nature of society, a deliberate return to the issues discussed during the first field visit. A second half-hour break followed, and the day was completed with a talk and handling session on tactics and weaponry led by another curator. This was intended to pull together the strands of the day's work, as well as providing a lighter touch – with a purpose – at the end of the day when students could try on armour to test weight and mobility.

The following week students visited the site of the battle of Towton, having prepared by reading primary accounts of the battle and historians' reconstructions. The site happily contains no signs marking hypothetical positions, but it is crossed by a road which means that tutor and students need to be aware of traffic. The major purpose of the visit was to evaluate the accuracy of historians' reconstructions, and to consider some of the military problems such as the difficulty of commanders in communicating with their armies. This was much clearer because the students could see the size of the battlefield and the lines of sight from strategic points, and stand on the spots suggested by historians for the armies and assess the logic of those positions.

Table 13.2 Student ratings of fieldwork in two courses

	4 (high value)	3	2	1 (low value)
House of Lancaster	4	5	1	
Parallel course	0	7	1	

At the end of the course, after examinations had been taken, students completed a questionnaire on the field visits, both for the course described above and for a parallel course. Students were asked to grade the value of the fieldwork for developing understanding and knowledge. As Table 13.2 shows, the number of students rating fieldwork as highly valuable differed substantially between courses. The reasons for this difference can be inferred from students' comments on other parts of the questionnaire. Several students following the House of Lancaster course echoed one comment that 'the visits were good, if not excellent, for the final examination'. None made comments such as those from the parallel course, that 'what we looked at was not really relevant' and 'as one nears the exam the importance [of the visits] dwindles'. This difference can therefore be ascribed to the degree to which visits have an explicit relationship to assessment. In addition, students on the parallel course regarded it as most successful for 'getting to know students/tutor', whereas students on the House of Lancaster course regarded 'adding to subject knowledge' as the objective most successfully achieved. A second reason for the difference may lie in the degree of structure to the visits. The House of Lancaster visits were closely structured, whereas the parallel course did not use structured activity sheets but relied on the tutor and students to observe and record in their own way. At this level it might be suggested that students would not appreciate closely structured work that has the tang of school worksheets, but the response from House of Lancaster students was positive because the tasks and the recording sheets gave students confidence and clarity of purpose, and also ensured that they had material at the end of the visit that they could use for future work. No activity sheet was used at Towton, eliciting the comment that 'Towton needed a sheet . . . as it was too much to take in and remember'.

Several possible improvements were suggested by students in addition to Towton needing an activity booklet. Two shorter visits to the Armouries could be used, as students felt that a visit early in the year would help them to understand more of the society and events, while a second visit would be retained as specific preparation for the visit to Towton. One change to a task could be that instead of asking a series of open questions such as 'What do the effigies tell you about the importance of loyalty?', alternative hypotheses are provided as answers to some of those questions for students to choose between, thus providing a variety of open questions and hypotheses from which to choose. The key elements to preserve will be a clear relationship between visits and assessment, clarity of objectives and preparation, variety and structure of tasks, and a variety of pace within a visit.

Conclusion

It seems that the historical community divides into those who regard work at historical sites as a natural and important part of a historical education, and those for whom site-work is either irrelevant, insignificant or a time-consuming intrusion on other priorities. Clearly, not every course can or should involve fieldwork. However, we would like to conclude by drawing attention to the wider value of fieldwork as part of a history degree.

One concern is about the impact on students' own teaching, should they go into teaching either in colleges or in secondary schools. Most history teachers in schools use fieldwork, and over 30 per cent of GCSE candidates follow the History Around Us unit of the Schools History Project GCSE course, which requires site visits and the interrogation of physical evidence. Are these teachers receiving models of good practice in their own experience as students? The experience of one of the authors of this article in helping to set up a new museum, and in particular in providing resources and activities for secondary schools, suggests that the 'Cook's tour' approach is being carried forward, sometimes with disastrous and nearly always with disappointing results in terms of the quality of work undertaken during the visit. Teachers who have used investigatory approaches have been much more successful in maintaining students' concentration and enthusiasm, and have elicited a greater volume of work from students.

In the longer term, history graduates will hopefully maintain their interest in history and visit sites, along with so many of the rest of the population. Will history graduates do so with a more informed eye than the general public for interpreting what they see, and be better able to learn from the site about the society that created it? Will they be more willing to question the heritage interpretations that they witness? If they do not, then has something important been missing from their historical education at university?

Notes

We would like to take this opportunity to thank those colleagues who took the time to complete questionnaires, many providing considerable detail.

1 C. Hallas, 'Learning from experience: field trips and work placements', in A. Booth and P. Hyland (eds), *History in Higher Education* (Oxford, Blackwell, 1996), p. 225.
2 M. Kent, D. Gilbertson and C. Hunt, 'Fieldwork in geography teaching: a critical review of the literature and approaches', *Journal of Geography in Higher Education*, 21:3 (1997), 313–32 provides a discussion of past and current practice and identifies key issues and problems for future development. This survey draws on over seventy articles and books in geography and closely related disciplines. Although it deals with geography it contains a great deal that will be of value to historians exploring the uses and value of fieldwork.
3 The research thus excludes oral history work and visits to record offices and other archives.

4 Examples of the range of sites visited by individual departments are: Lindisfarne, York, Fountains Abbey, Escomb, Jarrow and Antwerp by a northern university; and Dublin, Hadrian's Wall, York, Saltaire, Chipping, Wigan, Grange-over-Sands and Lancaster by a northern university college. Another university college makes use of the following: Walker Art Gallery, Liverpool; Quarry Bank Mill, Styal; Port Sunlight, Wirral; Ludlow Castle, local field systems and turnpike roads, the Grosvenor Museum in Chester and the city of Chester.

5 See Kent *et al.*, 'Fieldwork in geography teaching', p. 316.

6 Hallas, 'Learning from experience', pp. 225–6.

7 N. Lonergan and L. W. Andresen, 'Field-based education: some theoretical considerations', *Higher Education Research and Development*, 7 (1988), 70.

8 See Kent *et al.*, 'Fieldwork in geography teaching', pp. 315–17.

9 See, for example, A. Jenkins, 'Active learning in structured lectures', in G. Gibbs and A. Jenkins (eds), *Teaching Large Classes in Higher Education* (London, Kogan Page, 1992).

10 A. Jenkins, *Fieldwork with More Students* (Oxford, Oxford Centre for Staff Development, 1997), pp. 38–42, provides a list of sites and contacts. Useful starting points are the Computing in Teaching Initiative for History, Archaeology and Art history <http://www.arts.gla.ac.uk/www/ctich/homepage.html>. Try also Durham cathedral's virtual field trip <http://www.dur.ac.uk/~dla0www/c-tour/tour.html>, based on photographs rather than computer graphics.

11 See J. R. Gold and M. J. Haigh, 'Over the hills and far away: retaining field study experiences in large classes', in Gibbs and Jenkins (eds), *Teaching Large Classes*, for accounts of the development of group skills which, though based on residential courses, offer ideas which could be amended for day or half-day activities. See also G. Gibbs *et al.*, *Developing Students' Transferable Skills* (Oxford, Oxford Centre for Staff Development, 1994).

12 See, for example, A. Jenkins, 'Thirteen ways of doing fieldwork with large classes/more students', *Journal of Geography in Higher Education*, 18, (1994), 143–54; Jenkins, *Fieldwork with More Students*.

13 For ideas on alternative forms of assessment see S. Brown, C. Rust and G. Gibbs, *Strategies for Diversifying Assessment in Higher Education* (Oxford, Oxford Centre for Staff Development, 1994); and A. Booth's 'Changing assessment to improve learning' and 'Assessing group work', in Booth and Hyland (eds), *History in Higher Education*.

Part III

Learning and assessment

Reappraising and recasting the history essay

The academic essay, pedagogically speaking, presents us with a paradox that is uncomfortable as well as disconcerting. Within the humanities and the social sciences in general, but particularly in history, the essay has traditionally enjoyed a commanding position in the landscape of undergraduate education, where it owes its importance to its dual role. On the one hand, essay writing has been one of the principal pathways to learning, helping students to consolidate and enlarge their knowledge and understanding, while also sharpening their capacity to communicate information and ideas in the form of ordered statements. On the other, it has served as a powerful and pervasive tool of assessment. It has long been a commonplace of coursework assignments, as well as the hardy perennial of intermediate and final examination papers, and the processes of reading for, planning and drafting coursework essays – or preparing, via intensive revision, to write fluent essay answers under examination conditions – occupy a very substantial proportion of the academic workload of most students in these subject areas. Yet the undergraduate essay, as one historian observed two decades ago, presents us with an image of neglect.[1] Until quite recently, it had only very rarely been systematically surveyed or investigated by researchers, and received relatively scant attention in that large and still-burgeoning literature which seeks to offer budding lecturers a grounding in the fundamentals of university and college teaching.[2] Even in the darker corners of libraries and bookshops where the essay had not been altogether overlooked, it was to be found in the pages of 'how to study' guides which were largely preoccupied with the outward trappings of academic writing (style, grammar, punctuation, bibliographical finesse), rather than with its *raison d'être*, the intellectual demands and conventions of scholarship.

Happily, there are increasing signs that past neglect is now being remedied, and on two complementary fronts. Interest in how and what undergraduate students learn has blossomed, and has included a small but growing number of studies of essay writing which have grappled with its essential function in interpretation and the construction of meaning. At the same time – and as with virtually every aspect of teaching, learning and assessment in higher education – the practices and procedures of essay writing have been undergoing rapid and far-reaching changes, in response to a variety of stimuli which have included a heightened concern with graduate employability (and thus with communication, and interpersonal and other avowedly transferable skills); the new possibilities opened up by advances in computing and information technology; and a shift towards fuller documentation of course requirements and expectations, to meet the combined effects of larger classes, greater student diversity and diminished resources. This chapter considers developments on both fronts and their interrelationship: what are the research findings on the history essay; how is the history essay being recast (and cast off); and to what extent can we reconcile changes in learning–teaching strategies with an enlarged grasp of the nature of essay writing?

Research findings

The principal source of findings is a qualitative study which I carried out in the early 1980s of the essay-writing experiences of two groups of second-year undergraduates whose main courses were in history (seventeen students) or psychology (sixteen students).[3] The data comprised two sets of interviews with each student; essay marks and final degree results; a selective analysis of the students' essays; and their scores on a psychological inventory which sought to capture differences in approaches to studying in higher education.

The circumstances in which these students went about their essay writing will doubtless be familiar to most academic historians. The students were offered a choice of questions and generally had about four weeks in which to prepare and submit their essays, which were normally expected to be about 2,500 words in length. While they could draw appropriately upon their lecture and tutorial notes, they were expected to follow up lists of recommended reading and to track down further library material which might be germane to the questions set. The history students, unlike their psychology counterparts, were prolific essay writers, spending on average two-thirds of their working time on their essays; some had as many as 18–20 coursework essays to complete over the academic year as a whole. The average time spent on any one essay was 13–15 hours, though individuals' estimates ranged from a low of 6–8 to a high of 30 hours. Most of the students took extensive notes in preparing their essays, although here again practice varied widely from individual to individual: a small number took hardly any notes, while at the other end of the range, some took as many as 30–40 sides. Most – but not all – of the students worked from an essay plan, which took one of four forms: a rough sketch of initial thoughts and ideas; a basic plan which identified main points and the sequence in which they would be presented; an extended plan in which main points were linked to relevant material in students' notes; and an evolving plan which was progressively refined as work on an essay proceeded.[4]

Conceptions of essay writing

The major finding of the study was that the students differed in how they conceived of an essay in the subject concerned, and that these differences were evident in the ways in which they prepared and assembled their essays as well as in their sense of what they were trying to achieve. Among the history students, three qualitatively distinct conceptions were identified: the essay as *argument*, the essay as *viewpoint* and the essay as *arrangement*. To grasp the nature of these conceptions more precisely, each was also broken down into three sub-components which, as will become apparent, were also construed in different ways within contrasting conceptions:

- *interpretation*: the meaning or meanings given to essay material by the student;
- *organisation*: the structuring of essay material into a discussion of the topic which follows a particular sequence or order;
- *data*: the subject matter which provides the raw material or bedrock of essays.

The history essay as argument

This was the most sophisticated of the three conceptions, and is illustrated in the following comments by the students:

> Graham: [Essays] crystallise your ideas on a topic. You learn to put forward a logical argument.
>
> Chris: I try to aim that, come the end of the essay, that no matter what they thought before that, the logic of the argument and the evidence produced is such that, even if they don't agree with my interpretation, they've got to say it's reasonable, reasonably argued . . . Tutors aren't looking for sort of, eloquence of style and so on, it's more the argument you present, providing it's fairly clear.
>
> Will: You have to follow a coherent argument, basically. And that's the only time you have to – like in a lecture you don't and in a seminar you just usually state your point of view on a certain point. You don't form an actual, coherent argument, along a broad theme, really.

These students seemed to share a common definition of an essay, which could be summarised as *an ordered presentation of an argument well supported by evidence*. Within this conception, it was the interpretive sub-component which was uppermost: ideas had been moulded or 'crystallised' into a single entity, a distinctive position or point of view on a problem or issue. Organisation was also important but it was subservient to interpretation, since the point of view to be presented underpinned and informed the structural conventions of introduction, main text and conclusion and helped to make the essay 'coherent' and 'logical':

> Kate: Every paragraph, I sort of make sure I'm making a relevant point. Is it clear what point I'm making or am I just waffling?

> Edward: Conclusions are just, you've really got to just tie everything together then, you've got all your strands of argument. But then conclusions, since I've come to university they've become less important, I think, 'cos your argument should be developing all the way through the essay anyway.

Equally crucially, the third sub-component, data, was also viewed in terms of its potential as evidence, substantiating or refuting a particular position or point of view:

> Kate: I think I've got a balanced argument, a convincing argument, putting in enough facts, and reference points, to back up what you're saying . . . I suppose I could've written the essay saying that the court and country divisions were very pronounced by this time, and if I'd been able to back it well enough, then logically I should get the same mark, but I don't really think that that view is convincing enough to be able . . . to present it.
>
> Tom: [The tutor] will be looking for a very well-structured essay, very well balanced. [The tutor] likes you to, you know, weigh the evidence up and come to some sort of conclusion.

The history essay as viewpoint

At first glance the conceptions of argument and viewpoint might seem indistinguishable:

> Rick: It's a discipline to getting it, to getting your argument down on paper in a constructive and in a literate sort of fashion . . . If you didn't do an essay at all and just had tutorials, instead of essays, you'd then learn more but you wouldn't be able to express it so well.
>
> Alan: There must be a technique to writing the perfect essay. Um, I suppose you've got to have a clearly defined argument and a plan of what you're going to do, already written down, so you can always refer back to it, and then start from there.

Indeed, both conceptions shared an interpretive concern to present a distinctive point of view and an organisational concern with essays as integral wholes. What set them apart, however, was the way in which the sub-component of data was viewed. Where the viewpoint conception was to the fore, there was a general lack of concern with data, and only sparse acknowledgement of the role of data in evidential substantiation. In some instances, there were indications that reading was directed by a preconceived view of the line the essay would take:

> Martin: Well, I must admit, I had a set idea on the question. And so I went in with that attitude, I got the books, um, again, the same process of going through them, doing the reading, taking notes, analysing, condensing the notes down and then writing the essay out. I mean, it's much the same process, and I knew that it was what [the tutor] had thought as well . . . It was exactly what [the tutor] thought, but I believed in it myself as well.

In others, it seemed, the interplay of interpretive stance and supporting data was deliberately overridden:

> Rick: Usually, on the whole, I try and make the facts fit my argument anyway, sort of, or I try and start with the argument in my head anyway. I'll change [them], you know, the facts they [present].

The characterisation of this conception thus reflected the alliance of interpretation only to organisation: an essay was seen as *the ordered presentation of a distinctive viewpoint on a problem or issue.*

The history essay as arrangement

Within an arrangement conception, a history essay was seen as *an ordered presentation embracing facts and ideas.* Interpretation had an almost incidental status rather than a superordinate one: ideas were viewed disjunctively, as collections of essentially discrete thoughts. It was considered useful or important in an essay to express whatever ideas or opinions one might have, but there was no concomitant concern to marry related ideas to form a unified position or point of view:

> Donna: I think [tutors] are asking us to look at secondary sources and just see what we think about them. But – they do want our own ideas, but I think it's limited when you've only got secondary sources.
> Sue: What's distinctive is that I'm here expressing myself, and what I thought, and what my ideas are, in certain subjects, on paper. It's very important to know, it's a gauge [of] how well the course is going. Obviously if you're not coming up with the right ideas, or certain ideas, and aren't able to express yourself, then I think that obviously you've got problems.

Within this conception, questions of organisation and of data were seen in a characteristically flat and self-contained way, uninformed by a specific interpretive stance:

> Pattie: I usually start off with a quote, and then finish with a quote. I find that's the easiest way to start it. But I think the worst thing is starting an essay. Once you get halfway through you're alright. The first few pages . . .
> Frank: [I chose this question because] it was one that I could deal with systematically, in a way. I could deal with you know, Privy Council, financial administration, parliament, all these things in turn . . . So basically I was collecting the different things I was going to deal with; just put them down on a piece of paper. Then used the indexes of books, looked it up, and then I dealt with each in turn, collecting material from the different books. I did that . . . in rough, and then, when I copied it up, like this, you know, ironed it out a bit, and reorganised it, and put it how I wanted it.
> Donna: I usually get – probably not in the right order, but it's hard sometimes because various topics merge into each other and you never know how to separate it. Sometimes there's no distinct line, and you get, put bits in the wrong bits, and things like that.

Conceptions and academic conventions

What these findings suggest, then, is that the most telling characteristic of the students' essay writing was their particular conception of what constituted an undergraduate essay in history, and thus of what writing a history essay entailed. Indeed, which conception a student held was more significant than any given planning strategy adopted (since what was paramount was what their essay planning was directed towards), while a more sophisticated conception was associated with higher coursework marks.[5]

Since these findings stem from a single study involving a small sample, doubts inevitably arise about their validity and reliability. There is, nonetheless, a good deal of corroborative support from elsewhere. First, the findings are mirrored in the distinction between 'deep' and 'surface' approaches to learning now found in a large number of studies of student learning in higher education.[6] 'Deep' approaches share with the argument conception a concern with the constitution of meaning and the interplay between conclusions and evidence, while 'surface' approaches, like the arrangement conception, have a non-interpretive character in which facts, ideas and their structural scaffolding are only loosely interrelated. (The viewpoint conception seems to occupy an intermediate position between these two poles.) Second, similar differences have been identified in essay writing in a first-year sociology course,[7] in Australian case studies of essay writing in history,[8] and in an error analysis of essays on British history written by first-year Australian students.[9] They have also been echoed in a survey of essay writing in undergraduate psychology, where selecting material, focusing on the question set, keeping to a clear framework and presenting an argument emerged as major areas of difficulty.[10]

A further question which arises is that of how to account for the prevalence of conceptions of the essay such as 'arrangement' or as 'viewpoint' among second-year undergraduates, when these conceptions were manifestly at variance with the expectations of the students' tutors as well as with wider academic norms. In part, the answer would seem to be that such conceptions are resistant to conventional remedies. Increased practice in essay writing, injunctions to 'make a plan' or generalised instruction in the mechanics of writing would be as likely to reinforce an inappropriate conception as to wean students from it, for the daunting challenge the academic essay presents is that of learning how to think as well as how to write within the norms and conventions of a particular discipline.[11] Furthermore, the feedback tutors provide – at least in its traditional form of written comments on marked essays – may fail to connect because it relies on a complementarity of premises between tutors and students; that is, a shared understanding of what it means, for instance, to 'stick to the question' and avoid irrelevancies, 'marshal evidence', 'adopt a critical attitude to one's sources' or 'sustain an argument'.[12] The meaning of such terms is neither self evident nor subject free, but anchored to a given discipline at a specific level of academic study.

In part, too, such conceptions may thrive because the nature of academic discourse in history, as in other disciplines, has often been rooted in what Polanyi has called a 'tacit form of knowing'.[13] To the academic historian, the contours of good historical writing, and the norms and conventions on which it rests, are likely to be familiar, readily recognisable and implicitly understood. They are, however, hard to make explicit and thus are more easily invoked than straight-forwardly explained. The difficulties were strikingly evident in *First-Class Answers in History*, a series of reflections in the mid 1970s on the characteristics of outstanding essay answers in final examinations.[14] What was the aspiring history undergraduate, avid for enlightenment, to make of its editor's denial that there was any 'hidden mystery' about excellence in history writing, when seen alongside his equally pungent claim that the grounds for deeming an answer to be of alpha standard sprang from the experience and discrimination which examiners brought to their marking and could not be precisely articulated? Two-and-a-half decades on, university teachers of history seem much better equipped to guide their students, for there have been growing efforts in recent years to seek out practicable ways of helping students to master the conventions and challenges of communicating within the discipline. Among the variety of initiatives which have been pursued, four in particular stand out: greater explicitness about expectations of essay work; efforts to draw students into the assessment process; greater attention both to essay-writing skills and to an understanding of the fundamentals of historical study and enquiry; and the introduction of a much wider range of written and non-written forms of assessment tasks.

Clarifying expectations

One of the most fascinating developments in higher education over the last decade has been efforts to articulate much more clearly the criteria upon which students' work is to be assessed. Examples of these efforts are not confined to history, but can be found across a spectrum of disciplines and subject areas,[15] and seem to have been impelled by a range of interrelated considerations: concerns to ensure fairness and equity of treatment; a desire for greater openness about assessment processes and the judgements which arise from them; and attempts to achieve greater consistency across markers and across courses.

In its most basic form, achieving greater clarity about expectations usually involves drawing up a list of the criteria to be adopted in marking a given assignment, test or examination answer (which, in turn, hinges on securing consensus among course colleagues about what constitutes work of a given standard) and communicating these to students in written form – typically, via a course handbook – and through the medium of tutorial discussion. However, given the importance, as we have seen, of helping students to grasp the fundamentals of academic discourse, many such initiatives have not simply listed criteria but have also clustered or ranked them to indicate their relative weighting (thus signalling, for example, the extent to which the marks awarded are influenced by features

Figure 14.1: Essay assessment form

Name: Mark   %
Subject:

Marking Scale		Honours	*The letters below are not the direct basis*
70+	Excellent	I	*of your overall grade, but indicate your*
60–69	Very Good	II.1	*main strengths and weaknesses. A and B*
50–59	Satisfactory	II.2	*are good, C is satisfactory, but could be*
40–49	Marginal Pass	III	*improved. D and E indicate serious*
0–48	Fail	Fail	*weaknesses which you should work to*
			rectify

Knowledge — adequate reading – covers the subject with no serious omissions – concentrates on significant and relevant points   A B C D E

Analysis — answers questions asked directly and fully – grasp of historical issues and of period – understands arguments and interpretations of different historians – able to evaluate evidence and make a reasoned choice between arguments – takes objections and alternative views into account – able to handle concepts and abstract ideas   A B C D E

Structure — based on coherent essay plan – right balance of narrative and analysis – arguments in clear order and effectively linked – no irrelevance or repetition – arguments well supported by use of evidence, statistics, etc.   A B C D E

Presentation — clear English style – no major faults of grammar, etc. – structure of essay clearly indicated through use of paragraphs – effective introduction and conclusion – accurate use of references and footnotes – use of tables, maps or graphs where relevant – correct length   A B C D E

Some specific points on presentation which may need attention:
❐ Introduction   ❐ Conclusion   ❐ Use of paragraphs
❐ Grammar and sentence construction   ❐ Punctuation   ❐ Spelling
                                                        ❐ Length

such as style, grammatical accuracy or a command of bibliographic conventions relative to argument or the use and interpretation of evidence). Figure 14.1, which is taken from a course in European History at the University of Edinburgh, provides one example of the clustering of assessment criteria, but also illustrates how criteria can be integrated into an 'assignment attachment' or marking pro forma which is returned to students along with their marked essays, and therefore makes much more overt the extent to which any given essay has succeeded in meeting the criteria set.[16] The regular use of a pro forma of this kind also makes it feasible for a tutor or a course team to track, across a series of essays, those criteria which students have had most difficulty in fulfilling, and to take remedial action where appropriate.

Involving students in assessment

A further and more radical step in communicating expectations is to seek ways of more actively drawing students into the processes of reflecting on and applying assessment criteria, and thus enhancing the likelihood that they will internalise these and 'make them their own'. Student involvement in assessment is fast becoming a widespread and relatively commonplace practice. In a recent survey of Scottish higher education institutions, it featured in nearly one in four of the 310 assessment initiatives recorded.[17] However, it seldom entails students being asked to take on the full mantle of tutor-as-assessor. Generally speaking, it takes one or more of the following forms:

- encouraging students to comment in a relatively open-ended way on the quality of their own work or that of other students;
- involving students in dialogue and consultation about the criteria which are to be applied in evaluating and grading a particular assignment;
- inviting students to evaluate the quality of their own work, or that of other students, in relation to a set of predetermined criteria (but without proposing an overall grade or mark).[18]

In an American History course at Edinburgh University, for example, students have been encouraged to develop their capacity to appraise the quality of their written work by submitting, alongside a completed essay, informal evaluative comments on its chief strengths and weaknesses.[19] And in the European History course at Edinburgh from which Figure 14.1 is taken, the essay assessment form serves as a foundation for self assessment. In the second term of the course, the students are asked to evaluate their achievement in relation to the four ideal attributes of an essay set out in the pro forma (knowledge, analysis, structure and presentation), and to comment on how they have sought to address shortcomings pinpointed in previously marked essays.[20]

Enhancing writing skills and study strategies

A different but complementary approach is to strengthen the guidance given to students on the purposes and processes of essay writing in history. Happily, contemporary published guides on essay writing and other study skills have for the most part shrugged off a former preoccupation with idealised techniques and decontextualised advice,[21] and a number of handbooks are beginning to emerge which are concerned with the particular requirements and challenges of history as a discipline.[22] Yet worthwhile though it can be to direct struggling students to reliable written sources of advice, it is increasingly being argued that how to study and master a discipline, and how to communicate within it via essays and other media, should be an integral part of any undergraduate degree programme, and various examples can be found of initiatives in history courses which pursue this goal quite overtly. One such example is a series of writing workshops in Scottish history which aim not only to improve students' current writing skills but also to advise them on how to develop these skills independently, in ways that will match the increasing sophistication of the material they encounter throughout their academic careers as well as in their subsequent professional lives.[23] A compulsory first-year course at the University of Nottingham, Learning History, is concerned with fostering a range of learning skills (of which essay writing is only one) through a critical engagement with the nature of the subject that seeks to confront students with notions of truth and evidence and to challenge some of the preconceptions which they may have developed in their A-level studies.[24] And at Lancaster University, community-based projects help students to acquire a more reflective (first-hand) appreciation of the processes of historical research and scholarship, and their limitations:

> Through amassing and analysing their own primary material, students can become more aware of the structure, purposes, uses and limitations of data, and more conscious of the reliability and consistency of categories of information and of the nature of bias. But they are then also given an opportunity to formulate their own hypotheses and to question the assumptions which lie behind generalisations put forward in published works.[25]

Diversification in coursework assignments

Many of the history initiatives already described also exemplify a sea-change in coursework assignments which was also strikingly evident in the Scottish survey,[26] where almost three out of every four changes in assessment practices in higher education represented a shift away from reliance on the conventional stereotypes of essays (in the humanities and social sciences), laboratory and practical reports (in the natural sciences and engineering), and honours projects or final-year dissertations. One direction being pursued entails engagement not only with a much wider range of types of written work but also with oral and 'mixed mode' forms of presentation. Recent examples from undergraduate courses in history include: seminar presentations (Bath, Glasgow, Nottingham); reports by students on a placement, for example to a museum, conservation centre or company-records office (Aberdeen, Manchester); disk-based catalogues of historical records and archive collections, historical articles for company in-house journals, reports on placements, library displays and catalogues, and a biographical database on local philanthropists (Manchester); historical resource-packs for use in local schools (Lancaster, Manchester); and exhibitions, museum pamphlets and an audiotape and Braille guide to a working mill museum (Lancaster).[27] A second direction marks an equally significant break with the convention of the lone scholar and towards assignments undertaken by groups or teams of history students: for instance, contributions to a debate (Glasgow, Nottingham); collaborative and group oral presentations (Bath, Nottingham); group videos (Lancaster, Manchester); and group projects in which students prepare and produce an illustrated guidebook to a historical site on the Anglo-Scottish border (Lancaster).[28]

As I have argued elsewhere,[29] diversification on this scale represents much more than a readiness to break with convention, for it can help to enlarge students' communicative competence in constructive and challenging ways. Collaborative and group assignments stretch students' experiences of authorship, opening up opportunities for them to become much more familiar with the communicative strategies and styles of their peers and to learn how to review and revise what one has to say to accommodate and respond to their thoughts, ideas and observations. Similarly, rather than having narrowly to address their work to the 'tutor-as-examiner',[30] students are increasingly being encouraged to contend with the backgrounds, perspectives and needs of a wider constituency which may include, for instance, museum curators and archivists, visitors to historical sites and exhibitions, local community representatives, and pupils and their teachers in local schools. At the same time, developing a grasp of the requirements and conventions of a variety of types and modes of communication can help to nurture a keener eye for fundamentals – structuring, sequencing, pacing, clarity and economy of expression. And finally, pursuing possibilities such as these has been boosted by the advent of the personal computer and word processing, which liberates students from the drudgery of copying and re-copying by hand, and makes what they produce almost infinitely malleable: easier to amend, to adapt or to recast in a different form.

Means and ends

None of these developments need be seen as sounding the death-knell of the history essay. Indeed, one might reasonably contend that a much greater threat to its continued existence has lain in the habit of using it too often and too indiscriminately, with the consequence that the underlying purposes of essay writing have risked becoming obscured. Yet, as this chapter has sought to demonstrate, a fuller understanding of the nature of undergraduate essay writing is beginning to emerge alongside an imaginative array of teaching–learning initiatives, some of which aim to deploy the essay more effectively, while others venture far beyond the conventional boundaries of the coursework assignment. Developments on both fronts, I would suggest, prompt reconsideration of ends as well as means. The true measure of the essay, as of any other assignment or assessment, rests on its capacity to help students grasp the exacting demands of analytical and critical thought in history and to learn how to convey the fruits of their thinking in a clear, cogent and scholarly fashion. To the degree that these ends are achieved, long may the essay – and its successors – flourish.

Notes

1 D. Nimmo, 'The undergraduate essay: a case of neglect?', *Studies in Higher Education*, 2:2 (1977), 183–9.
2 D. Hounsell and R. Murray, *Essay Writing for Active Learning* (Sheffield, CVCP Universities' Staff Development and Training Unit, 1992).
3 D. Hounsell, 'Learning and essay-writing', in F. Marton *et al.* (eds), *The Experience of Learning* (Edinburgh, Scottish Academic Press, 1984), pp. 103–23; subsequently republished in a revised form under the new title 'Contrasting conceptions of essay-writing' in the second edition of *The Experience of Learning* (Edinburgh, Scottish Academic Press, 1997), pp. 106–25. See also D. Hounsell, 'Towards an anatomy of academic discourse: meaning and context in the undergraduate essay', in R. Saljo (ed.), *The Written World: Studies in Literate Thought and Action* (Berlin, Springer-Verlag, 1988), pp. 161–77.
4 D. Hounsell, 'Essay planning and essay-writing', *Higher Education Research and Development*, 3:1 (1984), 13–31.
5 Taking only the fourteen students who could be ascribed without qualification to one of the three conceptions, four of the five students with an arrangement conception had marks below 60 per cent, while all four students ascribed to the viewpoint conception had marks in the range 60–64 per cent. Only two students had marks of 65 per cent or more, and both held the argument conception.
6 See, for example, F. Marton, D. Hounsell and N. Entwistle (eds), *The Experience of Learning: Implications for Teaching and Studying in Higher Education*, 2nd rev. edn (Edinburgh, Scottish Academic Press, 1997); R. R. Schmeck (ed.), *Learning Strategies and Learning Styles* (New York, Plenum, 1988); N. Entwistle, *The Impact of Teaching on Learning Outcomes in Higher Education: A Literature Review* (Sheffield, CVCP Universities' Staff Development Unit, 1992).
7 M. Prosser and C. Webb, 'Relating the process of undergraduate essay-writing to the finished product', *Studies in Higher Education*, 19:2 (1994), 125–38.
8 J. Biggs, 'Approaches to learning and to essay-writing', in Schmeck (ed.), *Learning Strategies*, pp. 185–228.
9 G. Taylor and P. Nightingale, 'Not mechanics but meaning: error in tertiary students' writing', *Higher Education Research and Development*, 9:2 (1990), 161–75.
10 L. Norton, 'Essay-writing: what really counts?', *Higher Education*, 20:4 (1990), 411–42.
11 M. Prosser and C. Webb, 'Relating the process', p. 137.
12 D. Hounsell, 'Essay-writing and the quality of feedback', in J. T. E. Richardson *et al.* (eds), *Student Learning: Research in Education and Cognitive Psychology* (Milton Keynes: SRHE and Open University Press, 1987), pp. 109–19.
13 M. Polanyi, *The Tacit Dimension* (London, Routledge, 1967).
14 R. Bennett (ed.), *First-Class Answers in History* (London, Weidenfeld & Nicolson, 1974).
15 See, for example, G. Brown, J. Bull and M. Pendlebury, *Assessing Student Learning in Higher Education* (London, Routledge, 1997).
16 I am very grateful to Professor Robert Anderson of the Department of History, University of Edinburgh, for permission to reproduce this figure.
17 D. Hounsell, M. McCulloch and M. Scott, *The ASSHE Inventory: Changing Assessment Practices in Scottish Higher Education* (Edinburgh and Sheffield,

University of Edinburgh, Napier University, Edinburgh, and UCoSDA, 1996).

18 D. Hounsell, 'Learning, assignments and assessment', in C. Rust (ed.), *Improving Students as Learners*. Proceedings of the Fifth International Symposium on Improving Student Learning, University of Strathclyde, 8–10 September 1997 (Oxford, Oxford Centre for Staff and Learning Development, 1998), pp. 520–33.

19 'Student self-assessment as an aid to marking assignments' (A. Day, University of Edinburgh), in Hounsell *et al.* (eds), *The ASSHE Inventory*, p. 88.

20 'Structured feedback with limited self-assessment' (R.D. Anderson, University of Edinburgh), in Hounsell *et al.* (eds), *The ASSHE Inventory*, p. 90.

21 D. Hounsell, 'Learning to learn: research and development in student learning', *Higher Education*, 8:4 (1979), 453–69.

22 See, for example, M. Abbott (ed.), *History Skills: A Student Handbook* (London, Routledge, 1996); J. Black and D. M. MacRaild, *Studying History* (London, Macmillan, 1997); G. Pleuger, *Undergraduate History Study: The Guide to Success* (Bedford, Sempringham, 1997).

23 'Writing workshops in Scottish history' (R. Grant, University of Edinburgh), in Hounsell *et al.* (eds), *The ASSHE Inventory*, p. 66.

24 'A skills development course in history, using resource-based learning' (A. Booth, University of Nottingham), in J. Wisdom and G. Gibbs (eds), *Course Design for Resource-Based Learning: Humanities* (Oxford, Oxford Centre for Staff Development, 1994), pp. 52–4. For an outline of similar courses at other universities, see the newsletter *History 2000*, issue 2 (January 1997), pp. 3–4.

25 M. Winstanley, 'Group work in the humanities: history in the community, a case study', *Studies in Higher Education*, 17:1 (1992), 55–65.

26 Hounsell *et al.* (eds), *The ASSHE Inventory*.

27 The examples noted here and in the remainder of the paragraph are taken from the following sources: 'A skills development course in history, using resource-based learning' (A. Booth, University of Nottingham) and 'A divisional initiative to move all courses to resource-based learning' (P. Hyland, Bath Spa University College), which are to be found on pp. 42–5 and 52–4 of J. Wisdom and G. Gibbs, *Course Design*; 'A shift to continuous assessment of student-led seminars' (M. Moss, University of Glasgow) and 'An accredited museums and galleries training scheme' (J. Morrison, University of Aberdeen), which appear on pp. 40 and 131 of Hounsell *et al.* (eds), *The ASSHE Inventory*; D. Nicholls, 'Making history students enterprising: "independent study" at Manchester Polytechnic', *Studies in Higher Education*, 17:1 (1992), 67–80; Winstanley, 'Group work in the humanities'.

28 For further examples, see *History 2000*, issue 2 (January 1997), 4–5.

29 Hounsell, 'Learning, assignments and assessment'.

30 For a discussion of the problems of nurturing a sense of audience when pupils or students have to address their written work almost exclusively to the teacher-as-examiner, see J. Britton *et al.*, *The Development of Writing Abilities*, 11–18 (London, Macmillan, 1975); Hounsell and Murray, *Essay Writing*, ch. 2, pp. 5–13.

15   Susan Doran, Christopher Durston, Anthony Fletcher and Jane Longmore

Assessing students in seminars: an evaluation of current practice

Seminar assessment is increasingly a feature of the teaching of history within higher education. Although only approximately 15 per cent of departments in Britain are using this form of assessment, its usage is far higher than a decade ago and is increasing all the time.[1] This growing interest is due to many factors, including the requirement for more explicit skills development, the desire to improve student learning in seminars, the impact of a Teaching Quality Assessment (TQA) visit and the influence of the educational literature.[2] There is a need for more information on current usage as well as for guidelines on good practice.

This chapter is based upon a first-hand review of the practices of history departments in the UK undertaking this form of assessment. The sample is also representative of the full range of institutions within the UK system, being made up of nine 'old' (pre-1992) universities, five 'new' (post-1992) universities and four colleges of higher education. While one department visited had introduced oral assessment of seminars as early as the mid 1980s, all the others had done so since 1990, the majority during the early 1990s. A significant minority of departments visited were in the very early stages of this form of assessment, in that they had operated it for only one or two years, or at the time of the visit were only just introducing pilot schemes.

Varieties of current practice

Three main types of seminar assessment were in operation within the departments visited: assessment of oral presentations by individuals or groups; assessment of student-managed seminars; and assessment of general oral contribution to all the seminars of a course. In addition, some departments combined elements of the above by, for example, assessing students partly on their presentation to, and/or management of, one particular seminar, and partly on their more general contribution. This diversity seems to reflect *ad hoc* experimentation by individuals and departments within both their institutional context and curricular and pedagogic needs and experience.

Individual oral presentations frequently take the form of prepared papers which normally last for around ten minutes. Reading from a prepared text is generally discouraged in favour of elaboration based on written notes, but instances of reading from texts were observed. On some courses students are expected to use, and are marked on their use of, hand-outs and audio-visual aids. Presentations are usually given to student groups (of up to c. 20), but in a small minority of cases they are made only to the tutor or tutors. Assessment of group presentations is also common. In these cases, two or three students divide up a presentation on a particular topic and are given a group mark for their combined efforts. In one institution a number of timetabled seminar periods are given over to student preparation for more elaborate group presentations which occur later in the course and can last for up to thirty minutes. Here the presentations were delivered to one or more tutors and not the student peer-group. In a small number of departments, groups of two or three students are given full responsibility for running the whole of a seminar. In some cases they give a presentation and organise the discussion afterwards. In others they virtually assume the role of the tutor, by organising student preparation and allocating specific reading and other tasks beforehand, and by employing a variety of teaching methods, including primary-source analysis and role play, in the seminar itself. Here the tutor's role is to provide guidance and support for the student team, to draw out the salient points of the discussion, and to de-brief the students on their management of the session.

In a minority of departments students are marked on their overall contribution to all the seminars of a course. Contribution is taken to mean participation not only in whole-group discussion, but also in small sub-groups, and students are informed that quality of contribution is at least as important as quantity. In some cases, listening skills are also included as part of the assessment criteria. Some departments combine elements of the above methods, by assessing students partly on their presentation to, and management of, one particular seminar, and partly on their more general contribution to the seminar programme as a whole.

There is a wide spectrum of current practice in the area of assessment of oral contribution to seminars with regard to the percentage of modules and courses using seminar assessment, and the extent to which seminar assessment is voluntary or obligatory for students. Within some departments only a very small percentage of courses contain this form of assessment and only one or two staff operate it. At the other extreme, oral assessment is part of all, or the great majority of, the courses in several departments. In the former departments, only those staff and students who specifically wish to opt for this form of assessment need be involved in it, while those who are sceptical, unconvinced or hostile can easily avoid it. In the latter, both staff and students are obliged to participate; in some of these departments there appears to be a tendency for the more unconvinced tutors to operate it grudgingly and half-heartedly. Between these polarities, there are a significant number of departments where oral assessment is voluntary but practised by a significant group of committed tutors. Such departments offer students substantial numbers of orally assessed and non-orally assessed courses, while often allowing students to avoid any of the former.

Some departments operate oral assessment only at level one (first year), believing that it helps students to adapt to the higher education environment, while having no effect upon honours classification. Others include it at levels two and three, but deliberately exclude it from level one, believing that new and inexperienced students would struggle to cope with it. One institution operates it at level two but not three, on the grounds that by the end of year two it has achieved its goal of improving seminar quality. Several departments believe it to be an inappropriate form of assessment for Special Subject and dissertation work. In Scotland, one of the two institutions visited restricted it primarily to honours level (years three and four), while the other used it more widely across all four years.

Oral work is generally given a lower level of weighting than both written coursework and examinations, the average weighting being 10–15 per cent of the marks available for a course. In one department, however, it is weighted as low as 5 per cent, and in another as high as 40 per cent. However, given that in most departments oral assessment does not apply to all levels or all courses within levels, its overall weighting in terms of establishing degree classification is very low – rarely higher than 5 per cent.

Procedures for defining assessment criteria and for informing students of such criteria appear to be uncommon. The assessment of oral work is often regarded as an essentially impressionistic activity, with no formal grade-related criteria agreed for use by staff and/or students. Students in these departments are either given some informal verbal guidance by tutors or simply left unsure as to the basis on which they are being assessed. A sizeable minority of departments, however, provide their students with published grade-related criteria. Again, while some departments give their students little or no information about their results, or only informal verbal feedback, a minority have devised a standard feedback form, and some use this to discuss grades with students in individual de-briefing sessions. Several departments include an attendance element in their assessment criteria. This is done either by awarding a separate mark for attendance, or by establishing an attendance threshold and penalising students who do not meet it.

In most of the models of seminar assessment under scrutiny, both content and delivery are assessed, but usually without any formal mechanism for establishing the relative weighting of these two elements. Some assessors weight delivery more heavily, while others favour content over delivery on the grounds that they feel they are more competent to judge its quality. In a few cases students are encouraged in a preliminary seminar to decide the weighting of the assessment criteria for their individual assessments. Criteria taken into account with regard to delivery include audibility, speed, eye contact, use of audio-visual aids and ability to hold the attention of, and to interact with, the audience. Where students work in groups, a shared group-mark is often given. Some assessors, however, do give individual marks, and in one department the assessor awards a group mark, multiplies this by the number in the group, and re-allocates the total on an individual basis. Several departments have felt it necessary to introduce informal mechanisms whereby students can inform tutors if one or more members of the team have failed to pull their weight.

The responsibility for assessment is undertaken by the tutor in most departments. This may be either on his or her own or in conjunction with colleagues. In addition, there are plenty of examples of peer assessment of oral work, although a number of these schemes have been abandoned because of their unpopularity with students. Some of the tutors who continue to operate peer assessment systems find it necessary to moderate the results and to discount what they regard as obviously rogue marks. Self assessment is seen by some tutors as a useful contributory means of demonstrating to students the fairness and accuracy of the other elements of the assessment. Some tutors also find it helpful as part of the students' learning process to ask them to keep a seminar diary in which they make judgements about their individual levels of contribution. A few departments combine tutor, peer and self assessments to arrive at a composite overall mark for oral contribution.

Many tutors acknowledge the moderation of oral work to be a problematic issue. Some have encountered demands from institutional committees for the audio- or video-taping of seminars when they have first proposed its introduction, but there is evidence of only one – apparently not very successful – attempt to comply with these instructions. One department feels that its institution's regulations on moderation will make it impossible for it to assess general contribution to seminars as opposed to student presentations. While a few departments appear to have adopted the ostrich approach to the moderation problem by simply ignoring it, most are attempting to address it via various methods. Some are carrying out joint assessments of presentations with a colleague at the end of a course. In some institutions this is simply not practicable because it proves far too time consuming. A number of others are attempting to alleviate the problem by relying on the careful logging of the written material used by the student presenters (preparation notes, etc.) and/or by keeping their own full notes on each seminar. This material is then made available to external examiners. Externals have also been invited to attend seminars where oral work is being assessed, and in one department external examiners regularly attend at the point at which the assessments are made.

Where tutor, peer and self assessment are used in combination, this is also seen as a useful further means of moderating marks. Those departments in which a large amount of oral assessment occurs are able to moderate marks by comparing results across courses. However, most departments feel that the seriousness of the moderation problem is reduced by the low percentage of marks available for oral work. Many tutors are of the opinion that the benefits which stem from the assessment of oral work outweigh the undoubted difficulties over moderation.

Issues in seminar assessment

Just as there is diversity of practice, so there is a diversity of views about seminar assessment. Enthusiasts raise the following in support: employability; motivation; attendance; alignment of course objectives, teaching methods and assessment; whole-person education; diversity; depth of learning; and relationships among and with students. In all departments, a concern for the development of transferable skills is a major reason given for the introduction of some form of seminar assessment. Almost everywhere, tutors express a sense of responsibility for making students more employable by helping them to develop good oral communication and presentational skills. They believe that assessment patterns have an important role to play in this, as assessment signals clearly to students the skills, knowledge and understanding which a department considers important.

Most students appreciate learning transferable skills which will help them in the job market. Although shy students certainly find the experience of leading a seminar or giving a presentation 'traumatic', most recognise the value of seminars which focus on and assess their communication and presentational skills, and agree that it helps them to build up confidence over time. Some remark that it is better to learn to speak publicly among friends in a university seminar than in the more hostile or threatening environment of the workplace. However, only a small minority of students admit to selecting their courses on the basis of the form of assessment. For most, the topic and tutor are higher priorities in influencing their choice. Students are divided over whether or not they would also benefit from a level one study-skills module which includes guidance and training on giving presentations and managing seminars. As might be expected, it is the most confident and articulate students who do not feel in need of any explicit focus on oral communication skills. Although some tutors believe that self-assessment diaries or logs teach students to become more reflective learners, the students themselves are more sceptical. Many do not take them seriously and some confess to filling them in only at the end of the course.

In contrast, the introduction of seminar assessment appears to have had a positive effect on student motivation. For example, seminar assessment has usually brought about a marked improvement in student attendance in those departments where it has previously been something of a problem. Attendance has shown the greatest improvement in courses where a student's attendance record is built into the final mark. Students state that they work much harder for presentations which are assessed than for those that are not. They explain that, given all the pressures on their time, they have no choice but to be assessment driven in their work priorities. As a result of this increased attendance and preparation, the quality of seminars has improved. One head of department refers to the 'marvellous impact' on courses, as students now think more carefully about how to communicate material and are producing more imaginative presentations and more elaborate handouts. For their part, many students believe that the content of presentations is better in assessed seminars, as presenters have read in greater depth and have more ideas and information to impart. It is generally agreed by both tutors and students that far more work goes into presentations than the available marks actually warrant. The reason for this seems to be primarily that students want to avoid the 'public humiliation' of a poor performance in an activity which is thought important enough to be part of the assessment package. It may also be because many students have not worked out the actual percentage of the total degree mark that each presentation comprises. In those courses where the general participation of each student in every seminar is assessed, students are working more consistently; indeed, many complain about having to work too hard.

Many tutors have also been prompted to try out oral assessment as a response to a sense of dissatisfaction with the general quality of seminars, in the hope that assessment will encourage students to take seminars more seriously and put more effort into them. A significant number of tutors have found that levels of attendance at non-assessed seminars are unsatisfactory, and that the preparation and participation of those students who do attend is frequently inadequate. Some have also received complaints from their more committed students about 'freebooters' within seminars, and have been told by these keener students that they have become reluctant to share the product of their work with their less diligent peers. In several departments, the students have suggested some form of seminar assessment as a way of remedying this problem.

A few departments have been encouraged in this thinking by TQA teams, which have pointed out that they are highlighting course objectives such as oral communication skills, which they are not in fact assessing in any way. In addition, TQA teams have suggested to a few departments that they are using over-narrow and traditional assessment patterns – examinations and written coursework exclusively – and thus neglecting any evaluation of the 'whole person'. This criticism has led these departments to consider introducing more experimental methods, including oral assessment. In several cases, groups of students have complained that there is too much written assessment and have requested through staff/student committees that their seminar work be taken into account. In some other institutions, tutors themselves have independently come to the conclusion that assessment needs to be more varied so that it can reward the development of qualities which are valuable to employers but which may not be encouraged by the assessment of written work alone. A greater diversification of assessment methods is generally thought by its supporters to be fairer to students. In one institution, for example, seminar assessment has been introduced specifically to help those students who are keen and have a good understanding of history but who struggle to express their ideas on paper. The majority of students find assessed seminars more useful than unassessed ones, as the standard of presentations and quality of participation are usually higher. They do feel aggrieved when a student produces a weak presentation but at least they have the satisfaction of knowing that he/she will be penalised for it.

There is very often wider participation in those seminars where a group of students are assessed on their ability to manage the whole session and have assigned tasks to their peers. Equally, students participate more actively in those seminars where their own individual contribution to the general discussion is assessed. In both these kinds of assessed class, student solidarity as well as self interest ensure that the whole seminar group carries out preparation for each topic and becomes involved in discussion. Most students find these seminars more lively and interesting. On the other hand, when the presenters are being marked on the basis of their talk and handouts only, the audience of students tends to be passive. Students explain that they have less incentive to read for seminars in which they are not personally giving a presentation. Because of this, they also have less understanding of many subject areas. Many students, therefore, think they would learn more if they were given a mark for their general contribution to seminars as well as for their own presentation.

Some students feel that they are suffering from 'presentation overload', and express a weariness with listening to their peers' mini-lectures in seminar after seminar. In some cases, presenting or attending these mini-lectures is the only or primary learning activity experienced in a course. This is particularly true for seminars which have more than fifteen people in them, or where students are expected to do more than one presentation. It can also occur towards the end of a course if student presentations are re-scheduled as a result of earlier absence through illness. 'Presentation overload' often results in student passivity and boredom. Many students express a strong desire for a more diverse teaching and learning experience. In addition, some students feel that they are expected to give too many presentations, and complain that they have to prepare them for every course they are following in a term or semester. Students also want to know the explicit criteria by which their presentations and oral contributions will be assessed, as this will show them what is considered to be important and help them in their learning. In addition, all students feel that they would benefit from detailed and rapid feedback on their performance. They want private feedback in the form of either a written or oral report from their tutor as soon as possible after their presentations. Without such feedback, they argue, it is difficult for them to improve their oral communication skills by learning what they need to work on.

It is widely felt that seminar assessment is leading towards more student-centred learning. In many cases, student presenters/leaders are responsible for producing material for discussion to their peers, managing discussion and fielding questions. Some students have gained sufficient confidence in their independent learning to feel able to challenge the tutor on something approaching equal terms. In some seminars, tutors are behaving as simply another member of the group until the closing part of the session, when they lead a de-briefing or summary. As one tutor explains, in such cases seminar assessment is leading to the 'dethroning' of the course tutor. On the other hand, seminar observations reveal that this shift away from a tutor-dominated session can only take place when seminar assessment is fully integrated into the teaching experience. If only five or ten minutes of a seminar are turned over to a student presentation, there is a temptation for the tutor to resume control and conduct a mini-lecture for the remainder of the session. In several institutions, some tutors explain that they now think of seminars in a different way. No longer do they use them for transmitting information and covering the material. Instead, the detailed content of a course is left to handouts and lectures, while in seminars the process of student active learning is more important. Some tutors argue that this is leading to deeper levels of understanding. In addition, they are aware of acting as role models for student presenters and so pay more attention to the use of handouts, overheads and slides in their own lectures.

Very few tutors believe that seminar assessment has had a detrimental effect on relationships among students. On the contrary, most feel that students try to help presenters/leaders of seminars by participating more energetically in the discussion. There is often a more collaborative feel to a group, and students try to integrate shy or difficult members into the group. Students tend to bear out this impression and many spoke of a 'bonding experience' within the assessed seminar group. On the other hand, a few tutors are aware of some measure of competitiveness among students, but this is thought to be constructive since it leads them to put more effort into their presentations.

Students and tutors both consider that there is a greater onus on the course tutor to manage the group so that the more confident are prevented from dominating the session and all are given an opportunity to display their knowledge and understanding and to try out their ideas. At the same time, tutors have a responsibility to make the teaching environment safe, in order to encourage participation and risk taking. As one student comments, for seminars to work, tutors need to treat students with respect and not as inferiors. Tutors and students believe that this form of assessment helps tutors to know their students better. As one student explains, at the very least tutors are forced to learn their students' names. In many institutions, tutors find they have more individual contact with students, since they come to them for guidance before a presentation and for feedback afterwards. No students or tutors believe that seminar assessment has distanced students from their tutor. On the contrary, in seminars where students give presentations and manage the teaching session, tutors participate as equal members of the group or are friendly observers. Tutors are also seen as a support and resource for students, rather than treated as judges or gurus.

A number of tutors express worries about their personal competence to assess oral performance, believing that they lack the necessary experience and expertise in this field to make judgements in which they and their students can have confidence. Some express doubts about the advisability of oral assessment, questioning whether it is really their role to teach or assess 'social skills'. Other tutors comment that assessing oral work could lead to the 'commodification', management and professionalisation of education, and could hold dangers for intellectual 'free spirits'. They are far from convinced that it is the job of a history tutor to inculcate transferable skills. The more sceptical tutors focus on the problems of student risk taking, students dominating the seminar, equal opportunities, personality not knowledge, marking objectivity, impact on degree classifications, monitoring legal challenges and freeloaders. Some objectors believe that oral assessment can have an adverse effect on the learning environment. They fear that some students might be unwilling to take academic risks for fear of losing marks, while others might try to dominate seminars in an attempt to accumulate them. In one or two departments a concern has been expressed that it might lead to the domination of seminars by one form of teaching and learning activity; in particular an over-reliance on student presentations.

Another major concern relates to the question of equal opportunities: students with disabilities, such as a severe stammer or deafness, might, it is claimed, be disadvantaged; cultural factors might also intrude to the disadvantage of ethnic minority students; women might lack the confidence to assert themselves in seminars; and shy students will be penalised for an innate personality trait. Connected to this is the danger expressed by one or two tutors that a student will be marked on her/his personality rather than on a piece of intellectual work. Some of those with reservations express concern about the objectivity and comparability of marking. Students are not anonymous (as is now frequently the case with written papers) and likes and dislikes might affect the grade. They are also concerned that there could be no double marking or effective moderation of an individual's oral work, without excessive expenditure of staff time. Departments disagree over whether or not seminar assessment marks affect the final degree classification of a student. In some institutions the perception is that students achieve a slightly higher seminar mark than the overall module mark, leading to a slightly increased number of 2.1s in coursework. Others argue that seminar marks are broadly in line with written coursework marks, but that in a group of fifteen students there is a mismatch in around three cases. Most are satisfied that the introduction of seminar assessment has not led to grade inflation. Finally, some tutors are conscious of the possibility of students mounting legal challenges, and that there will be insufficient objective evidence of their performance if seminars are not audio- or video-taped.

The student view is, on the whole, very positive. They do, however, raise a number of important points. While most students express trust in their tutors' objectivity in marking their oral contribution, a few refer to worries about consistency in marking. Particular concern is caused when different tutors seem to follow different criteria. Some students suspect that tutors are harsher on presentations which come earlier in the course than on those given later. This anxiety is far more evident when the grade-related criteria are not made explicit to students or when tutors themselves are unclear about them. Few students note concerns about the issue of moderation, often because up to this point they have not given it any thought. When the issue is raised with them, some begin to see the difficulties of using unmoderated marks.

There seems to be little doubt that the use of explicit criteria limits the degree of subjectivity and impressionism in marking. Tutors are trying to overcome the problem of a lack of moderation by a variety of methods including detailed paperwork, students' self assessment, peer observation schemes and the use of external examiners. All tutors are well aware that some problems remain, but most argue that difficulties of subjectivity and impressionism exist with all forms of assessment and are not confined to oral assessment in seminars.

Many students express deep reservations about peer assessment. They are very uneasy about both marking and being marked by their peers. One particular objection is that students do not feel they possess the detailed subject knowledge necessary to evaluate the depth of preparation, coverage of a topic or accuracy of material. On the other hand, some tutors are enthusiastic about peer assessment and argue that it plays a role in empowering students and teaching them to be critical and reflective in their learning. At a practical level, however, a considerable number of tutors find peer assessment to be an unreliable and unfair marking system. Some marks, they complain, are 'absurd', while many tend to be higher than the tutor's own mark. One tutor argues that students are easily taken in by a slick performance, and others agree that students are more impressed with a confident delivery than careful research and a deep historical understanding. Another tutor points out that peer assessors are anonymous and therefore unaccountable. Some tutors disregard the peer marks which are furthest away from the mean, while others adjust the final grade to bring it more into line with their own assessment.

Many students like and value collaborative work, but some feel disadvantaged by assessed group-work. Those who live off-campus and those with family responsibilities or paid-work commitments note that it is difficult to attend preparatory meetings for group presentations out of normal class-time. Virtually all students argue that they should receive individual marks for a group presentation. A group mark is thought to be unfair and often causes considerable resentment when some members within the group are thought to be 'freebooters' failing to pull their weight. In general terms, students believe that it is fairer to have a diverse assessment package. They feel that seminar assessment gives many mature students the opportunity to compensate for their under-achievement in examinations by gaining marks for their more developed communication, analytical and research skills. Few students think that women are disadvantaged by seminar assessment, although complaints against dominant students are usually directed against men.

Keys to good practice

On the basis of the discussions and observations undertaken by the team the following recommendations and keys to good practice are offered.

Introducing seminar assessment

Before introducing seminar assessment to a department, it is important to discuss the issue fully with those students who are already on their degree course and to explain the rationale for the innovation. Students often feel anger and unease at a change in the rules in the middle of their higher education careers. For this reason it is probably better to introduce any changes into level one and thereafter work them through the system. Innovation at level one also allows teething problems to be ironed out without them affecting the degree classifications of students. The use of pilot schemes which can lead to modification of the assessment system at an early stage is also recommended. There are some clear disadvantages in students having a choice of diverse assessment practices within a single department – one being that they are able to complete their studies without being exposed to assessment methods that might help to develop new and valuable skills. On the other hand, many history tutors are still very suspicious about seminar assessment, and the attempts of some departments to force sceptics and opponents to tow a departmental line seem to have been counterproductive. At least at the outset, therefore, it is probably better to allow those tutors who wish to opt out of a system of seminar assessment to do so.

If seminar assessment is to be introduced, students might well benefit from the inclusion of presentational and oral communication skills sessions in a level one study-skills or 'learning history' module. If tutors want to use seminar assessment primarily to improve attendance, the evidence suggests that it is better to introduce a system of threshold marking, rather than to give a specific mark for attendance. It is also important to take steps to avoid the very real danger of 'presentation overload'.

Finally, oral assessment is easier when student numbers are not too great. With regard to assessment of presentations, the maximum comfortable number is around fourteen.

Types of assessment

Assessment of general contribution to seminars appears to have a greater impact on the quality of the learning experience than assessment of presentations only. Where presentations only are assessed, thought needs to be given to strategies for involving all the students in seminar classes. Our study has shown that peer assessment, used in isolation, is unpopular with students and problematic for tutors. If used, it needs to be openly moderated by the tutor. Probably rightly in many cases, students do not feel themselves competent to judge the content of a presentation. It would thus be more sensible and fairer to restrict their role to assessing communication and presentational skills. Alternatively, peer assessment might be used as an assessment guideline and evaluative aid for the presenter, while the awarding of the final mark is left to the tutor, who may take student views into account.

Criteria and clarity

It is vital that consistent, detailed and explicit criteria for assessment are fully discussed and agreed by the tutors within a department who are to be involved. Students need to be clear about the assessment criteria. Ideally, these should be discussed and formulated in consultation with the students, either in an introductory seminar for the course or within a level one study-skills course. At the very least, students should be asked to agree with the criteria. Grade-related criteria should also be given to students in written form. Tutors need to look very carefully at the balance of their criteria. If too much emphasis is placed on the content of a presentation it is questionable whether oral skills are being assessed at all. On the other hand, if delivery skills are given too much weight there is a danger that historical content and understanding will be overlooked. It is important that students' tasks should be just as well directed and focused for oral presentations as for their written assignments.

Role of tutor and students

Tutors considering the introduction of seminar assessment need to bear in mind that it brings with it a greater responsibility for ensuring that students are able to do themselves justice in seminars. The students and tutors interviewed considered that the course tutor had an important role to play in managing seminar groups in order to prevent a few individuals from dominating discussion and to encourage all to show their knowledge and understanding and to try out their ideas. Students should be encouraged to manage their own seminars. The team found the results of allowing them to do this to be very impressive. In one case, a seminar was observed in which three students beginning level two delivered a seminar of which many tutors would have been justifiably proud. It is clear that students should not be underestimated, for, as this and other observations made clear, despite their own doubts and misgivings, they commonly rise to challenges and gain great satisfaction from their achievements.

Weighting

The percentage of marks devoted to a presentation needs to reflect the amount of work that students are devoting to it. Five to ten per cent of the total module mark seems unfair to students who spend at least as long on a ten-minute presentation as they do on a short essay. Departments should consider achieving an equitable balance between the assessed elements of a course.

Individual and group

When group presentations are required, tutors should attempt to award some element of assessment to the individual. A composite mark for the entire group is probably best avoided, unless it is then shared out among the individuals either by the tutor or by the students themselves.

Resources

It is important that the physical environment suits the mode of teaching and assessment. Good oral presentations are best given in well-equipped rooms of sufficient size. Thought should be given to appropriate seating arrangements. Good discussion cannot, for example, easily take place in a room where students are forced to sit in rows.

Feedback

If oral assessment is to play a significant role in their learning, it is important that students are given meaningful feedback on their performance. Feedback might take the form of marks and comments on standard feedback sheets or be given in timetabled de-briefing sessions held soon after the presentation or student-managed seminar. This necessarily creates a heavier administrative burden for tutors which may be at least partly offset by a reduction in course-work marking.

Staff development

Many departments might benefit from some staff development input, either from institutional teaching and learning units or from external consultants, on how to assess oral skills and manage assessed seminars.

Conclusion

As history departments respond to such challenges as the introduction of 'bench-marking' and 'programme specifications', it seems likely that the emphasis on the acquisition of oral as well as written skills will continue to increase. It is hoped that the findings of this empirically based project will provide some practical help to departments as they both attempt and continue to tackle the complexities of seminar assessment.

Notes

1 History at the Universities Defence Group, *Submission to the National Committee of Inquiry into Higher Education* (Hull, University of Hull, 1997), p. 4.
2 See A. Booth, 'Changing assessment to improve learning', in A. Booth and P. Hyland (eds), *History in Higher Education* (Oxford, Blackwell, 1996), pp. 261–75; P. Hyland,

'Examining action research to improve seminars through assessment', in G. Gibbs (ed.), *Improving Student Learning: Using Research to Improve Student Learning* (Oxford, Oxford Centre for Staff Development, 1996), pp. 207–23; R. Lloyd-Jones and J. Allen, 'Group work, assessment and the journey to graduate employment: a survey of history students at Sheffield Hallam University', *Proceedings of a Humanities and Arts Higher Education Network Conference* (Milton Keynes, Open University, 1997); S. Brown and P. Knight, *Assessing Learners in Higher Education* (London, Kogan Page, 1994); G. Brown, M. Pendlebury and J. Bull, *Assessing Student Learning in Higher Education* (London, Routledge, 1997).

Assessing group work to develop collaborative learning

Group work has long been central to teaching in higher education, with various kinds of seminar occupying a pivotal position in the teaching of history courses. However, in Britain, the arrival of mass higher education and the appearance of a more heterogeneous student body, coupled with broader political and funding changes, have served to challenge traditional approaches to teaching. More students has meant that traditional seminar groups are less easy to justify in resourcing terms, and a more diverse student body, defined in terms of academic experience and qualifications, has required history programmes to address a greater number of individual learning needs.

This chapter discusses the experience of using assessed group work as a way of encouraging collaborative learning. It is based primarily on the experience of course development and teaching at the University of Teesside, where assessed group-work has been used extensively in the delivery of the history undergraduate programme. However, we have also sought to place this experience in a wider context, and have incorporated ideas and opinions from colleagues who employ similar approaches in a variety of British universities.

To contextualise our work, questionnaires were sent to sixty history departments throughout the country, eliciting thirty-eight responses. These data allowed us to establish a provisional overview of two main areas: first, they gave us an insight into the variety of assessed collaborative learning methods currently being used, including assessed seminars and class discussions, assessed written work produced by groups, assessed group-presentations and peer assessment; and second, they provided information on the perceived advantages and problems associated with such work. The questionnaire was followed by a number of semi-structured interviews with staff and second-year students at Teesside, as well as interviews with colleagues in seven other institutions, some with extensive experience of collaborative learning methods, some who are just embarking on their use, and some who remain sceptical of the practice.

The value of collaborative/group-based learning

At the outset, it will be useful to identify the perceived advantages of group work which have been used to advocate its more systematic and widespread application within universities. The following claims have been made:

- Group-work can develop the individual student's critical and analytical skills. It can be used to develop more active and 'deep' approaches to learning, thereby developing greater levels of understanding.
- Communication skills are developed within groups, particularly those involving debate, discussion and the formulation of an argument.
- Personal insights and interpersonal qualities are developed by working with others (e.g. greater sensitivity, self confidence).
- Participation in groups enables students to develop a greater understanding of the dynamics of team working (group roles, group behaviours) (an experience that could be useful in later employment.
- Group-work can also serve a broader social function (developing staff–student relationships, mutual student support and friendships).[1]

Several studies have offered convincing testimony that particular intellectual qualities may be enhanced by discussion and cooperative learning.[2] Such studies have rarely been grounded in the discipline of history, although a recent project at Sheffield Hallam University, *The Assessment of Group Work and Presentations in the Humanities,* is based on the particular experience of history students and offers a pedagogic rationale which is consistent with that of earlier studies: 'Group work provides an opportunity for more variety in the learning process by shifting the focus away from the student as a passive recipient of knowledge and encouraging a more proactive independent approach to learning.'[3] This chapter is not concerned to offer a critical review of the relevant educational literature. Instead, it seeks to gauge the effectiveness of this approach, as perceived by students and tutors within a number of history departments where assessed group-work now forms a significant element in undergraduate teaching and learning programmes.

The main rationale for promoting group-based learning which emerged most strongly from the responses to our questionnaire highlighted the social benefits of such work. Almost 80 per cent of respondents felt that group-work helped to build social networks among students – an important feature in the current academic world. In our own institution, for example, where a significant proportion of students are home based, and where mass higher education and modularisation tend to increase student isolation and militate against a sense of discipline-based identity, there was evidence both from students and staff that group-based learning fostered friendships and social contacts. These networks not only enriched the overall student experience, but also helped to underpin more effective and confident approaches to academic work – a culture that academics from an earlier generation might have called 'collegiality'.

In our survey, tutors pointed to the increase in the size of the student body and its more heterogeneous composition as key factors which challenge traditional patterns of delivery and assessment. In this regard, tutors and university managers often look to group-based learning as a way of managing scarce university resources. However, only one out of seven of our interviewed respondents offered group-work as an 'easy' way of teaching and assessing more students, and questionnaire respondents were split almost equally over this issue; 58 per cent thinking that group-work offers some potential resource gains, and the remaining 42 per cent downplaying this supposed advantage. Our own experience would tend to confirm the latter view. The resource advantages of cutting down on class-contact time are usually offset by greater demands in the preparation and monitoring of group-based activities. Group-work rarely requires extra resources compared with more traditional courses (almost 70 per cent of questionnaire respondents felt this to be the case), but the argument for adopting group-work because it promises to ease pressure on tutors and university managers is not always borne out by experience.

The third main advantage that most respondents associated with group-work is the development of 'transferable skills', still a contentious issue within academic culture, but one which recognises the importance of generic skills – effective communications, time management, team working – which are valued by employers, and which history courses are increasingly being asked to foster. Over 80 per cent of questionnaire respondents saw this as one of the main benefits of group-based learning, and in several interviews tutors identified the promotion of transferable skills as an important reason for introducing such methods. Indeed, there was evidence from one respondent working in the traditional university sector that students themselves called for the use of group-based learning as a skill necessary for future employment. At Teesside, most of the second-year students interviewed, including those who found group-work difficult and sometimes disagreeable, recognised the importance of transferable skills, and saw team-working experience as a potentially valuable feature of undergraduate experience which they could incorporate within their CVs.

Undoubtedly there is a widespread acknowledgement that assessed group-work plays an important role in enhancing the employability of history students, but the recognition often comes reluctantly and with a sense of regret. Behind such uncertainty lies the familiar question: to what extent should any history degree identify and promote employment skills? There are several responses that might be offered, but two are worth stressing. First and most obviously, only a small minority of history graduates pursue their historical studies to postgraduate level and beyond; most approach their undergraduate studies as a sensible route into other areas of work and are concerned to make that transition successfully. If employability matters to students, then it should matter to their tutors. Second and more fundamentally, a false opposition tends to be drawn between core academic work and 'employment-related skills'. Thus group-based work is often represented as a necessary but disagreeable medicine which history students are strongly advised to take, yet group discussion and debate have always occupied a central place in historical practice, where they play an important role in the generation of new ideas and understandings. Presumably, this is why we keep persevering with things such as conferences and seminars. Group work does have advantages in terms of making history students more employable, but its implementation need not drag us into unpalatable academic compromises; it remains, as it always has been, a core defining feature of historical method.

Not all respondents were willing to claim categorically that group working led to gains in historical understanding, pointing to the impossibility of disaggregating the group-work from the broader educational experience. However, exactly half of questionnaire respondents felt that collaborative work did indeed lead to gains in historical understanding. Fifteen per cent saw no gains compared with other teaching and learning methods, and the remainder signalled their unwillingness to decide on this complex issue. Several students talked very positively about a greater sense of ownership and pride in completing group-based projects independently of the tutor, and several tutors were convinced that real gains had been made in historical understanding: 'I can't prove it, but I was struck by the heightened levels of engagement which developed within the group once I began to let them push things along by themselves. The quality of the ideas and thinking improved dramatically.'

The widespread use of seminars represents an enduring commitment to the use of group-work, if not always to its assessment. One assumes that the underlying justification for their use centres on a desire to encourage active, independent and collaborative learning among students, leading to greater levels of historical understanding. Seminars have always provided an important alternative dimension to the more didactic methods associated with lectures and private reading, where the authority of the lecturer and the author can sometimes weigh heavily on the fragile confidence of students. In the relatively open pedagogic spaces offered by seminars, students have an opportunity and responsibility to play more active roles in the learning process. In this sense, most of us have been practising collaborative learning methods for a very long time. Yet almost all of us bemoan the problems associated with such work: the familiar complaints of seminar papers being gabbled through, only to be met with sullen silence from other group members; the predictable nucleus of conscientious students who prepare for classes and contribute to discussions, set against a rump of others who do and say almost nothing. These are familiar horror stories.

There may be several factors which contribute to such problems – the unfortunate chemistry of certain student groups, inappropriate seminar rooms, unhelpful attitudes on the part of some tutors – but two key issues of course design play a crucial role in determining the success or otherwise of group-work. First, it should be introduced into degree programmes in a structured and progressive fashion. Students need to be given a clear rationale for working in groups, as well as being trained in the necessary skills required for such work.

Second, experience suggests that students are more inclined to invest time and effort in work which counts towards a final degree classification than in work which carries no such value, and in this situation it seems sensible to give an assessment weighting to group-work. However, finding effective ways in which to assess collaborative projects has always posed a severe challenge to anyone venturing into this field, and many colleagues have avoided such approaches simply because assessment problems seem so daunting. While we would not want to ignore the seriousness of this issue, it also needs to be emphasised that a range of assessment strategies has been developed and refined in history departments over the last few years which offer practical and successful solutions to most, if not all, of these problems.

Structuring and progressing group work in degree programmes

At Teesside, the history department's first experiment with assessed group-work came with the development of community-based group projects. All second-years were required to take this module, and were organised into groups of between four and seven members. Groups worked towards the preparation of materials for a variety of organisations, including primary and secondary schools, museums and the local media. The main impetus behind this work was twofold: first, money was available from the university's Enterprise in Higher Education fund to develop community-led projects which involved working with external clients; and second, some colleagues believed that such work would save on resources and demonstrate engagement with a broad political agenda which was currently valued both internally and externally. Group projects were there-fore more a response to contingent factors than a carefully planned element in a coherent and progressive curriculum. The result was that students encountered assessed group-work in the second year, when traditional working patterns were already well established, and this 'thing' called History Group Projects was widely perceived as an alien growth on the traditional corpus of lectures, semi-nars and essays.

Our experience of this work and its subsequent fate may serve as a useful exemplar of the perils associated with an unsystematic approach to course design and curriculum change. Even before the project work began, many students were worried by the prospect of working in groups. Partly this was the product of previous negative experiences of group working; in part it was fear that individual grades would be affected by the presence of 'freeloaders'; and partly it arose from the sheer novelty of the exercise. Although these anxieties tended to lessen over the four years in which the innovation ran, particularly as we developed assessment models which allowed the diligent student to be rewarded and marginal performers to be penalised, levels of student anxiety and hostility remained uncomfortably high throughout much of this period.

Evaluations of the course soon highlighted two key factors which contributed to this unease. The introduction of a radically new form of group-based learning and assessment into the second year of a degree programme proved to be a fundamental mistake. Students complained, quite rightly, that they were approaching a major part of their second-year studies without any adequate first-year preparation. However, anxieties were not just the product of these structural factors but were also generated by the prevailing culture of the department. Many tutors, for example, were unable to play an active role in the design and delivery of the course because its local, community-based nature provided no platform for their particular expertise and interests. This lack of involvement led to tensions and suspicions which played their own part in heightening the resistance of some students.

However, one consequence of introducing group projects was its contributory effect in promoting a more systematic development of the first- and second-year curriculum. Having recognised that students only encountered collaborative working and its assessment in year two, we set about introducing a significant element of group work in a first-year core module. This course was designed primarily to develop first-year students' understanding of historical interpretation, as well as of wider academic skills such as essay writing. Throughout the first six weeks of a twelve-week teaching programme, six themes were introduced using lectures and classes. Students then elected to focus on one of the six themes, and groups of between three and five members were established, based on these choices. Offering this element of selection was an important motivational factor, since it gave students a chance to study the topics which most interested them, and also helped to reconcile the potential tensions between individual and group-work. An overarching group question provided the focus for the preparation and delivery of group presentations, whilst five satellite essay questions encouraged individual students to channel their work into the group effort. Throughout the last six weeks of the course, groups worked towards a presentation, meeting their tutor for short monitoring tutorials each week. As part of their preparation for this element in the assessment strategy, students were introduced to group working and presentation skills by, *inter alia*, contracting with each other and the tutor, and undertaking structured activities and receiving feedback on their performance.

In order to encourage a greater degree of involvement among all tutors within the department, a new second-year core module was introduced which retained a strong element of group-work, but which provided a wider framework in which all history tutors could make a contribution. While several colleagues still approached such work with scepticism, these changes helped to embed group-work within the prevailing culture of the degree programme.

It will be obvious from this brief account of curriculum design that there was a strong element of the *ad hoc* in these developments and that they were driven, particularly in the early phases, by a combination of resource pressures and personal enthusiasms. In retrospect, there was a need for greater coherence and congruence in our curriculum, and a need for a broader sense of ownership among colleagues. The opportunity to address these issues came when the history department was chosen to pilot the university's Teaching, Learning and Assessment Strategy.

Among other things, this Strategy advocated the design of degree programmes around learning outcomes, developed for significant points of a course (e.g. end of programme, end of each year); the use of teaching strategies which promoted intellectual autonomy; and assessment methods which were both broad and balanced. This approach not only allowed the history programme to achieve greater coherence, but it also permitted the foregrounding and development of particular pedagogic activities such as group-work.

In surveying the development of group working for students at Teesside, from induction through to the end of the second year, we would identify the following as being of value in effective educational development. The purposes of group working need to be identified clearly and communicated to students; hence the importance we attach to clear learning outcomes and to the provision of programme and module guides. The rationale for group working needs to be underpinned by a teaching strategy that foregrounds collaborative group-work in seminars, and uses a range of group-working techniques such as pyramiding, buzz-groups, brainstorming and syndicate work. These need to be reinforced and underpinned by dedicated activities designed to identify the characteristics of effective group work, individual contributions to groups, and reviews of personal strengths and needs. These should not, we believe, be developed independently in courses divorced from historical studies. Indeed, while group-work was introduced into first- and second-year modules for a variety of reasons, some to do with social networking and some concerned with the development of transferable skills, the main rationale behind its use centred on our belief that it fosters deeper levels of historical understanding. Put simply, students engage more effectively with historical issues when they are able to learn from each other via discussion. Such projects allow students to bring their individual knowledge and different perspectives to bear on a given topic, and the whole is, therefore, greater than the parts. It is only when students are aware of some of the dynamics associated with group-work that they can use these insights to work with a greater level of independence in later stages of the programme. One fundamental issue which underpins these developments is assessment, and it is to that critical area of course design that we now turn.

The challenge of assessment

Assessment practice in higher education has been criticised in the past for its dependence on a relatively narrow range of methods; typically in the humanities, a diet of exams and essays. Nevertheless, things are changing under the influence of the spread of modularisation, the changing nature of the student body, and the wider demands coming from both the economic and political arenas. At

Teesside, we would add to these the effects of an outcome-driven approach to course design, which, when combined with the assessment principle of validity (that programme aims and objectives should match assessment methodologies) has led to a broadening and deepening of the assessment strategies practised within our undergraduate degree programme.

Assessment is a fundamental element of the student experience. Most students are clearly assessment driven, and the ethos and aim of a programme, as Rowntree has argued,[4] may be discerned by its assessment strategies, which in turn play a major role in determining the approach that students take to learning. Given this centrality, there is great force in the contention that if you wish to alter the way students learn, alter the way they are assessed. Often, however, proposed changes to assessment methods present a challenge to assumptions which are deeply rooted in staff and student cultures. Therefore, not only do we need a powerful rationale for introducing group-work into the curriculum, but also new assessment practices which are perceived both by tutors and students to be fair, effective, open and manageable. Doing this is not easy. All of our respondents identified the design of effective assessment methods as the main problem facing the successful implementation of group-work in history undergraduate courses. A predictable range of concerns was identified, clustering around two main issues.

The individual and the group

The most common concern raised by students and tutors involved freeloading students who might inhibit a group's effectiveness, and 'weaker' students who might reduce the grades of the diligent and able. Essentially, these concerns are the product of a fundamental clash of cultures. By introducing assessed group-work into history programmes, we place a collective exercise within a prevailing culture of intense individualism. Students study and compete as individuals and are graded accordingly, while most tutors operate at various depths of scholarly independence and isolation. In such a context, both tutors and students are often worried by the prospect of individual grades being raised or lowered by what are perceived to be extraneous and unfair factors. These anxieties need to be taken seriously, and a range of measures put in place which will help to reassure students that the assessment system is indeed fair. There are several possible ways of addressing this problem[5], but having spent seven years experimenting with different approaches at Teesside we have settled on a well-established and relatively simple method which has proved successful. The system works as follows: If a group is given an overall mark of 60 per cent, then this is multiplied by the number of members in the group. In a group of five members, this would produce an overall total of 300 marks, which the tutor would then allocate according to the varying contributions of individual students. Sometimes, this is done on an equal basis, but sometimes the disparities can and should be dramatic. There have been several cases, for example, where outstanding group members have received first-class marks while very weak group members have been failed. So, for example, the pattern of the five marks in our notional group might be: 75 + 68 + 65 + 55 + 37 = 300 marks.

Partly in response to the problem of the freeloader, but also as a way of increasing student awareness of effective group working, we experimented with various forms of peer assessment. However, whenever 'pure' forms of peer assessment and marking were introduced, in which students were required to allocate final marks to each other, high levels of student resistance and alienation were generated. Interestingly, most students were willing to engage in very searching forms of self assessment, but were reluctant to mark their peers in a similar fashion. Informal methods of peer assessment continue to be used as part of a background evaluation of projects, but the final allocation of grades is now the exclusive responsibility of tutors.

The weighting which may be given in modular systems to assessed group-working, and the bearing that this may have on final degree classifications, also need to be considered carefully. Too high a weighting can produce anxiety among conscientious and able students who fear that their final grades may suffer as a consequence; too low a weighting can communicate the message that group-work is not valued. Finding an acceptable balance is particularly important in core courses where all students are compelled to engage in such work, and where a significant number may approach it with anxiety and perhaps even hostility. At Teesside, we have come to the conclusion that group marks in core courses should be weighted at between 20 per cent and 30 per cent. Indeed, all of the sixty-five second-year students who were interviewed considered this weighting to be appropriate; anything lower than 20 per cent, might lead some students to treat the exercise less than diligently; anything more than 30 per cent runs the risk of heightening levels of anxiety among conscientious students.

In order to arrive at individual marks, students submit a portfolio of work showing their overall contributions. A group portfolio is also submitted; this may include a set of ground rules for the group which have been agreed collectively by its members, project plans, individual contracts, minutes of meetings (including attendance schedules), monitoring and evaluation pro formas, and a diary of 'critical incidents'. The final group 'product' varies: in one module, it takes the form of a group presentation; in another, a 'reader' is researched and compiled, comprising both group and individual contributions; in another module, an eclectic range of community-based projects is produced based on client specifications. Students are offered a range of criteria to support their work and to guide tutors in final assessments. Criteria cover essay writing, presentations and the monitoring of group work.

Assessing a process

The second main area of concern surrounding the assessment of group-work centres on a range of practical and management issues. How can we design assessment strategies which adequately measure dynamic collective processes (e.g. discussions, planning, managing and delivering group-based projects) as opposed to tangible individual products (e.g. essays, exam scripts, projects)? Apart from the problems of defining assessment criteria – 'What skills are being fostered and assessed?' – and the problems of devising assessment strategies which measure these qualities effectively, we also face the problem of generating a reliable record of such work which can be given to second markers and external examiners for moderation.

Some of the methods mentioned in the previous section help to record and assess this dynamic process; minutes, diaries, plans and contracts have all been developed and refined by colleagues working in this field, and gradually, over the course of the last ten years, a sophisticated range of strategies has been assembled. One of the most exciting recent developments has been the role which e-mail and electronic seminars can play in facilitating and assessing this kind of exercise. At Teesside, one group of students involved in group-work took part in a project to test the possible applications of e-mail to collaborative learning. Each student was provided with an e-mail address and was given a short training session in its use. An electronic seminar site was provided which kept a structured record of all contributions between group members, including the group tutor. In this particular case, the tutor initiated seminar discussion by posting several questions on to the site, each question having its own sub-site. Members of the group were then able to enter the site using computers in the university or in their own homes. Each contribution was recorded, so that students could begin to debate ideas and issues among themselves, rather than responding only to questions posed by the tutor. By the end of the process (which ran for a two-week experimental period) a body of written text had been generated which could be printed and passed to second markers within the institution, as well as external markers outside it.

This method is particularly useful in creating an assessable record of a dynamic process, and promises to resolve many of the problems encountered thus far: less confident students, for example, can find a distinctive voice in e-mail discussion which they often struggle to find in more conventional seminars; less motivated members of groups can be more effectively monitored, and penalised for poor or non-existent contributions. It provides valuable feedback for all concerned, allowing the tutor and the group to analyse and reflect on how the collaborative process is working. It also provides external examiners with a formal record of the discussion process, overcoming one of the perennial problems of moderating collaborative work.

This review of assessment problems and methods does not claim to offer perfect solutions. By the same token, we would argue that traditional forms of assessment have their own problems; there is sufficient evidence to suggest, for example, that essays and examinations are open to criticism, with variability between markers and the elevation of content over analysis being two of the most obvious areas of concern. This is not to disparage the essay or the exam, but merely to recognise that all assessment is to some degree imperfect. Although the challenge of assessment remains the main problem facing the development of group-work in higher education, it is important to stress that such problems are no longer as intimidating as once they were; a number of methods have been developed, based on the practical experience of tutors working in a range of history departments, which offer an effective range of solutions to such problems.[6]

How do we start?

If someone were to ask us how to initiate new approaches to group-based learning, we would stress the following:

- Be clear about objectives and outcomes: why are you introducing this assessment approach?
- Start small: don't do anything overly ambitious in the first instance, or anything which is radically out of step with the culture of the department.
- Work with the grain: point to the increasing emphasis on particular teaching, learning and assessment strategies promoted by the Dearing Report, Quality Assurance Agency, Higher Education Funding Council and others.
- Be careful when and where you introduce group work: don't introduce it for the first time in the second or third years of a programme. Prepare students for working in teams, either by progressively building group working into the curriculum (the preferred option) or by organising introductory workshops.
- Talk to colleagues who have used these approaches: key into the network.
- Communicate with students and staff: explain why you are adopting this strategy.
- Ensure that you have departmental support: at best, the positive engagement of colleagues, at worst their acquiescence.
- Balance group-based assessment with individual work.
- Monitor the course as it progresses and be ready to take remedial action.
- Evaluate the course and learn from the staff and student experience.

Notes

1 See, for example, D. Jacques, *Learning in Groups* (London, Kogan Page, 1992); L. Thorley and R. Gregory, *Using Group-Based Learning in Higher Education* (London, Kogan Page, 1994); N. Entwistle and P. Ramsden, *Understanding Student Learning* (London, Croom Helm, 1983); D. Bond, *Developing Autonomy in Learning* (London, Kogan Page, 1981).

2 See, for example, B. C. Dart and J. A. Clarke, 'Helping students to become better learners: a case study in teacher education', *Higher Education*, 22 (1991), 317–35; V. S. Higgins *et al.*, 'Identifying and solving problems in engineering design', *Studies in Higher Education*, 14 (1989), 169–81.

3 J. Allen and R. Lloyd-Jones, *The Assessment of Group Work and Presentations in the Humanities: A Guidebook for Tutors* (Sheffield, Sheffield Hallam University, 1998). See also A. Booth, 'Assessing group work' and 'Changing assessment to improve learning', in A. Booth and P. Hyland (eds), *History in Higher Education* (Oxford, Blackwell, 1996).
4 D. Rowntree, *Assessing Students: How Shall We Know Them?* (London, Kogan Page, 1987), p. 1.
5 See Allen and Lloyd-Jones, *The Assessment of Group Work*, pp. 9–11, for a useful listing of different assessment approaches.
6 For further reading on assessment methods, see G. Brown, J. Bull and M. Pendlebury, *Assessing Students in Higher Education* (London, Kogan Page, 1997); S. Brown and P. Knight, *Assessing Learners in Higher Education* (London, Kogan Page, 1994); G. Gibbs, *Assessing More Students* (PCFC, 1992); S. Brown, C. Rust and G. Gibbs, *Diversifying Assessment in Higher Education* (Oxford, Oxford Centre for Staff Development, 1994); G. Gibbs, *Learning in Teams* (Oxford, Oxford Centre for Staff Development, 1995).

Assessing learning outcomes: tests, gender and the assessment of historical knowledge

In this chapter we examine how one institution in the United States is addressing external demands of accountability. For years, higher education in the United States enjoyed unfettered public support. The value of college for students and the country was 'an almost righteously unexamined premise – the "great self-evident" of higher education'.[1] But in the late 1970s critics started complaining, often deservedly, that greater access to higher education had eroded the quality of learning.[2] Diverse constituents began to demand that colleges and universities objectively demonstrate how they were serving the needs of their students, their communities and the nation. By 1990, some forty states had embraced the assessment movement and its focus on student outcomes.

Today, more than 90 per cent of US institutions of higher education conduct formally defined assessment activities to demonstrate student learning outcomes.[3] While there is no direct equivalent for this development in Britain, the current interest in trying to establish national benchmark standards for student learning springs from a similar concern for greater public accountability. In the United States there is a dual emphasis on knowledge and skills developed within the discipline and across the curriculum. In Britain benchmarking of student learning is being piloted for each subject or discipline. Australia's accountability movement, in contrast to that of both the United States and Britain, concentrates largely on faculty research output and, as yet, pays no appreciable attention to assessing student outcomes.[4]

In the United States, the public's call for accountability in higher education needs to be answered seriously and directly. But we should do so through intellectual engagement and established research standards. In this chapter, we introduce issues that should be at the forefront of calls for accountability. These issues are developed in a review of the assessment movement in the United States and a case study of one institution's assessment of general historical knowledge. Our focus in the case study is on general education and history at a single institution, but the discussion relates to all disciplines and applies to all institutions of higher education.

A national context of assessment

State mandates and accreditation boards have advanced the assessment movement in the United States. Tennessee initiated the movement in 1984, when it provided incentives for demonstrated increases in student performance. Colorado and Virginia soon followed with their own versions of mandated assessment. Currently, at least twenty-seven states legislate rigorous accounting by public colleges and universities.[5] One accrediting agency, the Southern Association of Colleges and Schools, requires each institution to 'have a strategic plan and an internally developed assessment program to measure progress toward the performance goals in the plan', and all six regional accrediting agencies in the United States require some form of assessment.[6] The movement continues to gain momentum, as evidenced in political agendas and the popular press.

Within this climate, colleges and universities have adopted and developed a number of approaches and specific instruments to address assessment issues. Initially, many states proposed assessment efforts based upon state-wide testing. This format offers credible measures that are easy to score, have high reliability, and can cover many topics efficiently.[7] In the United States, institutions of higher education have used entrance examinations such as the Scholastic Assessment Test[8] and advanced placement examinations for years as admission criteria, and to place students and award credit for prior learning and achievement. Advancement or exit tests are a natural continuation of these established practices and provide an ostensibly objective way to measure student learning in college. But as Peter Ewell points out, 'pure political opposition on the part of higher education leaders and sound reasoning about what might really cause campus-level change' led most states to adopt a decentralised approach to assessment.[9]

In its varied forms, this new approach emphasised the importance of grounding assessment in local missions and cultures. Colleges and universities were given flexibility in the methods they could use to address assessment mandates. Unfortunately, the new focus did not address a primary concern with the initial embracement of large-scale testing. While *centralised* testing was denounced, institutions were still encouraged to use national and local tests in their assessments of student learning. The ability of tests to measure students' knowledge and learning experiences accurately was not seriously questioned.

The research on bias in test content and performance suggests that we need to re-think what tests measure. Sadker and Sadker,[10] Scheuneman and Gerritz,[11] and others[12] have proposed that tests measure factors other than intrinsic knowledge of subject material. Because tests measure both 'intrinsic difficulty' of subject material and the 'personal attributes of the examinees . . . which may affect their test performance', Scheuneman and Gerritz argue that performance declines as the characteristics of the people taking the test become less congruous with the characteristics of the test itself.[13] Furthermore, a number of scholars have argued that multiple-choice tests are gender biased[14] and lead to negative consequences for women and minorities.[15]

These concerns relate directly to other issues that should be considered in discussions of assessment. For example, recent studies have suggested that history instruction may be gender biased. Fournier and Wineburg asked fifth- and eighth-grade students to project themselves into historical roles.[16] Gender differences reflected the central, if not exclusive, role of men in history. In another study, Ferree and Wienand found that some history and English instructors include topics about women in history while others do not.[17] The authors showed that biased instruction has an impact both on students' interests and knowledge about certain topics in history. We should expect measures of student outcomes to detect such curriculum biases. Indeed, studies have documented performance bias on tests of historical knowledge. For example, Zwick and Ercikan identified gender differences in performance of the history sections of the National Assessment of Educational Progress, and found that women tended to do better on questions that concern women's rights or slavery and segregation, while men performed better on questions concerning war or identification of event dates.[18] Breland *et al.* report similar gender differences on Advanced Placement European and American History exams.[19]

Such issues complicate assessment. There are countless methodological and theoretical concerns that should be addressed by educators, politicians, the public and assessment professionals. But in trying to keep up with the demands for data and for broad interpretations, we have simplified the research process. In the remainder of this chapter, we present a case study that illustrates how an institution addressed state mandates to assess general education outcomes.

An institutional assessment case study

The case study presented below reports findings of gender differences on a test of historical knowledge. The test was administered to seniors at the College of William and Mary, a highly selective state-assisted university in Virginia. William and Mary was established in 1693 by British royal charter, making it the second oldest university in the United States. Today, the university has schools of arts and sciences, business administration, education, marine science and law. There are over 5,500 undergraduate students. These students can earn degrees in thirty-four areas of concentration within the school of arts and sciences, and four areas of specialisation within the school of business administration.

Findings from the case study were important to the institution because they contributed to a discussion of the College's goals of a liberal education and forced us to reflect on how we assess our general education curriculum. Ultimately, that reflection led to changes in general education requirements. In the newly adopted general education curriculum, all students complete a set of general education requirements. The requirements cover analytical, writing and computing skills, as well as knowledge areas including mathematics and quantitative reasoning, social sciences, history, creative and performing arts, natural sciences, and philosophical, religious and social thought. The case study is a testimonial for other institutions in their searches for appropriate ways to assess student outcomes that result in meaningful changes.

In the past decade, Virginia institutions have been afforded considerable latitude in defining appropriate goals and assessment methods. At the same time, the State Council of Higher Education for Virginia held institutions to fairly rigorous standards. These standards were outlined in a set of nine principles published in 1992 by the American Association for Higher Education. Generally, the principles emphasised the importance of: (1) defining educational values; (2) understanding learning as a multidimensional, integrated experience revealed in performance over time; (3) explicitly stating goals; and (4) giving equal attention to outcomes *and* experiences. The principles also called for assessment programmes: (5) to be ongoing; (6) to involve representatives across the campus; (7) to address issues that people care about; (8) to do so in an environment supportive of change; and (9) to meet responsibilities to students and to other constituents.

Some institutions in Virginia resisted assessment mandates; others responded by creating assessment programmes that were almost exclusively the domain of university administrations. Our institution's response differed from most because we structured our programme in a manner that ensured that faculty, not administrators, became its chief architects. Consequently, we designed a programme that would not only fulfil state mandates but would also provide us with important answers to curricular concerns. In addition, because faculty members who were sociologists played key roles in creating and maintaining the programme, appropriate social science research standards have always been applied to each project. After ten years of formal evaluation, the programme is well regarded in the state. It continues to be faculty driven and directed towards institutional needs.

In Virginia, institutions of higher education have been required to implement local plans for assessment that addressed 'basic skills, general education, major-field outcomes, and alumni follow-up'.[20] The university had developed an assessment plan that called for the use of surveys and tests to evaluate general education objectives. The initial intent was to develop a test of historical knowledge and, over time, to develop different tests for each area specified by the university as important to its educational mission.

Timing of the initial assessment mandates was fortuitous: the university was in the thick of a debate about its general education curriculum. A self study associated with re-accreditation required that we review the curriculum, and, in doing so, the faculty realised that the requirements had drifted from their original intent. The curriculum was loosely defined, whereby students were required to take nine courses distributed among the humanities, the social sciences and the natural sciences. Two additional courses (in sequence) had to be taken in one of these general areas that was outside the student's major subject. Under this system, a student could graduate from the university without taking a single history course, even though the university specifies as one of its goals that students will acquire a general historical knowledge of seminal events, movements and ideas that have shaped Western civilisation and the United States.

The historical knowledge test[21]

As part of a state-mandated programme to evaluate general education, a faculty subcommittee on curriculum assessment developed a multiple-choice test of historical knowledge. The test was designed to reflect the university's general education objectives by focusing on important historical and geographic knowledge that students with a liberal education ought to know as responsible citizens in a democracy. The goals provided a general guide for constructing the test, but it was by no means an easy process to define important historical knowledge. The subcommittee included historians and faculty members from other disciplines. It was thought that by involving non-historians in the process, we would emphasise knowledge of *general* historical importance and avoid developing a test relevant to a particular history course.

The subcommittee felt that responsible citizenship implied the ability to place current public issues in the historical settings/contexts from which they had emerged. For example, discussions of gender relations should be informed by knowledge of women's movements and when women received the right to vote. Debates about oil dependency should be based on knowledge of where it is produced. And so on. Test items needed to cover important events, movements and ideas that have shaped Western civilisation and the United States. If students in large numbers could not answer these questions correctly, then there would be some cause for concern. The subcommittee also included some items on the test so that national comparisons could be made. In 1989, the National Endowment of the Humanities (NEH) conducted a test of knowledge on history and literature for a representative sample of seniors in American colleges and universities, and eleven NEH items were selected for inclusion in this test. The items concerned important historical figures, specific events, significant authors and literary works.

Based on the university's general education goals and a review of the NEH test, the principal architects of the William and Mary test (three male faculty members from History, Philosophy and Psychology) constructed questions in three general areas: world history, with a focus on Western civilisation; American history, from the origins of the nation to the present day; and world geography, with a focus on the locations of countries and bodies of water in Europe, Asia and the Middle East. The team consulted with members of the history department and other disciplines. Each of the three faculty members independently developed a set of questions. They then came together to review and revise the questions and to develop a test that could be taken in a fifty-minute class period. A working draft of the test was reviewed, revised and approved by two larger faculty groups, the General Education Subcommittee and the entire Assessment Steering Committee (both groups including male and female faculty members).

The final test of 71 items included 11 taken directly from the NEH test and 60 items constructed locally. Some of the NEH items asked students to locate Voltaire, Montesquieu and Benjamin Franklin in the Enlightenment; to identify the Reformation as the rupture within Christianity that resulted in the first Protestant churches; to recognise the purposes of *The Federalist* papers and the Monroe Doctrine; and to associate the Scopes trial with teaching evolution in schools. Locally constructed items covered such topics as the founding of Jamestown, the Magna Carta, the US Declaration of Independence, the Constitutional Convention of 1787, the time period of World War I and US allies in World War II, the Renaissance, the Ottoman Empire, the Iron Curtain and Vietnam. Students were also asked about historical figures such as Julius Caesar, Marie Antoinette, Marie Curie and Mahatma Ghandi. Geographic items asked students to locate on maps countries in Asia, Europe and the Middle East, as well as the English Channel, Strait of Gibraltar, and the North and Mediterranean Seas. In addition to the test questions, we also asked students about the number of history courses taken in college, whether they had received credit based on the advance placement test, and their gender. We thought exposure to college-level history might affect test scores. We were also interested in possible gender differences. After many meetings and much discussion and debate, the test was approved by members of the university faculty.

The subcommittee was not particularly interested in determining *when* students acquired their historical knowledge. It assumed that many students at this highly selective university already possessed much of the required skills, values and knowledge before coming to college. The historical knowledge being tested was assumed to be sufficiently basic and important that graduating seniors would have retained it, regardless of when that knowledge was acquired. This model is quite different from the popular value-added model of educational performances that looks at changes, and from the student-based models that look at individual learning outcomes. The test was administered during regularly scheduled classes that were balanced between the humanities, social sciences and natural sciences. Initially 31 seniors took the test. It was then administered to a larger group of 300 seniors (about one-third of the graduating class).

Findings and evaluation of results

When we administered the test, we thought that greater exposure to history would lead students to better performance on the test. We found this to be the case. On average, students who were awarded advanced placement credits or who took a history course in college scored about five points higher on the historical knowledge test than did students without these types of exposure. We also thought that men might have more exposure to history, but this was not the case. Men and women were, on average, about equally likely to have received advanced placement credits in history, and they were equally likely to report taking some history classes in college. However, we did find some interesting course-selection patterns. Men were more likely to have taken more than three history classes, and women were more likely to have taken one history class. But well over a third (37%) of the people who took the test indicated that they had taken no college history courses.

We also found that men, on average, answered about six more questions correctly on the seventy-one-item test than did women. This is true even when we take exposure to history into account. In seeking an explanation for this difference, we reviewed the test content and identified twenty-four of the seventy-one questions that are normatively associated with men. Many of these items share a common focus on power relations, such as wars, treaties, occupations of territory, coercive tactics, physical force and images of powerful individuals. We reasoned that some portion of the difference between men and women on this test may have resulted from the extent to which they were more or less interested in these relations. When we removed the twenty-four gender-sensitive items, the difference between the scores of men and women became insignificant.

In summary, we found that exposure to previous historical knowledge helps predict test performance, but we also found that men and women were about equally likely to take advanced placement history classes or history exams. While exposure to historical knowledge contributed to test performance, it did not explain gender differences in test performance. In contrast, we found that by removing biased test content (as determined *a priori*), we removed a significant portion of gender differences in test performance.

Reviewing the general education curriculum

At the time the test was administered, the university had a loosely defined general education curriculum. The experienced curriculum had drifted from the intended curriculum. This was quite evident given the findings of the test. Even though historical knowledge is specified in the goals of the general education curriculum, 37 per cent of the students who took the test indicated that they had not taken a college-level history course. This concerned faculty and reinforced the decision to replace the existing general education system with seven specific knowledge-based requirements.

The overall test scores were hard to interpret, especially because the test was designed to measure basic historical information appropriate for graduates to know as citizens in a democracy. On average, students scored 79 per cent on the seventy-one-item test. Over half the students scored above 80 per cent and over three-quarters scored 70 per cent or above. But 21 per cent (12 per cent of the men and 31 per cent of the women) received scores of less than 70 per cent. In a sub-analysis of the NEH items, university seniors outperformed the national sample on all eleven items included in the test, with an average difference across the eleven items of about seventeen percentage points. These differences are substantial, but not surprising because the university is a highly selective institution.

Clearly, the historical knowledge test raised more questions about assessing student learning than it answered. It was difficult to evaluate student scores, in part because the test was not norm referenced; nor were anticipated and acceptable scores discussed before the test was administered. In the eleven items for which comparative data were available, students at the university fared well. But a more appropriate comparison would be with students from other highly selective schools with equally rigorous admission standards. Beyond the difficulties of interpreting test scores is the serious charge of test bias. The test was developed locally by three male faculty members and reviewed by men and women. In hindsight, there were clear content issues related to gender and broader curricular issues. Of concern was the extent to which test results replicate biases in the curriculum. Alumni pointed to other biases as well (e.g. no items addressed western US history, some alumni cohorts had lived through recent history and questioned how important events were selected).

The new general education requirements reflect concern about the results of the historical knowledge test. The old general education curriculum required no history courses. The new general education curriculum requires three history courses (one in history and culture in the European tradition, one outside the European tradition, and one on cross-cultural issues). Changes to the curriculum will expose all students to college-level history courses and, as shown above, such exposure is associated with higher test scores. The question faced by faculty was whether this methodology offered the most appropriate measure of basic historical knowledge and skills, especially when course content and pedagogy vary substantially and multiple-choice test results are affected by individual attributes.

Alternatives to tests

Our university has explored alternative methods for assessing the new general education curriculum. Two methods are described briefly here. The first includes surveys of students and faculty, and the second includes course portfolio analyses.

Surveys

Survey questionnaires are a mainstay in social science research generally, and in assessments specifically. Questionnaire-based assessment strategies are very efficient, relatively inexpensive and have considerable face validity. However, questionnaires provide only indirect evidence of knowledge and skills, and are therefore considered less credible than other approaches to assessment.[22] A less recognised concern is how perceptions often reflect gender stereotypes.[23] The resulting biases are rarely accounted for in interpreting survey results. With these drawbacks in mind, we illustrate one way in which survey questionnaires can provide useful information about programme and institutional effectiveness.

A broad array of courses are designated as meeting each general education requirement. To be designated as meeting one of the requirements, a course must meet certain criteria. When the new curriculum was implemented, we developed seven questionnaires based on the criteria for each of the general education requirements. We asked students enrolled in fifty-one designated courses to rate the extent to which the course addressed the relevant criteria. Instructors were asked to complete a parallel questionnaire so that student and faculty perceptions of course content and its relation to general education requirements could be compared collectively. Similar questionnaires conducted at the university have pointed to consistency among student and faculty responses, although faculty tend to rate certain areas (e.g. amount of class discussion) higher than do students.

In the initial study, our goal was to evaluate the strengths and weaknesses of a survey for assessing the general education curriculum and to get student and faculty feedback about individual questionnaire items. Results emphasised important methodological considerations, such as when and how to administer the questionnaire and how to distinguish the general education assessment questionnaire from a course evaluation. Another, more fundamental issue concerns the defining of clear learning goals associated with curricular requirements and clear assessment goals. Through the pilot study (and the ongoing general education assessment) we identified particular goals that were difficult to interpret empirically. A survey allowed us to look at potential variation in how goals were being interpreted, by looking at variation within and among classes.

We have implemented the first round of general education assessments, and in preliminary findings students and faculty suggest that courses designated as meeting a particular general education requirement are exposing students to the theoretical and methodological concepts specified in the requirement objectives. The curriculum is new and such compliance is not surprising. Over time, however, courses might drift away inadvertently from the specific goals of the broader general education curriculum. A survey lets us track the curriculum over time.

In addition to a survey that measures perceived exposure to knowledge and skills, the university explored the use of course portfolios for assessing the general education curriculum. Course portfolios provide authentic assessments of student knowledge and skills and complement questionnaire data.

Portfolios

Portfolio assessments are often associated with individual student performance. Portfolios differ in terms of their purpose, but generally students build collections of their work that document acquisition and command of the knowledge and skills associated with an academic domain. It is beyond the scope of this chapter to review the many applications and techniques associated with portfolio-based assessments, but there are numerous examples in the educational literature.[24] We use the term 'course portfolios' to refer to examples of students' work that meet predetermined levels of performance in a course. The resulting portfolio represents one course, but can include several students' work.

In our case study, course portfolios were collected from the same classes in which the surveys were conducted. Instructors submitted a single portfolio containing examples of student work. Examples were from more than one student, and represented exemplary and satisfactory student performance on class assignments and tests. Members of a faculty subcommittee evaluated the contents of each portfolio and determined the extent to which student work related to the objectives of the general education requirement associated with the course. This methodology was especially appealing to faculty. Portfolios provide a performance-based evaluation of the knowledge and skills developed in the new general education curriculum. Faculty saw many advantages in this method, especially when there were multiple indicators of knowledge and skills in the portfolios. However, such large-scale portfolio analysis has several drawbacks, most notably time commitments and rater reliability issues. Portfolios take some time for faculty to construct, and scoring them is a major commitment on the part of faculty volunteers. It is important for each of the volunteer raters to share a common understanding of the criteria used to score portfolios. Because we intentionally include both experts and non-experts on the scoring team, a common understanding cannot be taken for granted.

Using a single portfolio to represent a class average reduces the amount of time involved in using this strategy to assess curricular requirements. When hundreds of courses are involved, it might be possible to sample courses without misrepresenting the general findings of the study. Faculty members found scoring of the portfolios to be fairly quick because they were looking for evidence that each criterion was met and were not trying to evaluate the course or individual student. We also monitored rater reliability. Our raters (faculty members) were carefully trained and participated in calibration exercises to determine differences in rating criteria. Each portfolio was rated by at least two faculty members on a series of criteria used to designate a course as meeting a general education requirement. Given these adjustments, the portfolio methodology promises to provide informative results.

Conclusion

In this chapter, we have shared our experiences in assessing historical knowledge as a component of the general education curriculum. Generally, we point to four significant lessons we have learned from over a decade of conducting formal assessments, and from this study specifically: (1) *learning goals* must be clearly specified; (2) *assessment goals* must be clearly specified; (3) *multiple methodologies* should be used to enhance our understanding of, and confidence in, assessment results; and (4) assessment results should have *practical implications*.

Learning goals are often difficult to establish for a general education curriculum, especially when courses from different disciplines share core criteria but differ in substantive content. But even within individual departments and courses, goals frequently look more like philosophical statements than testable objectives. We have found that establishing assessment goals concurrently with the learning goals helps to define more clearly what we want to accomplish and how we will know when or if we have accomplished it.

We have also learned to be patient, to experiment with different approaches to assessment, and to conduct pilot studies that inform curricular and assessment decisions. Although we did not discuss differences in pedagogical or learning styles in this chapter, they should be considered in deciding what types of measure to use in assessment. For instance, a portfolio might be less appropriate for a course with 250 students, no written assignments and an emphasis on learning facts, whereas a test might be inappropriate in a small seminar where the emphasis is on critical thinking and research skills. What is important in an assessment of student learning is to know what questions you want to answer; what methodological options are available; the strengths and limitations of those options; and potential biases in the curriculum, in pedagogies and in assessment methods.

Finally, assessment results that are not anchored to meaningful change are ineffective. The methods illustrated here have led to curricular changes and have informed resource allocation decisions. But the curricular evaluation is also informative to instructors. Surveys are returned to instructors with summaries of results for the individual course and for all courses collectively. Portfolio results are also distributed to instructors. This practice allows instructors to place their courses in the broader institutional context, but avoids reducing the assessment to a course- or instructor- evaluation process.

Are multiple-choice tests appropriate for assessing student learning outcomes of a general education curriculum? The case study presented here suggests that enrolment in classes is only one factor that is related to test scores and, as a result, tests measure more than exposure to material. This argues strongly against the use of tests as measures of competency. The institutionalisation of minimum achievement tests would serve only to support and reproduce the current biases in the curriculum. Instead, test results are useful in indicating the divergence between curriculum interests and student interests. Given this interpretation, we suggest that tests are useful in indicating biases in curriculum material and faculty viewpoints. In short, tests measure not only student achievement, but also what is important to faculty.

The broader goal of this chapter was to document the evolution of a general education assessment programme. We believe that assessment, in practice, should be formative and summative. It should lead to improvements and meet demands for accountability. To do this requires careful and thoughtful planning. Course results must be available to individual instructors, and aggregate results must be available to faculty and administrators. Finally, we need to hold assessment practices to rigorous standards. We need to evaluate those practices regularly, and we must recognise how multiple methods to some degree defuse potential problems inherent, but not always recognisable, in any research method.

Notes

1 P. Ewell, *Information on Student Outcomes: How to Get It and How to Use It* (Boulder, National Center for Higher Education Management Systems, Inc., 1983), p. 1.

2 G. Gaither, 'The assessment mania and planning', *Planning for Higher Education*, 24 (Spring 1996), 7–12.

3 T. W. Banta and Associates (eds), *Making a Difference: Outcomes of a Decade of Assessment in Higher Education* (San Francisco, Jossey-Bass Publishers, 1993).

4 D. A. DeBats and A. J. Ward, *Degrees of Difference: Reshaping the University in Australia and the United States* (Sydney, The Australian Centre for American Studies, 1998), p. 70.

5 Mark Clayton, 'States turn generous eye to universities', *Christian Science Monitor*, 12 January 1998, p. 7.

6 Gaither, 'The assessment mania', p. 7.

7 D. T. Erwin, *Assessing Student Learning and Development* (San Francisco, Jossey-Bass, 1991).

8 Originally named the Scholastic Aptitude Test.

9 P. Ewell, 'The role of states and accreditors in shaping assessment practice', in Banta and Associates (eds), *Making a Difference*, p. 343.

10 M. Sadker and D. Sadker, *Failing at Fairness: How America's Schools Cheat Girls* (New York, Macmillan, 1994).

11 J. D. Scheuneman and K. Gerritz, 'Using differential item functioning procedures to explore sources of item difficulty and group performance characteristics', *Journal of Educational Measurement*, 27:2 (1990), 109–31.

12 See, for example, G. Ben-Shakhar and Y. Sinai, 'Gender differences in multiple-choice tests: the role of differential guessing tendencies', *Journal of Educational Measurement*, 28:1 (1991), 23–35; M. Zeidner, 'Sociocultural differences in examinees' attitudes toward scholastic exams', *Journal of Educational Measurement*, 25:1 (1988), 67–76; S. F. Chipman, 'Word problems: where test bias creeps in', paper presented at the Annual Meeting of the American Educational Research Association, New Orleans, 5–9 April 1988, pp. 1–40.

13 Scheuneman and Gerritz, 'Using differential item functioning procedures', p. 109.

14 See, for example, J. Anderson, 'Sex-related differences on objective tests among undergraduates', *Educational Studies in Mathematics*, 20 (1989), 165–77; N. Bolger and T. Kellaghan, 'Method of measurement and gender differences in scholastic achievement', *Journal of Educational Measurement*, 27:2 (1990), 165–74; H. M. Breland, 'A study of gender and performance on advanced placement history examinations', *College Board Report*, no. 91–4 (New York, College Entrance Examination

Board, 1991); H. M. Breland, D. O. Danos, H. D. Kahn, M. Y. Kubota and M. W. Bonner, 'Performance versus testing and gender: an exploratory study of an advanced placement history examination', *Journal of Educational Measurement*, 31:4 (1994), 275–93; Sadker and Sadker, *Failing at Fairness*; K. F. Slevin and D. P. Aday, Jr, 'Gender differences in self-evaluations of information about current affairs', *Sex Roles: A Journal of Research*, 29 (November 1993), 817-28; FairTest: The National Center for Fair and Open Testing, 'FairTest Fact Sheet: The SAT' <http://www.fairtest.org/facts/satfact.htm>.

15 See Ford Foundation, *Gender Bias in Testing: A Public Policy Dialogue* (New York, Ford Foundation Office of Communication, 1991); L. Sperling, 'Can the barriers be breached? mature women's access to higher education', *Gender and Education*, 3:2 (1991), 199–213.

16 J. E. Fournier and S. S. Wineburg, 'Picturing the past: gender differences in the depiction of historical figures', *American Journal of Education*, 105:2 (1997), 160–85.

17 M. M. Ferree and A. Wienand, 'Does ignorance breed contempt? The balanced curriculum survey, fall 1986', unpublished report, Women's Studies Program, University of Connecticut, 1987.

18 R. Zwick and K. Ercikan, 'Analysis of differential item functioning in the NAEP history assessment', *Journal of Educational Measurement*, 26: (1989), 55–66.

19 Breland *et al.*, 'Performance versus testing and gender'.

20 Ewell, 'The role of states', pp. 343–4.

21 For a more complete discussion of the methodology and statistical analyses, see R. S. Gossweiler and K. F. Slevin, 'The importance of gender in the assessment of historical knowledge', *Research in Higher Education*, 36:2 (1995), 155–75.

22 P. Ewell, 'Establishing a campus-based assessment program', in D. F. Halpern (ed.), *Student Outcomes Assessment: What Institutions Stand to Gain*, New Directions for Higher Education Series, no. 59, 15:3 (London, Jossey-Bass Limited, 1987), pp. 9–24.

23 See S. Beyer and N. Gross, 'Inaccurate gender stereotypes regarding GPAs and representation of female students by major', paper presented at the Annual Meeting of the American Psychological Society, San Francisco, 1996; L. J. Bornholt, J. J. Goodnow and G. H. Cooney, 'Influences of gender stereotypes on adolescents' perceptions of their own achievement', *American Educational Research Journal*, 31:3 (1994), 675–92.

24 See, for example, T. W. Banta, J. P. Lund, K. E. Black and F. W. Oblander, *Assessment in Practice* (San Francisco, Jossey-Bass, 1996); T. F. Slater, J. M. Ryan and S. L. Samson, 'Impact and dynamics of portfolio assessment and traditional assessment in a college physics course', *Journal of Research in Science Teaching*, 34:3 (1997), 255–71; E. M. White, *Teaching and Assessing Writing* (San Francisco, Jossey-Bass, 1994).

Learning from feedback on assessment

That learners need feedback in order to understand, develop and improve upon their accomplishments is probably a commonplace in education. Indeed, high-quality feedback can be regarded as a 'critical condition of excellence' in the teaching of undergraduates,[1] whereas a lack of feedback raises serious questions about the ethics of assessment. Feedback on learning may be given to groups and individuals, within or outside normal teaching sessions, and at various times or stages of a teaching programme. It can be used for many purposes: to grade achievements, to identify and correct errors, to diagnose strengths and weaknesses, to develop students' understanding and skills, to motivate students, to promote progression, to help students to learn how to learn, to encourage independent learning and, of course, to impress colleagues and external assessors. It is also a key component of any activity in which there is an emphasis upon the interaction of learners and teachers (as in seminar discussions), rather than on the teacher's transmission of knowledge and information. In these interactive sessions the feedback that learners receive is usually developmental and diagnostic, for its aim is to encourage learners to reflect upon their knowledge, skills and values with a view to developing these, and addressing any shortcomings before presenting work for marks or grades that count towards more formal reckonings of progress and achievement. To facilitate this process and enhance the prospect of improvement is therefore a fundamental goal of learner-centred education. But even under these conditions, the *process* of transformation and development of students' learning is seldom deliberatively tracked. So it is to the feedback given upon particular *products* of learning (typically the essays, examination scripts and other items required for summative assessments) that students are most inclined to look for evidence of what it is that tutors actually rate of great importance in the curriculum and in the discipline, and what they really think of each student's particular achievements.

As most tutors probably know from their own experiences, assessment is in many respects the driving force of student learning. It clearly exercises a powerful influence on what it is that students learn within a course or programme, and how they approach learning; most students are selectively negligent about those elements of the curriculum that are not thought worthy of assessment, particularly when there are too many to be studied deeply. Assessment also plays a major role in defining how students spend their time outside the classroom, which in turn affects much of their experience of learning. From a vast array of educational research, we also know that assessment exercises a powerful influence on the actual quality of students' learning. Thus tasks and methods of assessment that seem to encourage students to adopt a 'surface' approach to studying – in which they do not seek personal and conceptual understandings, but see their studies as consisting of lots of unrelated bits of knowledge to be memorised and reproduced under stressful conditions – cannot be expected to advance the kinds of critical thinking and independence that we generally associate with higher education. These can be advanced, however, when assessment tasks and methods are designed to reward a 'deep' approach to studying – in which students seek personal understanding, relate new ideas to previous knowledge and experience, look for underlying principles and patterns, examine the evidence and logic behind arguments, and practise problem solving and critical reflection.[2]

What skills and knowledge students learn, how they spend their study-time and the quality of their achievements are thus all closely related to what is generally referred to as 'the assessment system': usually expressed as the number, form, timing and relative 'weighting' of all the tasks required to pass a course or programme. On any course/module or programme, that 'system' may or may not be closely related to what actually happens in the classroom. So some students may be able to pass or attain high marks on certain courses without actively participating in, or even attending, the teaching sessions. In such cases, the teaching may be, or may be thought to be, of little relevance or value to students in terms of the learning outcomes that are formally assessed. And it is unlikely, therefore, that the impact of classroom feedback on students' learning will be great. Even where teaching sessions are closely related to assessed learning outcomes, feedback on the development of students' learning may be slight. This may be due to many factors, such as a lack of attention to the processes and progress of students' learning, or class sizes that seem too big to permit feedback being focused on individuals' abilities and needs. Yet whatever the relationship between teaching and the assessment system, in most cases each student's sense of personal achievement, motivation, and hopes and prospects of improvement will be directly related to the nature and utility of the feedback that they receive on their assessed performances. For it is this feedback that has the capacity to turn each item of assessed work into an instrument for the further development of each student's learning; providing in the process a unique insight into the values and attitudes of tutors.

Clearly, feedback on assessment may be delivered in many different ways and forms, and be designed to serve a variety of functions. Holding tutorials to return assignments, leaving work to be collected from general offices or student pigeon-holes and posting students' grades on notice boards are all common practices – though each is likely to signal quite different things to students. Moreover, even in its simplest and most emphatic form – the solitary grade or mark returned on an assignment or exam script – feedback is replete with meanings. For the mark or grade must either refer students to something that offers explanation, or signal the assessor's failure to declare anything about the criteria, standards, values and conventions by which the judgement has been reached. Even the choice of materials to deliver feedback – institutional pro forma, computer print-out, criteria-assessment sheet, individual correspondence – sends signals about the educational values embedded in the assessment system. So, of course, does the tone of the assessor's comments. What students learn from feedback is thus much more than just their reading of the particular marks and comments that are placed upon each piece of work. From the text and contexts of the feedback given, they will form opinions about a host of factors (such as the extent to which their tutors prize each student as an individual, and what particular aspects of performance a tutor most values) that will affect not only their motivation and the kind of learning that is undertaken, but also their ability to manage their own learning – not least with regard to improving the quality of future work.

While all feedback on assessment should be clear, fair, accurate and appropriate to the student, it may not always be primarily designed to serve a developmental function. Indeed, a great deal of feedback is often principally concerned with informing students about the standard of their performance, rather than with enabling them to make improvements. This is clearly evident in relation to practices normally associated with the publication of individuals' course or exam achievements, but it is also evident in much of the feedback that is given on progress tests and course assignments. Thus students may receive very detailed statements about their particular attainments in a piece of work, but little guidance about how to realise improvements; comments such as 'this essay lacks an analytical structure' or 'you didn't select the best books available', even when fully understood, do not in themselves offer much practical advice. Similarly, where students receive a set of grades or scores for their performances under particular headings or criteria, marks for, say, 'the use of primary sources' or 'the management of seminar discussions', may help students to identify their strengths and weaknesses, but do little to show students how to build upon them or address them.

To be effective, developmental feedback therefore needs to encompass more than an appropriate explanation or justification of the assessment given. It needs to be perceived as timely and relevant to a student's future studies, focused on valued and attainable objectives, aware of students' own perceptions, and sensitive to the range of responses that various kinds of criticism and advice might prompt. Yet, in some senses, even this is not enough. For in order to help students to become deep, autonomous and life-long learners, capable of managing and evaluating their own learning and accomplishments within and beyond their academic studies, feedback must also assist students to take greater responsibility for their own learning. Enabling students to learn how to learn (metacognition), to develop their abilities of self-critical reflection and assessment, and to practise and gain confidence in the range of skills that will help them to direct and sustain their own learning, are thus key objectives that need to be recognised not only in the design of teaching and learning programmes, but also within the assessment system and feedback given.[3] This is a tall order, even for the experienced tutor. Yet it is not a new one, for in many respects it reflects a long-held goal of higher education: to produce critical, flexible and successful independent learners. Moreover, in disciplines such as history the importance of that goal has long been recognised through, for example, the emphasis placed on the development of students' critical thinking and, more particularly, the assessment value often attached to students' final project-work and dissertations. In the general context of growing numbers and diversity of students in normal teaching sessions, and the reduction of time for tutorials on students' individual progress and achievements, it is worth considering what is now happening in the use of feedback as an instrument for the development of students' learning.

With the assistance of colleagues at seventeen history departments around Britain,[4] a survey was conducted of students beginning the second, third or fourth (Scotland) year of their undergraduate history programmes in the autumn of 1998. The aim of the survey was to gather information in relation to two sweeping questions: (1) What do students taking history courses learn from the feedback that they receive on their assessments?; (2) How, within current resources, might we as history tutors set about enhancing the quality and utility of the feedback that we are giving? The survey consisted of an anonymous questionnaire in which students were asked fifty questions under four broad headings: 'Receiving Feedback', 'Value of Feedback', 'What Tutors Value' and 'Improving Feedback'. Forty-six questions called for rating-scale (tick-box) responses and four asked students to compose their own answers. Students were also asked to provide information about their age, sex, nationality, degree route, year and mode of study, and educational qualifications. Following pilot studies, most questionnaires were issued at the end of seminars in the various departments and collected by class tutors, who returned 674 usable (plus 11 substantially incomplete) questionnaires for analysis. To assist with the reading/interpretation of individual responses and general findings, a series of *ad hoc* meetings and conversations was then held with small groups of students, and some tutors from the seventeen departments.

What emerges from this survey is that, while there are important differences in the responses of particular types of student and between departments,[5] there are also many common patterns of response. These can be used both to illustrate some of the underlying congruences of history students' experiences and perceptions of feedback in the discipline, and to indicate several possible avenues for development and improvement. In what follows here, I have given foremost attention to the examination and interpretation of these general patterns, pausing to consider variations in the responses of the many sub-groups of respondents (e.g. by age, gender, place of study) only where these are so great that they suggest substantial differences in the experiences and perceptions of particular kinds of student.

Learning from feedback on assessment

Although a majority of students have some experience of receiving feedback on assessment during teaching sessions, their chances of receiving regular tutorials on their work would appear to be quite slim. Only one in ten state that they often receive tutorials on their assignments; and while half the students in one small department evidently do, this is well above the norm for all other groups. Indeed, over 40 per cent of all students claim never to have received a personal tutorial on their assessed work; and though the proportion is often lower in some of the older (pre-1992) universities, it rises to over 90 per cent in one of the 'newer' (post-1992) departments. Here, as at most other new universities, students are even less inclined than elsewhere to ask for a tutorial. A quarter of all students say that they have occasionally requested one, but only 3 per cent have evidently done this often. Far from being a widespread practice, the use of tutorials to return assignments has thus become quite rare in many departments; a 'regrettable but necessary' trend, and the inevitable consequence of increases in student numbers and staff workloads, according to some tutors. Whether this reflects a broader change in the importance that history tutors have traditionally attached to the personal and intellectual development of students as individuals is difficult to determine. But it would be surprising if a lack of individual tuition did not affect many students' motivation and approaches to studying.

As the great majority of history students do not receive regular tutorials to discuss their learning problems and achievements, and gain face-to-face advice about how to make improvements, it is through written feedback that they usually learn about their performance. On return of an essay, most students take less than twenty minutes (35 per cent take less than ten) to read and think about the comments, but a large majority will re-read them at a later date, and 44 per cent will do this 'often'. Most students will also, at least occasionally, use the marker's comments to help with future assignments, though there are considerable variations according to the student's place of study. The idea of feedback for reflection and development is thus well embedded in most students' thinking, and in this respect it is worth noting that students with high traditional entry qualifications (at least twenty-four A-level points, or equivalent) are both generally more likely to re-read comments and three times as likely to ensure that they read tutors' remarks on other students' scripts. Even allowing for departmental differences, the fact that 70 per cent of all students share their feedback suggests that more could be made of the learning opportunities that this affords. But first we would need to know much more about what is happening on these occasions; particularly the kinds of things that students learn from their private peer-discussions. From the anecdotal evidence that I have gathered, it seems that, aside from the social bonding, support and a little 'crowing', many students believe they learn as much (and sometimes more) about their tutor's way of thinking from reading the comments on other students' papers as they do from the comments on their own.

Since the traditional essay-examination remains the key item of assessment for most history students (as it is the one that usually carries the highest value in

...t be expected that feedback on exams would be well
...s of most departments. Yet 70 per cent of all students
...have received any kind of feedback (other than a grade
...performances; a figure that would be significantly higher
...holly untypical returns from two departments where feed-
...ent. Excepting students in these two, very different depart-
...per cent of all other students gain feedback 'often'. Why this
...se rests primarily upon long-held habits of, and opinions about,
a... ...t cannot be untangled here. But in general it appears that proper
concer... ...stablish rigorous, verifiable, accurate and impartial procedures for
the testing of achievements in exams has been thought to obviate the need to tell
students *why* they attained a certain mark or grade, and what might be done to
make improvements. Thus close focus on standards has tended to divert attention from the goal of improving student learning; and good practices of summative assessment in relation to exams have appeared to be at odds with
developmental and diagnostic work – even though this does not need to be the
case. Yet, whatever claims are made about the value of the learning that is undertaken for and tested by traditional examinations,[6] there can be little doubt that
in terms of gaining individual advice about how to make improvements in this
vital work, most history students are still kept largely in the dark.

The value that history students place on feedback is well illustrated by the fact
that over 90 per cent believe that it can help them to identify their academic
strengths and weaknesses, to feel a sense of achievement in their studies, and to
raise their marks for future work. About three-quarters of all students also
believe that feedback helps them to deepen their understanding of what they
have learned and to appreciate its importance; though there are significant variations here not only between departments but between students according to
their entry qualifications and year of study. Thus second-year students and those
with low traditional entrance-scores (between one and eight A-level points) are
particularly likely to believe that assessment feedback helps them to appreciate
the importance of what they have learned. And while 70 per cent of all students
say that feedback helps them to understand the potential uses and applications
of their knowledge, this figure rises to over 80 per cent among 'low entry' groups
and falls to just over 50 per cent for those with the highest entry-scores. Of
course, there may be many reasons for these and other variations noted, and far
more research and corroboration of these findings would be needed before any
firm conclusions could be drawn. Yet from the evidence reported here, there is at
least a *prima facie* case for suggesting that, notwithstanding the form and
purpose of the feedback given, its perceived utility will vary considerably
between different kinds of student. Thus, for example, in reflecting on the feedback they receive, mature students (aged twenty-five and over) are generally most
likely to say that they find it very useful, while 'high entry' students are least
likely to do so – which appears to be contradicted by their distinctive tendency
to re-read tutors' comments on their own and other students' scripts.

As a tool for encouraging students to develop their abilities to monitor and reflect upon their progress, feedback on assessment serves a vital function. So the fact that 93 per cent of history students (with very little variation) believe that it helps them to review their own progress is very pleasing, particularly as this should provide a good platform for the development of independent learning. However, a substantial number of many kinds of student – 38 per cent of 'old' university students (23 per cent of new), 34 per cent of males (22 per cent of females) and 32% of under-twenty-five year-olds (18 per cent of over-twenty-fives) – either 'don't know' or disagree with the proposition that feedback helps them to become more independent learners. It may be that many of these students always possessed a strong sense of their autonomy, or even that in some cases feedback actually increases reliance upon tutors. And in this respect it is worth noting that when history students enter their final year, and are often embarking on their dissertations, there is a marked decline in support for the idea that feedback promotes the growth of independent learning. Similarly, by their final year, some 35 per cent of students (26 per cent of second-years) either 'don't know' or disagree with the proposition that feedback helps them to contribute to teaching sessions. While there may be many reasons for these figures, it appears that what may be happening is that, by their final year, some students are using feedback more selectively (and strategically) to ensure that they gain higher marks for their essays and other assessed assignments, rather than to develop greater independence and raise their level of participation in the classroom.

Although in recent years there has been a notable diversification of assessment tasks and practices in higher education, essays and essay-examinations still constitute the fundamental items of assessment in most history programmes. For students, this means that most of their study time is devoted to the usually solitary activities of reading, preparing and writing essays and revising for examinations; and for tutors, that most of the time spent on assessment is dedicated to the grading of essays and exam scripts. Most feedback is provided by tutors' written statements, in summary advice and comments, and various kinds of marks and marginalia on coursework. What students learn from these and the contexts in which they are framed, therefore, largely determines the effectiveness and efficiency of the feedback process – whatever tutors believe to be its major purposes. Moreover, although student views about what is required in the writing of a history essay may be informed by many factors (such as prior experience, class discussions and peer reflections), we could expect feedback to exercise a particularly powerful influence on students' perceptions of what tutors really value. So, working from a selection of assessed essays, as well as marking criteria and essay guidelines issued by departments and some published works offering study-skills advice to students, a list of seventeen features of essays was compiled and put to students to ascertain their views about how important they thought each of these features would be to tutors when marking a history essay. Table 18.1 shows the percentage of all students who rated the feature as 'very

Table 18.1 Student views of what tutors value when assessing history essays

Essay feature	All-student assessment of importance[a] (%)	Range of student response, by department[b] (%)	Student assessment by age of university[c]	
			'Old' (%)	'New' (%)
Answer to the question set	91	84–100	91	91
Clear line of argument	90	81–94	93	89
Clear structure/organisation	83	62–95	83	83
Wide reading	79	62–89	75	80
Analytical thinking	69	56–95	75	66
Understanding of historical debates	63	36–80	63	63
Footnoting and referencing	57	25–89	38	64
Personal insights, views and judgements	51	27–77	62	47
Appraisal of historians' works	46	31–63	44	47
Correct use of English	45	34–69	37	48
Use of historical theories/concepts	38	22–62	28	42
Use of knowledge from teaching sessions	30	11–67	20	34
Use of primary sources	29	18–41	22	31
Skills in use of visual material/sources	9	0–22	6	11
Skills in use of numerical/statistical data	8	0–23	8	8
Knowledge drawn from other disciplines	8	0–21	4	9
Skills in use of C and IT-based data	7	0–13	5	8

[a] Average percentage of all (674) students who rated the feature as being 'very important' to tutors.
[b] Lowest and highest percentages of students who rated the feature 'very important', by history department (min. qualification: twenty-five student responses). 'Old' universities in italic.
[c] Average percentages of students at 'old' (pre-1992) and 'new' (post-1992) universities and university colleges, who rated the feature 'very important' to tutors.

important' to their tutors, the range of responses by department, and the student responses from 'old' and 'new' universities and colleges.

How far the student ratings in the table match the importance that tutors actually attach to each of the selected features raises many questions; not only about the feedback that students are receiving, but also about the kind of learning that undergraduate history programmes are aiming to promote. Thus, for example, the ranking order suggests that tutors place a higher value on footnoting and referencing than they do on the correct use of English or the personal insights of their students. And for some students these priorities are even more pronounced: the importance of footnoting rises to 73 per cent among 'low entry' students (40 per cent for 'high entry'), and to 89 per cent for students in one department where the figure for personal insights is just 27 per cent. Similarly, while 62 per cent of all female students think that footnoting is highly valued, only 48 per cent believe that this is equally true for their personal insights, views and judgements. According to the table, student skills in the handling of visual, numerical and computer-based data are also held in low regard by tutors, at least insofar as essays are concerned. These lowly ratings fall even further as students enter their final year, and in one typical department the use of visual sources, numerical data and computer-based skills is reckoned by 49, 33 and 66 per cent of students respectively, as being of no importance at all to tutors when assessing essay work. Such figures pose a challenge to tutors who believe that history education should be enhanced by greater attention to the development of these and other skills, and in some departments this has led to a notable diversification of assessment tasks and practices, particularly with regard to the assessment of students' oral communication skills. Yet this has done little to reduce the hegemony of the essay and essay-examination in most assessment systems, even though the practice and development of skills in essay writing is seldom the subject of attention in the classroom.

Considering the diversity of history students and degrees in higher education, it is not surprising that the relative importance of particular essay features should vary somewhat between departments. But the fact that many students believe that tutors actually attach little or no importance to the knowledge acquired from teaching sessions (at least when they are regularly assessing student learning) suggests that either there is some failure of communication or that many tutors expect their students to place a higher value on the learning that takes place within the classroom than they themselves are prepared to credit. Moreover, while mature students and 'low entry' students are twice as likely as under-twenty-five year-olds and 'high entry' students (the ratios are 45 to 23, and 34 to 17 per cent) to think that tutors will reward knowledge acquired within the classroom, the most critical influence upon student perceptions of the importance of this and most other essay features is the student's place of study. Thus while 11 per cent of students in one 'old' department think that their tutors place a high value on classroom knowledge, in a 'new' department this figure reaches 67 per cent. And in the same departments, while 22 per cent of the 'old' university students think that their tutors value the use of historical theories and concepts when marking essays, the corresponding figure in the 'new' department is 62 per cent. To some extent such differences can be traced in the overall responses of students from 'old' and 'new' departments. So, for example, students in the former are more likely to believe that evidence of analytical thinking will be well rewarded in their essays, and twice as likely (by 16 to 8 per cent) to believe that the use of primary sources is of no importance. Yet most of the major variations of responses between departments are not due to differences of age or size of institution. Nor, from a cursory view, do they appear to be closely related to differences in the marking criteria and essay guidelines issued by departments. So it is not unlikely that in each department students quite reasonably form their views about what their tutors really value in large part from the feedback that they actually receive upon their work.

How far this information enables students to understand the merits and limits of their achievements, and how to make improvements, are questions that lie at the heart of providing effective feedback on assessment. In both cases, students need to be able to conceptualise what constitutes a good essay in the discipline, for, as Hounsell's seminal work has shown,[7] unless students understand the principles and practices of academic discourse in a discipline, they will be caught in a cycle of feedback deprivation – no matter how voluminous the comments and corrections made upon their scripts. At a pragmatic level, this means that students need to understand what their tutors mean by such terms as 'structure', 'argument', 'analysis', 'interpretation' and 'evidence' in history writing, so that they know the kinds of question that historians ask when reading, and can organise their material and direct their writing to address a topic in a way that meets the particular requirements of their tutors. In the process of learning the codes and conventions of what constitutes academic literacy in history (from the questioning of texts and sources to the rules of scholarly citation), students become initiated into, and empowered within, the dominant modes of discourse for the discipline. Yet that learning may also prove unsettling, and even alienating, for some students as they learn that the dominant paradigms for undergraduate history writing (such as inclusion of personal interpretation but omission of the first-person pronoun) are cultural constructs that have been developed primarily to serve the needs of professional historians rather than all kinds of history student.[8] Following up feedback with face-to-face discussion should therefore help students to come to terms with the metalanguage of the discipline, and enable tutors to maintain an open dialogue about the kinds of writing that may be deemed appropriate for the demonstration of historical knowledge and understanding in the undergraduate curriculum. Since students are always looking for ways in which they can raise the grades of their assignments, tutorial discussion should also help them to appreciate what is most important in the written criticism; thereby helping to counteract the use of various stratagems (such as reciting the tutor's particular opinions and compiling artificially extended bibliographies) which are believed (with some justification) to lead to higher marks, even though they encourage the adoption of a 'surface' approach to learning.[9]

Reading students' comments in answer to the question, 'What is the most important thing that you have learned from feedback on your work?', there can be little doubt about either the value that most students attach to feedback or its potential impact on their learning. Thus one third-year notes that feedback has shown her 'how to construct an essay in a way that includes analysis, evidence and structure', and a second-year notes that it has shown her 'how to go about analysing my work myself, so that I can assess it and make it better before I hand it in'. Yet for the great majority of students, including those who sing its praises, feedback clearly poses many problems. Aside from comments such as, 'I don't believe that I have ever received any constructive feedback – a remark of "satisfactory" tells me nothing', most responses seem to signal that the art of writing a good history essay is principally about the avoidance of mistakes. Thus most students seem to learn 'where I went wrong', 'what went wrong', 'where my weaknesses lie', 'my personal limitations', 'all my bad points', 'what my problems are', 'things not to do', 'my faults' and 'my mistakes' . . . usually without complaint. And these mistakes or 'personal weaknesses' are usually associated with tutors' remarks about poor essay structure/organisation, lack of argument and analysis, errors in the use of English and failure to footnote properly. So, typically, the most important things that many students say they learn are that 'the structure of my essays is always commented on', 'I'm not analytical enough', 'I can't spell or understand what I've done wrong' and 'my system of referencing is still giving me problems'. Such knowledge may be an essential requirement for improvement, but it seldom seems sufficient to most students.[10] Moreover, their difficulties are compounded by the belief that 'different tutors have different requirements and personal preferences'. Not only is this disconcerting but, as students move from course to course and from essay to essay, it is often quite discouraging: 'Improving my work is practically impossible. Tutors are not willing to provide time to help, and the standards within my department vary drastically!' The fact that so much written feedback appears to students to be primarily judgemental rather than developmental, and to reflect a 'deficit' model for measuring their learning and achievements, may help to explain why only a minority speak of it as encouraging, stimulating or confidence building, and why one in six admit to having left some coursework uncollected. Yet, however disappointing feedback often is to students, they never seem to lose faith in its potential value.

When asked about what tutors can do to make feedback more helpful, by far the most frequent call is for individual tutorials; though students also stress that tutors shouldn't 'make you feel you only have three minutes to discuss the essay', but should 'explain how the essay can be improved – a factor I feel tutors find difficult to do'. 'Drop-in sessions, when students can talk about the difficulties they are having with their work' are also recommended as an aid for students who lack the confidence to ask for a tutorial. And in this respect it is worth noting that many students feel that 'tutors are very busy people who could do without the hassle of paperwork' and 'don't seem to like being pestered for information and advice'. The illegibility of some tutors' handwriting is also evidently a common problem, and one for which no student has any patience. Above all, however, in relation to written feedback, students call for much clearer and more precise advice about what to change and how to make improvements. They repeatedly say that they need to know 'exactly what the comments mean', 'exactly what I need to improve on', 'specifically what I can improve or change' and have 'specific advice on how to improve, instead of "Think about structure"', 'a path which I can follow, rather than take pot luck'. The importance of precise advice is also signalled, particularly by female students, in responses to a set of propositions about what tutors might do to make improvements. Table 18.2 shows large majorities in favour of most of the proposed activities, and even a very small majority of students in favour of using each other for peer discussion

Table 18.2 Student views of what tutors can do to improve feedback

	All-student response[a]		Range of student 'agreed' response, by department[b]
	Agree (%)	Disagree (%)	(%)
Provide more-precise advice on scripts	95 (47)	4 (0)	88–100
Hold a tutorial during preparation time	85 (30)	9 (1)	63–95
Fully explain the standards required	85 (26)	11 (0)	72–97
Write more comments on scripts	81 (27)	16 (0)	69–92
Show marks against assessment criteria	81 (26)	12 (1)	62–92
Circulate model/excellent answers	79 (34)	17 (2)	69–92
Take more account of individuality	71 (21)	19 (1)	54–87
Use teaching sessions to give feedback	64 (11)	29 (1)	53–75
Comment on student's own assessment	63 (13)	23 (1)	51–75
Encourage peer feedback on work	48 (10)	42 (5)	39–62
Take less time to mark and return work	44 (15)	53 (9)	28–75

[a] Average percentages of all (674) students who agree or disagree that the activity will improve feedback. Figures in parentheses indicate percentages of students who 'strongly agree' or 'strongly disagree'. 'Don't know' responses omitted here.
[b] Lowest and highest percentages of students who agree that the activity will improve feedback, by history department (minimum qualification: twenty-five student responses). 'Old' universities in italic.

and feedback on their work.[11] Moreover, although there is a considerable range of responses by department, in general there is little variation of response by age, degree route, sex and year or mode of study. Entry qualifications do, however, make a difference: 'high entry' students placing greater emphasis upon the need for precise guidance, advisory tutorials, more written comments and model answers; and 'low entry' students stressing the potential benefits of tutors commenting on students' self assessments and taking less time to return assignments. But even these are only matters of emphasis within a strong overall pattern that shows that most students are very keen to obtain both more general and more individual guidance than they currently receive.

In the final section of the survey, students were asked to identify the biggest problem that they faced in trying to improve their work. Just over half of all responses were concerned with feedback issues, as students re-stated and elaborated points that they had made in an earlier response. Thus many students stressed that while they were 'always trying to achieve a higher standard', they rarely knew 'how to set about it'. And this was due primarily to 'not knowing what is meant' when tutors use such terms as 'structure', 'analysis' and 'original thought' in criticism of a history essay; not receiving clear, precise and practical advice about how to make improvements; and not having the benefit of tutorials to talk about learning problems and achievements.

In most other responses, students identified a range of personal factors that they believed were major obstacles to their progress. The ten most frequently cited 'personal' factors identified by all (561) students who answered the question, 'What do you think is the biggest problem you face in trying to improve your work?', are listed in order as follows:

- shortage of study time;
- poor self management/organisation;
- need for greater self reflection;
- limited academic literacy;
- need for more work/effort;
- making good use of own ideas;
- not knowing/selecting what is most important;
- lack of enthusiasm, and laziness;
- fear of making mistakes in coursework;
- general lack of self confidence.

While shortage of study time due to work and family commitments is by far the most widely cited problem, it is worth noting that the next two major obstacles are closely related to the development of students' skills in self management and reflection. These skills are vital to the attainment of student autonomy in learning, so it is important that they are valued and developed not only in assessment tasks and practices, but also in the way that feedback is considered and delivered as an essential part of the whole process of improving student learning.[12] That students want and need to develop these skills is well illustrated by the table rankings and by the way in which many students describe their biggest problems. Thus a second-year sees her problem as 'Getting out of the habit of what I keep doing wrong. I guess I'm just forgetful and get carried away with what I'm doing, and I write an essay without really thinking of what went wrong in the last one'. And a third-year student defines her biggest problem as 'Having the time to complete a piece of work, then stand back and reassess what I have done. Often when I am handed back my work and reread it I notice how I could have improved the structure/argument etc, but at the time I was so caught up in what I had actually done, and moving on to the next issue, that I did not see this.' In these and other cases, what students learn from feedback in terms of learning to manage and reflect upon their work may well be more important than what is actually learned from undertaking the assignment.

In thinking about how to improve the quality of feedback on assessment, this survey of student experiences and perceptions raises many questions about the effectiveness of current practices and conventions. Above all, it confirms the need for further research and reflection on the goals and methods of assessing and providing feedback in history education. And it highlights the importance of developing a much deeper dialogue with students about their learning problems and achievements. In this respect, one student's tiny comment on what she regarded as her greatest challenge is probably pertinent to almost everyone: 'I could do with more help, to be honest.'

Notes

1 See K. P. Cross, 'Improving teaching and learning through classroom assessment and classroom research', in G. Gibbs (ed.), *Using Research to Improve Student Learning* (Oxford, Oxford Centre for Staff Development, 1996), pp. 3–10. For a general discussion of the importance of feedback on assessment, see G. Brown, J. Bull and M. Pendlebury, *Assessing Student Learning in Higher Education* (London, Routledge, 1997) and P. Knight (ed.), *Assessment for Learning in Higher Education* (London, Kogan Page, 1995).

2 See F. Marton and R. Saljo, 'Approaches to learning', in F. Marton, D. Hounsell and N. Entwistle (eds), *The Experience of Learning: Implications for Teaching and Studying in Higher Education* (Edinburgh, Scottish Academic Press, 1997, 2nd edn), pp. 39–58; J. B. Biggs, 'Approaches to learning and essay writing', in R. R. Schmeck (ed.), *Learning Strategies and Learning Styles* (New York, Plenum Press, 1988); N. Entwistle, *Teaching and the Quality of Learning* (London, CVCP/SRHE, 1994); G. Gibbs, *Improving the Quality of Student Learning* (Bristol, Technical and Educational Services Ltd, 1992), ch. 1; P. Ramsden, *Learning to Teach in Higher Education* (London, Routledge, 1992).

3 D. Boud, 'Assessment and the promotion of academic values', *Studies in Higher Education*, 15:1 (1990), 101–11; 'Experience as the base for learning', *Higher Education Research and Development*, 12:1 (1993), 33–44; *Enhancing Learning through Research and Development* (London, Routledge, 1995).

4 In addition to colleagues at Bath Spa, I should like to thank the following historians for their assistance in this survey: Alan Booth (Nottingham), Peter Brickley (Chichester), Peter Davies (Huddersfield), Simon Ditchfield (York), Jeremy Gregory (Northumbria), Roger Lloyd-Jones (Sheffield Hallam), Don MacRaild (Sunderland), Alex Murdoch (Edinburgh), John Peters (Worcester), Philip Richardson (Bristol), Roger Richardson (Winchester), Graham Rogers (Edge Hill), Adrian Smith (Southampton), Sally Sokoloff (Nene), Chris Williams (Cardiff) and Mike Winstanley (Lancaster). I am also very grateful to George Brown (Ulster), Graham Gibbs (Open) and James Wisdom (London Guildhall) for their support and advice. Finally and foremost, I should like to thank Nicky Wilson (Bath Spa) for her constant and invaluable assistance.

5 For the profound effect that academic departments have upon students' approaches to studying and their learning outcomes, see P. Ramsden, 'Student learning and perceptions of the academic environment', *Higher Education*, 8 (1979), 411–27.

6 See the interesting discussion on history students by N. Entwistle, 'Frameworks for understanding as experienced in essay writing and in preparing for examinations', *Educational Psychologist*, 30:1 (1995), 47–54.

7 D. Hounsell, 'Contrasting conceptions of essay-writing', in Marton, Hounsell and Entwistle (eds), *The Experience of Learning*, pp. 106–25; 'Essay writing and quality of feedback', in J. T. Richardson, M.W. Eysenck and D. Warren Piper (eds), *Student Learning: Research in Education and Cognitive Psychology* (Milton Keynes, SRHE/Open University, 1987), pp. 109–19.

8 See M. Prosser and C. Webb, 'Relating the process of undergraduate essay writing to the finished product', *Studies in Higher Education*, 19:2 (1994), 125–38; T. Lillis, 'New voices in academia? The regulative nature of academic writing conventions', *Language and Education*, 11:3 (1997), 182–99; M. R. Lea and B. V. Street, 'Student

writing in higher education: an academic literacies approach', *Studies in Higher Education*, 23:2 (1998), 157–72; D. Smith, J. Campbell and R. Brooker, 'Developing students' essay-writing skills', in C. Rust (ed.), *Improving Students as Learners* (Oxford, Oxford Centre for Staff Development, 1998), pp. 250–61.

9 L. S. Norton, 'Essay-writing: what really counts?', *Higher Education*, 20 (1990), 411–42; L. S. Norton, T. E. Dickins and N. McLaughlin Cook, '"Rules of the game" in essay writing', *Psychology Teaching Review*, 5:1 (1996), 1–13; P. Osmond, S. Merry and K. Reiling, 'Students' and tutors' perceptions of "a good essay"', *Research in Education*, 58 (1997), 81–4.

10 See G. Dohrer, 'Do teachers' comments on students' papers help?', *College Teaching*, 39:2 (1991), 48–54; M. L. Hirsh and S. L Gabriel, 'Feedback strategies: critique and evaluation of oral and written assignments', *Journal of Accounting Education*, 13:3 (1995), 259–79.

11 C. L. Keh, 'Feedback in the writing process: a model and methods for implementation', *English Language Teaching Journal*, 44:4 (1990), 294–304; G. Mowl and R. Pain, 'Using self and peer assessment to improve students' essay-writing: case study from geography', *Innovations in Education and Training International*, 32:4 (1995), 324–35; S. Brown and P. Dove (eds), *Self and Peer Assessment* (Birmingham, SCED Paper no. 63, 1991); H. Somervell, 'Issues in assessment, enterprise and higher education: the case for self-, peer and collaborative assessment', *Assessment and Evaluation in Higher Education*, 18:3 (1993), 221–33.

12 Skills-development courses for history students are discussed in E. Martin and P. Ramsden, 'Do learning skills courses improve student learning?', in J. A. Bowden (ed.), *Student Learning: Research into Practice* (Parkville, Australia, University of Melbourne, Centre for the Study of Higher Education, 1986), pp. 149–65.

Select bibliography

There is now an extensive and rapidly growing literature on teaching and learning in higher education. We have therefore confined ourselves to those works which will be of most practical use to university history teachers wishing to think through their practices or seeking answers to teaching issues. Many other references, including those to journal articles, can be found in the end notes to individual chapters, and by searching the lists of the major publishers of higher education texts, such as Open University Press and Kogan Page in the UK and Jossey-Bass in the USA.

The American Historical Association publishes numerous bibliographical pamphlets on various aspects of history, and *Perspectives*, its newsletter, contains a regular 'teaching innovations' section with short, practical articles on disciplinary teaching and learning in higher education. In the UK, the Historical Association journal, *Teaching History*, while schools focused, also contains ideas relevant to teaching at degree level. *History and Computing* carries a wide range of articles on all aspects of development and practice in this important field. More generally, in the USA the *AAHE Bulletin* (American Association of Higher Education), *Change*, *College Teaching*, *The Teaching Professor* and *Journal of Excellence in College Teaching* carry informative articles on many aspects of teaching relevant to university history teachers. So too in the UK, the magazine the *New Academic*, and the more scholarly *Studies in Higher Education*, *Teaching in Higher Education* and *International Journal of Academic Development*, contain much valuable material on teaching and learning issues. *Research into Higher Education Abstracts*, published by the Society for Research into Higher Education in the UK, provides a survey of articles and periodicals relevant to the theory and practise of higher education with an emphasis on Britain and Europe, and *Higher Education Research Abstracts*, published by Claremont Graduate School, California, offers a similar service for the United States.

General works on teaching and learning in higher education

The twelve volumes published by the Committee of Vice-Chancellors and Principals (CVCP) in its 'Effective Teaching and Learning in Higher Education' series (Sheffield, CVCP, 1992) cover most aspects of teaching and learning, as more briefly do the five volumes in the Polytechnics and Colleges Funding Council 'Teaching More Students' series (Oxford, Oxford Centre for Staff Development, 1992). Also useful are the many titles in the '53 Ways . . .' series, edited by G. Gibbs, S. Habeshaw, and T. Habeshaw, and published by Technical and Educational Services, Bristol, and the annual volumes from the Improving Student Learning Conference proceedings, *Improving Student Learning* (1994 to date), published by the Oxford Centre for Staff Development.

Bonwell, C. & Eison, J., *Active Learning: Creating Excitement in the Classroom*, ASHE–ERIC Higher Education Report, No. 1 (Washington, DC, George Washington University, 1991).

Booth, A. & Booth, J., *Enhancing Teaching Effectiveness in Humanities and Social Sciences* (Sheffield, UCoSDA, 1997).

Brown, G. & Atkins, M., *Effective Teaching in Higher Education* (London, Routledge, 1990).

Davis, J., *Better Teaching, More Learning: Strategies for Success in Postsecondary Settings* (Phoenix, Oryx Press 1993).

Entwistle, N., *Teaching and the Quality of Learning* (London, CVCP/SRHE, 1994).

Gross Davis, B., *Tools for Teaching* (San Francisco, Jossey-Bass, 1993).

Halpern, D. *et al.*, *Changing College Classrooms: New Teaching and Learning Strategies for an Increasingly Complex World* (San Francisco, Jossey-Bass, 1994).

Lowman, J., *Mastering the Techniques of Teaching* (San Francisco, Jossey-Bass, 1995).

Marton, F., Hounsell, D. & Entwistle, N. (eds), *The Experience of Learning: Implications for Teaching and Studying in Higher Education* (Edinburgh, Scottish Academic Press, 1997).

McKeachie, W., *Teaching Tips* (Lexington, D.C. Heath, 1994).

Meyers, C. & Jones, T., *Promoting Active Learning in the College Classroom* (San Francisco, Jossey-Bass, 1993).

Ramsden, P., *Learning to Teach in Higher Education* (London, Routledge, 1992).

History teaching and learning

Texts with a higher education focus

Blackey, R. (ed.), *History Anew: Innovations in the Teaching of History* (Long Beach, California State University Press, 1993).

Booth, A. & Hyland, P. (eds), *History in Higher Education: New Directions in Teaching and Learning* (London, Blackwell, 1996).

Stearns, P., *Meaning over Memory: Recasting the Teaching of Culture and History* (Chapel Hill, University of North Carolina Press, 1993).

Schools-focused texts containing material of interest to university teachers

Ankeney, K. *et al.*, *Bring History Alive! A Sourcebook for Teaching United States History* (Los Angeles, University of California, National Center for History in the Schools, 1996).

Bourdillon, H. (ed.), *Teaching History* (Buckingham, Open University Press, 1994).

Dunn, R. & Vigilante, D. (eds), *Bring History Alive! A Sourcebook for Teaching World History* (Los Angeles, University of California, National Center for History in the Schools, 1996).

Husbands, C. *What is History Teaching?: Language, Ideas and Meaning in Learning about the Past* (Buckingham, Open University Press, 1996).

Nash, G., Crabtree, C. & Dunn, R., *History on Trial: Culture Wars and the Teaching of the Past* (New York, Knopf, 1998).

Percoco, J., *A Passion for the Past: Creative Teaching of U.S. History* (Westport, CT, Heinemann, 1998).

Phillips, R., *History Teaching, Nationhood and the State: A Study of Educational Politics* (London, Cassell, 1998).

Teaching and course design

Boud, D. & Feletti, G., *The Challenge of Problem-Based Learning* (London, Kogan Page, 1996).

Brown, S., Armstrong, S. & Thompson, G., *Motivating Students* (London, Kogan Page, 1998).

Diamond, R., *Designing and Improving Courses and Curricula in Higher Education* (San Francisco, Jossey-Bass, 1989).

Duffy, D. & Jones, J., *Teaching with the Rhythms of the Semester* (San Francisco, Jossey-Bass, 1995).

Ellington, H. & Race, P., *Producing Teaching Materials* (London, Kogan Page, 1993).

Gibbs, G. & Jenkins, A. (eds), *Teaching Large Classes in Higher Education* (London, Kogan Page, 1992).

Jaques, D., *Learning in Groups* (London, Kogan Page, 1991).

Laurillard, D., *Rethinking University Teaching: A Framework for the Effective Use of Educational Technology* (London, Routledge, 1993).

Rowntree, D., *Preparing Materials for Open, Distance and Flexible Learning* (London, Kogan Page, 1992).

Schoem, D. *et al.* (eds), *Multicultural Teaching in the University* (Westport, CT, Praeger, 1995).

Weimer, M., *Teaching Large Classes Well* (San Francisco, Jossey-Bass, 1987).

Wisdom, J. & Gibbs, G., *Course Design for Resource Based Learning: Humanities* (Oxford, Oxford Centre for Staff Development, 1994).

Assessment of students

Anderson, G., Boud, D. & Sampson, J., *Using Learning Contracts: A Practical Guide* (London, Kogan Page, 1996).

Assiter, A., *Using Records of Achievement in Higher Education* (London, Kogan Page, 1993).

Brown, G., Bull, J. & Pendlebury, M., *Assessing Student Learning in Higher Education* (London, Routledge, 1997).

Brown, S. & Knight, P., *Assessing Learners in Higher Education* (London, Kogan Page, 1994).

Cross, P. & Angelo, T., *Classroom Assessment Techniques: A Handbook for Faculty* (San Francisco, Jossey-Bass, 1993).

Dary, E., *Assessing Student Learning and Development: A Guide to the Principles, Goals and Methods of Determining College Outcomes* (San Francisco, Jossey-Bass, 1991).
Miller, A., Imrie, B. & Cox, K., *Student Assessment in Higher Education* (London, Kogan Page, 1998).

Developing students' skills

Transferable skills

Assiter, A. (ed.), *Transferable Skills in Higher Education* (London, Kogan Page, 1995).
Bardrow, I., Evers, F. & Rush, J., *The Bases of Competence: Skills for Lifelong Learning and Competence* (San Francisco, Jossey-Bass, 1998).
Bligh, D. (ed.), *Teach Thinking by Discussion* (SRHE/NFER-Nelson, 1986).
Gibbs, G., *Learning in Teams* (Oxford, Oxford Centre for Staff Development, 1995).
Gibbs, G., Rust, C., Jenkins, A. & Jaques, D., *Developing Students' Transferable Skills* (Oxford, Oxford Centre for Staff Development, 1994).
Guirdham, M. & Tyler, K., *Enterprise Skills for Students* (London, Butterworth-Heinemann, 1992).
Mcyers, C., *Teaching Students to Think Critically: A Guide for Faculty in All Disciplines* (San Francisco, Jossey-Bass, 1986).

Study skills

Abbott, M., *History Skills: A Student's Handbook* (London, Routledge, 1996).
Benjamin, J., *A Student's Guide to History* (New York, Bedford/St. Martin's Press, 1998).
Black, J. & Macraild, D., *Studying History* (London, Macmillan, 1997).
Fairbairn, G. & Winch, C., *Reading, Writing and Reasoning: A Guide for Students* (Buckingham, Open University Press, 2nd edn, 1996).
Northedge, A., *The Good Study Guide* (Buckingham, Open University Press, 1990).
Pleuger, G., *Undergraduate History Study: The Guide to Success* (Bedford, Sempringham, 1998).
Storey, W., *Writing History: A Guide for Students* (Oxford, Oxford University Press, 1999).

Computing and information technology skills

Greenstein, D., *A Historian's Guide to Computing* (Oxford, Oxford University Press, 1994).
Lewis, M. & Lloyd-Jones, R., *Using Computers in History: A Practical Guide* (London, Routledge, 1996).
Maier, P., Barnett, L., Warren, A. & Brunner, D., *Using Technology in Teaching and Learning* (London, Kogan Page, 1998).
Mawdsley, E. & Munck, T., *Computing for Historians: An Introductory Guide* (Manchester, Manchester University Press, 1993).
Schick, J., *Teaching History with a Computer* (Chicago, Lyceum, 1990).
Stein, S., *Learning, Teaching and Researching on the Internet: A Practical Guide for Social Scientists* (London, Longman, 1998).

Student support and guidance

Chickering, A. & Rosser, L., *Education and Identity* (San Francisco, Jossey-Bass, 2nd edn, 1993).

Earwaker, J., *Helping and Supporting Students* (Buckingham, Open University Press, 1992).

Peelo, M., *Helping Students with Study Problems* (Buckingham, Open University Press, 1994).

Raaheim, K., Wankowski, J. & Radford, J., *Helping Students to Learn: Teaching, Counselling, Research* (Buckingham, Open University Press, 1991).

Wheeler, S. & Birtle, J., *A Handbook for Personal Tutors* (Buckingham, Open University Press, 1993).

Wisker, G. & Brown, S. (eds), *Enabling Student Learning* (London, Kogan Page, 1996).

Developing as a teacher

Developing reflective practice

Brookfield, S., *Becoming a Critically Reflective Teacher* (San Francisco, Jossey-Bass, 1995).

Brown, S. & Race, P., *Assess Your Own Teaching Quality* (London, Kogan Page, 1995).

Cowan, J., *On Becoming an Innovative University Teacher* (Buckingham, Open University Press, 1998).

Schon, D., *Educating the Reflective Practitioner* (San Francisco, Jossey-Bass, 1987).

Researching into teaching and student learning

Ashcroft, K. & Palacio, D., *Researching into Assessment and Evaluation in Colleges and Universities* (London, Kogan Page, 1996).

Bennet, C., Foreman-Peck, L. & Higgins, C., *Researching into Teaching Methods in Colleges and Universities* (London, Kogan Page, 1996).

Cohen, L. & Manion, L., *Research Methods in Education* (London, Routledge, 1994).

Cross, K. & Steadman, M., *Classroom Research: Implementing the Scholarship of Teaching* (San Francisco, Jossey-Bass, 1991).

Hammersley, M. (ed.), *Educational Research: Current Issues* (London, Paul Chapman, 1993).

Jones, M., Siraj-Blanchard, J. & Ashcroft, K., *Researching into Student Learning and Support* (London, Kogan Page, 1997).

McKernan, J., *Curriculum Action Research: A Handbook of Methods and Resources for the Reflective Practitioner* (London, Kogan Page, 1991).

Zuber-Skerritt, O., *Action Research in HE: Examples and Reflections* (London, Kogan Page, 1992).

Index